I BOUGHT A H/

A diary of the life of
NEVILLE DILKES

Oxford Publishing Services

Published in 2021 by

Oxford Publishing Services

34 Warnborough Road

Oxford, OX2 6JA

www.oxfordpublishingservices.com

Republished on Amazon in 2024

ISBN: 978 0 9955278 8 1

Copy-edited and typeset in Garamond by Oxford Publishing Services.

I BOUGHT A HALL

"It's not the music ... it's the inconvenience!"

Dedicated to my dearest Pamela, late wife and the mother of our four daughters who were all present at the precise moment I decided to write this book 52 years ago. Pamela had a love and an inscrutable understanding of me, happily apparent throughout all our too few years together.

Thanks to:

To my dear young wife Christine who, in spite of the competition she must have felt was completely up to all the challenges which have included concerts as a flautist and of course the inevitable sailing. More recently I cannot ignore the time she has spent in our attic gathering press cuttings, programmes and photographs together and putting everything in order, (including my life.)

My thanks to Keith Diggle for his brilliant management in my early days and later for introducing me to Philomusica where I shared my time as associate conductor with David Littaur. David was more than a colleague and we came to be close friends. Also the many musicians with whom I worked, some from the beginning to the end. Their loyalty and abilities are beyond measure. Thanks also to David Cound, Treasurer for the Sinfonia throughout my time with the orchestra, and a colleague from my earlier days when he was principal tenor with Opera da Camera.

To Jo Wild for her help sorting through all the photographs, and a big thank you to Oxford Publishing Services whose patience and friendship has been invaluable.

Finally to Glenn my son in law, married to my youngest daughter Rebecca, for his desire to create a film and sound track of my life which resulted in me having to delve into my past providing me with much of the material needed to write this book.

CONTENTS

FOREWORD

This book is inevitably about music, conducting and forming first an amateur orchestra, then an opera company and finally a professional orchestra, each at the request of the musicians with whom I was working at the time. However, there is more to life than that.

I first thought of writing this book when I bought and moved into Tixover Hall in the county of Rutland in May 1968. While dining with my wife Pamela and our four daughters, Clare, Rachel, Gré and Rebecca, on our first Saturday evening in our new and beautiful surroundings, I suddenly felt so proud that I was prompted to announce that one day I would write a book to commemorate this important achievement in our lives. Little did I then know what the future would really hold.

They say that all first books are biographical, even novels I am informed. I was determined that this would not be a biography and thought that memoirs was a better description, but on the advice of my editor settled for diaries (less emotional I suppose). The reader is invited to share my interests, which, apart from music, include offshore sailing, flying, antiquarian horology, philosophy, cars and, in recent years, cosmology. A cynic might add, 'and wives', but that was as a result of a sudden bereavement.

From time to time, Pamela would remind that the book was still waiting to be written, and later, after Pamela's death, my present wife Christine who, with her characteristic humour, made it a condition for her coming to live with me in France. In 2018, precisely fifty years later, Glenn McMillan, my son-in-law married to my youngest daughter Rebecca and living close by in France, asked if he could record my life story in vision and sound, to which I agreed. This resulted in searching through diaries, programmes, scrapbooks and newspaper cuttings in the attic and followed by researching the internet, much of which was carried out by Christine. Glenn, knowing about the book, was prompted to present it in the form of a DVD under the same title, which he has now completed. I decided that it would be factual and not express the sorts of comments and opinions I have included in the book. However, to keep up with Glenn, my interviewer, I inevitably needed to make copious notes, which expanded and now make up this book. Writing it would now be easy – famous last words!

My father lived for 97 years and was astonished by the amount of changes he witnessed during the course of his lifetime. Progress we know is exponential and successive generations have to keep up with the race, so to speak, but it has to be said this has always been easier for the privileged classes.

I was not privileged and only got to know anything about the real world in which I was living through doing my National Service. It was a very different world compared with that of my sheltered working-class upbringing and, being an only child, I was perhaps a little spoilt. New seeds were then planted and they flowered when I emerged as a civilian.

First, now aged 21, I had to catch up on the time I had lost due to National Service, particularly the changes that were made with regard to access to subsidized advanced education.

I thought I heard someone say in the past that there were only two ways to live this life, (i) as tramp or (ii) as a king. Google refuses to tell me who it was, so it could just be me! From renting council properties in Corby, to buying three cottages in the country, which we converted into a spacious country house, and then a lovely period property in the middle of Stamford, we finally reached our pinnacle, so to speak, with the purchase of Tixover Hall – and all this coinciding with my move from teaching to conducting.

Now, writing this book and looking back, I think it was probably a mistake to buy the hall, although not for obvious reasons. We did not lose a single friend or relative as a result of the move, and indeed it was in many cases the complete reverse, as we made countless new friends and continued to do so in spite of it perhaps ruffling a few feathers.

There were three reasons why I later chose to retire to and live in France, namely *liberté, égalité* and *fraternité*. In short, I favour a republic over a kingdom and am at heart a socialist. Having said that, I still feel English and continue to enjoy my visits to the country of my birth, which sadly, apart from the countryside, I now find increasingly difficult to recognize in cultural terms. 'Ye know, er, ye know' the lingo has changed, and many sentences starting with 'so' – and sad to say, notably by the BBC, which at one time set the standard we all recognized as 'King's English'.

Not surprisingly, I was on the side of the remainers when the Brexit referendum was launched in 2016. When the serious negotiations reached boiling point I never ceased to be amused by the number of times the phrase, 'but we are a *sovereign* state', was used in the reported Brexit negotiations of 2020, which seemed to imply that we were special. (Did our negotiators not know that nearly all countries in the world are sovereign states?)

The word sovereign of course has another meaning, which stems from the class system that is still so fundamental to people's thinking in England. No other country in the world has such a complicated aristocracy, not to mention, further down the scale, the Honours list ranging from knighthoods down to the British Empire Medal. The result is that we live with a class system that would better be handed over to the National Trust.

Following the decision to leave Europe, I see Britain's future in danger of becoming four independent countries – England, Scotland Wales and Ireland – and later all four separate countries rejoining Europe to become part of a United States of Europe. These are just a sprinkling of my thoughts before the diary begins.

Even before National Service, I was aware of the 'gay' community, known to my generation as 'Nancy boys', but until I moved into elite musical circles, I never foresaw how much it would affect my progress. Thankfully, the world (or should I say the law) finally woke up to the fact that there was nothing new about homosexuality and, almost overnight, about the time of my retirement, everything changed. Soon, many well-known personalities began to make their sexual orientations known on the media and, as a result, the world is now a better place. For me and others during this period, the change came too late. It was common knowledge that the BBC music department, Royal Opera and Ballet, Glyndebourne and other leading organizations in the music world not surprisingly look after their own kind to protect their futures. It could frequently be observed that if two candidates of equal ability but with different sexual orientations were interviewed or auditioned for a position, the outcome would be a foregone conclusion. So, unless an artist was already well known, the chances of starting or enhancing a career in this field were formidable. I remember my father on many occasions asking why there were so many foreigners conducting our concerts? Already famous, I suppose; they were not of course auditioned!

I will relate a story following a dinner party in Nottingham at which our host and his wife invited Pamela and me to meet another married couple with an interest in music. I subsequently received a telephone call at home from the other guest who, knowing that I had spent time in London, asked if we could meet there as he thought he could provide some help with the Sinfonia. We met and he took me to a restaurant for dinner. I suddenly noticed that the conversation was gradually veering towards sexual matters and was beginning to get 'personal', and that this came to a head when he said, 'If you invited me to sleep with you tonight I could not refuse you.' Apart from being astonished by the suggestion, I wondered why on earth he would think that I wanted to and realised that, because I was an artist, he had assumed that I could not be anything other than homosexual.

I can say in all sincerity that I have never at any time been opposed to same sex relationships provided they did not include me, but may have been guilty of making my heterosexuality too apparent.

Following my mid-life interest in philosophy, in later life I found myself becoming fascinated by the progress that was being made in space travel and science in general. The recognition of global warming and the threat to the planet's existence prompted me to think about who we are, what purpose our lives fulfil, and what the future might hold. There was nothing new to this question, but in view of the advancement of scientific knowledge, were we getting any nearer to answering it? Landing on the moon was a significant moment in our lives as it proved that we could, in a very small way, escape our immediate environment.

As a sailor, I was among the first to use GPS, which was a formidable step on from RDF (radio direction finding). We now have satellites circling our planet locating where we are, and more recently have landed a research station on Mars. Science in my lifetime has advanced at an incredible pace and continues to fascinate me. I have read about quantum physics, parallel universes and am basically left with the lonely thought that we know with certainty that humanity only exists on one planet and in our solar system. If we needed to escape from it, we cannot, as according to Einstein, nothing can travel faster than the speed of light, which makes it impossible to reach another world in our lifetime. (Science fiction has created 'Warp' speed in Star Trek so that may be the answer.) Furthermore, and closer to the point, many scientists believe that life does not exist anywhere else in the universe. The latest 2016 Drake equation would seem to agree with this. We know that our evolution on planet Earth took four and a half billion years to develop to its present intelligent level, which I understand is used in the equation. I leave readers with this thought. Already knowing that we are alone in the solar system makes one feel even more alone in the universe.

Chapter 1

How It All Began
1930–1940
Birth, parentage, musical beginnings

Although I have no recollection of the event, I emerged to see this planet in the early hours of 28 August 1930. My birth certificate indicates this was at an address in Howard Street, Derby. I was told I cried a lot and my parents had many disturbed nights. Modern thinking would probably attribute this to the unconscious sense of awe shared by many in those days, despite the experience of this miracle having lasted for the previous 150,000 years or more. The reader will have quickly realized my present interest in, not history but science! However, to continue, as I am writing a diary, I will stick to the point. First a word about my background.

Parentage

Both my parents were born in Derby. My mother's father was born in Portsmouth but went to Coventry to serve his apprenticeship to become a clockmaker afterwards moving to Derby where he married my grandmother. My father's father, Albert Dilks (note the spelling) was born in Ilkeston near Derby, moving there for reasons of work.

My father, following in his father's footsteps, worked in a factory but as a pattern maker. After his apprenticeship he moved in this capacity to Bennet & Sayers a foundry making castings for brick machinery and, I understand, he was very competent at this work. Making patterns is one thing but I am told there were occasions when he would go down to the foundry and carve the required mould in the sand by hand allowing the molten metal to be poured directly into it, therefore dispensing with the pattern. There is no doubt in my mind that his real talents lay in art and music. There are few walls in our house, and indeed in my daughters' houses, that are not evidence to this claim. His violin playing I accompanied and heard!

1

My mother was well organised and, like most women of the period, never went out to work until the war when she helped in a school kitchen. My parents had a good relationship – my father would arrive home on Friday evening with his pay packet, which he would hand to my mother unopened. She was in charge of the finances, which suited my father as he would just happily take his pocket money. I do not think he spent much, but he was very generous when he could be. He was the middle of three sons. His eldest brother Horace worked as a clerk eventually becoming chief clerk at the Silk Mill in Derby. His brother Eric, 13 years younger, also had a clerical job first in a solicitor's office and later in the county education office where he too later became chief clerk. None of the three boys had a grammar school education, but each of their futures at the point of leaving school were influenced by events of the period. Horace born at the beginning of the century (1900) was able to start his working life in an office and had probably shown promise in maths and English at school. Arthur, born in 1903 had talents in art and music that would be difficult to measure at any time but particularly so at the time he left school during the 'general slump'. The family, now with Eric a small baby, probably needed money and I have no doubt his mother was oblivious to his talent and would have adopted the attitude of 'what's good enough for your father should be good enough for you.' In the event, he did not have to leave school to work in a foundry, but started an apprenticeship to become a pattern maker. I imagine working with wood was deemed to be an improvement on the heat and dust of a foundry.

It is interesting how the middle child of three frequently seems so different. Here we have a situation in which the eldest boy is a keyboard player, of the piano and organ, as was the youngest. My father, in the middle, chose to play the violin, but also wanted to draw and later paint. He was a natural string player and in terms of technique and intonation had the makings of a professional. He played in an orchestra in Derby and I have heard there was talk of him becoming leader. I believe he received lessons from the conductor who was also a violinist. In Derby, the only professional music, apart from teaching, was limited to the theatre. Theatre orchestras existed in the provinces, whereas symphony orchestras only existed in London and perhaps one or two larger cities (only a few now in the twenty-first century); unless you had an exceptional talent there was little opportunity to get on the musical ladder. Large towns had a theatre and a theatre orchestra so there were local musicians who could make a living out of playing, but it was mainly evening work. Some would have other work, others perhaps would teach. It was going to be many years before peripatetic music teaching was introduced.

My father had considerable technical ability and never ceased to surprise me with the repertoire he played. At a very early age he would ask me to accompany him, which was good for my sight-reading. His favourite phrase to me was, 'Can we have a tune?' He could play almost anything but was not very disciplined. I discovered a large repertoire of violin music including concertos, overtures, and solo works such as the Elgar Chansons. We played the Mendelssohn and Beethoven violin concertos and I must smile when I think back to how the last movement of his Mendelssohn must have sounded as it got faster, a challenge to me that I just had to meet! His love of drawing and painting was probably dominant, in fact I do not think I ever saw my father without a pencil in his hand throughout his entire life. Drawing everything he saw was second nature to him. He attended art classes in Derby after school and, in my opinion, his caricatures of people, instantly recognizable, are outstanding. His pencil work was supreme. I believe the classes he

attended were cut short when his dear mother discovered nude drawings he had done from live models while at school!

My paternal grandfather Albert, played the organ. They had a street house with a piano in the dining room and an organ in the living room, an impressive instrument known as a 'harmonium'. Two foot pedals pumped the bellows to provide the air for the reeds – pipes not being used for household instruments. It was large but a beautiful piece of furniture. I believe he was highly thought of at the foundry, so perhaps bought the organ new, but the piano could only be described as 'honky-tonk'. He played and encouraged his sons to play, so Horace, the eldest, eventually became a keyboard player and organist at the local Baptist church.

I have vivid memories of my grandparents. I can remember my paternal grandfather, Albert standing on his head in his seventies. He was always showing me interesting things and, on one occasion, demonstrated how to fry an egg with a magnifying glass. Bright sunlight outside meant he put an egg on a plate on the window sill, got his magnifying glass and used the sun to cook the egg, I was most impressed! He also had an interesting brother, my father's uncle, also Arthur, after whom I presume my father was named. He sometimes came over from Ilkeston and was able to play the musical saw. This is a long saw that you sit with, the blade on the ground and draw a bow across it, by flexing the saw the note changes and it is possible to play a tune.

My paternal grandmother was a strong minded woman and I always felt she disliked me, but on reflection I think I was probably quite cheeky, perhaps very cheeky. Their house had electricity, most still only had gas, but they had had theirs converted and of course electricity was an expensive commodity in those days. I was encouraged to go to my grandparents for tea on Tuesdays after school, so while my mother chatted I would do my homework and, later at grammar school, I needed to sit at the table to do it, which required light. My grandmother always complained when I put the light on and, on one occasion, I remember her saying, 'Do you know you are an evil boy putting on the light.' I remember replying, 'Surely it is evil people who like the dark because they commit burglaries and I do not,' so adding that she was wrong. She said this was being cheeky. I would have thought it was being intelligent; I never looked forward to Tuesdays but could not break the routine.

My maternal grandparents were charming. My grandfather Charles was much older. After his first wife died, he married her sister, so he married two women from the same family. My mother was from the second marriage. Not only did she have two sisters, she was the eldest, she had a step brother and three step sisters. I saw quite a lot of Lill and her husband Charlie James. They had a street shop in Normanton and when they went on holiday for a week or more we would go over and stay there so that my mother could run the shop, which included an off licence. This meant that my mother had to pull pints of beer in the evenings, to which my father was theoretically opposed because of his strict Baptist background, but my mother was more relaxed.

From my earliest days my mother was concerned about my education; she made sure that I knew my times tables and could spell so, I had to learn very long words. Even as a small boy I could spell words like encyclopaedia. She would buy me books on general knowledge and we had a whole set of volumes called *Peoples of all Nations*. The emphasis was very much on I MUST be clever. She really did encourage that and she was determined to get me to a grammar school. Nobody else in the family had been near a grammar school and I was in fact to be the first.

What do I remember of my early years?

I have been asked many times, what is the earliest thing you remember? I think it was being pushed in my pram by my father. I distinctly recall seeing him in the framework of the pram hood and him exciting me by running at a great speed. Shortly after I was born we moved to a council rented property in a southern part of Derby and then to Findern Street where they bought a street house just outside the town centre and close to my father's employment. I was then two or three years' old and have memories of lying on the floor in the living room, discovering the staircase and eventually moving from crawling to walking. I remember being taken to the doctor around the age of five with a sore throat for which he took a swab, and being told I may have to have my tonsils taken out. I had been worried about this possibility as I was aware of other children having that operation. Our doctor surprisingly turned up at the house in the early evening and announced the swab had revealed I had diphtheria and that an ambulance would shortly turn up and take me to the isolation hospital outside Derby. My parents could not visit me, but my father would cycle a very long distance to see me through the window. When I eventually returned home after several weeks he would massage my legs every night to ensure I returned to normal, which I did. However, I did develop a stutter, which was to haunt me until I left Derby to do National Service when approaching the age of 19.

Musical beginnings

I attended an infant school on the main Ashbourne Road, which meant quite a long walk, first in my mother's company, but later when I had friends to a meeting point from where we walked together. Well before the age of seven I was able to look after myself, for there were no main roads to cross. Even before starting school my mother gave me my first piano lessons. Coming from a musical family, my father had already bought a piano, a Rogers upright, which I inherited and only eventually sold in my twenties when I bought a Bechstein, one down in size from a concert grand. This piano, which had belonged to the composer and pianist Franz Reizenstein, was advertised in London. It was only one of two pianos I ever owned until well after my retirement. Returning to my mother, she could not play the piano but sang soprano in the Baptist chapel choir and could read the treble clef. She could find the notes on the piano keyboard and was able to play and learn the soprano line in hymns and anthems. She would encourage me to play the piano and taught me what she knew, but she did not know the difference between the lines and spaces of the treble and bass clefs. So what I was able to play in the treble clef did not sound quite right when I tried to play the left hand as well. I remember solving the problem by thinking if the note above middle C was D, the note below must be B. (The piano is the only instrument on which you can not only hear the sound of the note but can actually see it.) That being the case the top line of the bass clef must be A. It worked! The 'floating' line, so to speak, is called a ledger line and I was to discover later that composers cheated by putting another one below C, thus borrowing the bass clef A indicating it was to be played by the right hand, and vice versa in the left hand. My mother later bought me a piano tutor, which confirmed my thinking. I will digress at this point to say that music, although having existed since time immemorial, is the youngest of all the art forms. This is because it took until the middle ages to find a satisfactory way of indicating pitch and length of sounds that would enable the inventor of a tune, perhaps with words, to pass it on for everyone's benefit. We know that, even in the nineteenth century, many centuries-old songs had only been passed down through memory, which was what inspired composers like Vaughan Williams to collect and arrange them for performances in our time.

Regarding friendships, there was an older boy, Michael Hinks, living further up the street and Denis Evans (about whom more later) who visited an aunt once a week, but I was happier playing with two sisters who lived next door. We played and shared secrets together. I was taken to Sunday school every week at Junction Street Baptist Church, which was within a 20-minute walk. I had solved the problem of making the left-hand notes sound right on the piano and by the age of six was able to play simple hymns at the Sunday school, which provided me with female class mates who liked to come and sit by me.

I started having piano lessons with my uncle Eric, father's younger brother, at the age of six. In 1937 we moved to St Albans Road where they were building new houses. My father had saved sufficient money to pay the deposit on a three-bedroomed semi with a very long garden backing onto Ryckneld Recreation Ground. Uncle Eric had married before we moved, I was a page boy at the wedding, and he had already bought a street house close to our new one. My new school was Firs Estate, one term in the infants department, then to the junior school next door in the autumn. I continued my lessons with my uncle Eric and progress was rapid. Eric was a fine pianist, incredibly good at sight-reading and I never understood why he had not chosen music as a career. As I was to discover in my later years, the reasons were clear as such choices were not readily available, but he was a formidable challenge to me. He took an enormous interest in my talent and I provided him with the excuse he wanted to take me to concerts in Derby; Iris, his wife, perhaps a little less interested. I remember a recital by Colin Horsley in which he played Liszt's 'La Campanella'. Uncle Eric confessed when we left the concert, 'Now you know why I do not practice,' to which I remember replying, 'But uncle that is why, from now on, I *will* practice!' I asked my mother to buy me a copy of the music, which she did, and I still have it today. I was reminded of this comment when we came to France and subsequently recorded the piece on a DVD in our music room in Nalliers.

At junior school I had a teacher, Eric Maunder, whom I greatly admired. He was a Derby man and had won a scholarship to go to university, a rare achievement in those days. He was my hero because he could answer any question I put to him. Another boy in the class was Peter Flixon, with whom

I constantly battled for first place. My father became interested in puppets and not only built a model theatre but also eventually carved his own puppets. The theatre became my Christmas present and I remember, with lead models of Snow White and the Seven Dwarfs plus my father's help, produced the story on stage from a script read from a book he edited. The theatre had draw curtains and battery lighting. I took it to school after Christmas to give a pantomime performance to the class, which impressed Mr Maunder. That year Uncle Horace, organist and choirmaster at Junction Street Baptist Church, was preparing the oratorio *Olivet to Calvary* for a performance at Easter. As both my mother and father were members of the choir, I attended rehearsals and followed the score. I immediately noticed the composer was Maunder, so excitedly asked Mr Maunder if they were related. I cannot recall his exact answer but guess it was something like, 'Well I suppose we must be.' Excitedly I told my father and as a result he was invited to talk about the work before the performance from the pulpit. Meeting Eric, my father discovered he played the viola and he quickly became a family friend and frequent visitor to our house. When Uncle Horace assembled the Sunday school and chapel choir, as he did each year for two performances of an anniversary concert, my father assembled a string ensemble for him which now included Eric Maunder. Uncle Horace conducted, Uncle Eric played the organ and the ensemble accompanied the anniversary choruses and the congregational hymns.

War on its way

At this time I became aware of the possibility of war and in 1939 it became a reality. Eric Maunder was among the first people we knew to be called up, which cut short his visits to our house until he appeared on leave and, of course, in uniform. He had been given a rank in the early stages and I seem to remember he was in the Royal Army Ordnance Corp.

My father was deemed to be in a 'reserved' occupation, so at least for the time being was not called up. Fortunately, his age increased faster than the age limit of the call up so he remained in the reserve category. Frantic work started all over the country to prepare for the war. We had an Anderson air raid shelter delivered for which my father had to dig a large hole at the bottom of the garden, insert the metal structure and bolt the sections together. It was an oblong domed building six foot high in the middle and stood in the hole, which was quite deep. The soil dug from the ground was then thrown over the top and sides. Whenever the rapid up and down pitch of the warning siren sounded, usually in the middle of the night, we hurriedly got out of bed and ran down the long garden path (shaded torches were allowed) and renewed our sleep in the shelter where there were two bunk beds, one either side. My mother thoughtfully always had a flask of tea or cocoa at the ready. There were barrage balloons in the sky all over Derby to keep the enemy aircraft from flying low to see their targets, and usually a lot of ante aircraft fire from the ground when enemy planes flew over. There was in fact more danger from falling shrapnel from the artillery guns than bombs if you were outside. For this reason, we were each issued with protective head gear (tin hats) and also had gas masks in case the enemy resorted to this low level of attack. That falling shrapnel was a real danger was clearly indicated by the amount found on the pavements and roads the next day. We collected these on the way to school!

The war obviously seriously disrupted the food chain and we were given ration books to ensure fairer distribution, though some people, particularly the wealthier ones, cheated, with transactions on the recently-termed 'black market' becoming more commonplace and the 'Land Army' recruiting women from all walks of life. This was to help increase the food supply and anyone with the semblance of a garden was expected to 'grow at home'.

As time went by, more and more teachers were called up and eventually Firs Estate junior school had to close. Most of the pupils stayed at home, but my mother, who was very aware of the importance of education, did everything in her power to get me a place at another school. She succeeded and I was given a place at a school in the centre of Derby. This meant a daily bus ride into town, which was more vulnerable to bombing than the suburb in which we lived, but the new school worked out well, even to the point of discovering that my new teacher, Sidney Brace, lived opposite Ken Fitzhugh, a close friend of my father's at Bennet & Sayers. Ken, a skilled draughtsman, lived in Mickleover just outside the Derby boundary close to our home in St Albans Road, and he and my father admired each other's artistic abilities. We frequently visited their house after the evening service on a Sunday night. On one occasion I excitedly spotted my teacher watering his flower garden in the front of the house opposite. Being friendly with him, Ken duly introduced my parents and I soon found myself with another friendly teacher. I mentioned my speech defect earlier and this had already caused some concern at my junior school. More positive action was now taken and I was sent to the children's clinic in Derby for speech therapy. I remember hearing myself described as being 'highly strung', which meant little at the time, but my treatment involved a period of lying on a bed and being encouraged to relax. I fell in love with my nurse and remember the shape of her legs, which loomed above me. I must have had a thing about nurses, as I had a passing interest in the nit nurse who visited the junior school from time to time. However, she was much more active as she thrilled me by running her exploring fingers up my short trouser leg! Returning to speech therapy, there were breathing exercises, particularly when reading long sentences, and probably more that I have forgotten. I never stammered with friends and relations, but my main problem was starting a sentence. For example, I had great difficulty giving my destination to the conductor on a bus. I usually circumnavigated this by changing my first word at the very last moment, which could, and did, put me into several difficult situations, often to the amusement of my listeners.

My parents, wishing me to follow in the footsteps of my two uncles, decided at the age of nine that I should learn to play the organ. I should have organ lessons with my other uncle, Horace. By this time my father was a deacon at the church, so there was no difficulty gaining access to an organ on which I could practice. It was a two manual pipe organ with a straight pedal board and about ten hand drawn stops. At that time, it had not been fitted with an electric blower so had to be hand pumped. For Sunday services, a youth was paid sixpence to be imprisoned in a small chamber under the pipework where he moved a long wooden lever up and down to fill the bellows with air. The bellows would hold the air until a note was played. The amount of air needed naturally increased with the number of notes being played together, the number of pipes in use at the time and the number of stop pulled outs. The capacity of the bellows was thus severely challenged when the organist played a full chord involving every stop – the manuals and pedal board coupled together, and it was a full time job for the pumper to keep up. A lead weight hanging from the bellows dropped down on a scale when the air was pumped in, and would ascend at a rate dependent on the number of stops in use and texture of the music. Not only did my mother accompany me to the church, there was a main road to cross, but she also pumped the organ for me while I was practising. It was not long before I was playing a voluntary before and after the evening service, and later for the congregational hymns, and also accompanying the choir that my uncle conducted. I sat with the three tenors when not playing, alongside the organ trying to join in singing the tenor line.

Chapter 2

Early Years
1941–1948
Education, after leaving school, meeting Pamela

1941

At the age of 11 I took the education committee's scholarship, later called the 11+. If I passed I would go either to the Central School, originally in the centre of Derby, or to Bemrose School, a completely new institution close to where we were living on the outskirts of the town. It was a foundation trust school with both free and fee-paying places. There was also Derby School which was entirely private. (At my invitation, Sir Max Bemrose, a descendant of the printing family after which the school had been named, became the first chairman of the Midland Sinfonia Concert Society.)

Being solely fee paying, there was no question of me going to Derby School, but there was a two-fold chance of getting a place at one of the other two by taking both the education department's scholarship and the entrance examination for a fee-paying place at Bemrose. Thus, failing the education department scholarship but subject to passing the entrance exam, I could still secure a grammar school place but not without some strain on our finances. As it transpired, I passed both the education committee's scholarship for the Central School with no fees and the Bemrose entrance exam with fees. My parents thought I should be given a choice, but it was obviously going to help them if I chose the Central School. They offered me a new bicycle if I chose the cheaper option, so I did. Ironically, 12 months later, as a sign of the times, fee paying at the Bemrose School was abandoned!

The Central School building, along with its laboratories and lecture theatre, was literally in the centre of Derby, but at the start of the war it was evacuated to a large Georgian house in Darley Park in the country, which was very, very beautiful. Interestingly, it remained a school until 1958, despite a fire in 1948 from which it took three years of work to recover. In 1962, sadly it was pulled down as it was deemed unsafe, with the exception of one room, now a café, and the last remaining room of the mansion. Darley Park is a large picturesque and popular park within walking distance of the city centre, so a peaceful haven. Located on the banks of the River Derwent the area is now part of a World Heritage Site.

We were taken to school every day by a free bus service and, while aesthetically inspirational, going there meant being deprived of facilities such as laboratories, physics or chemistry labs, a carpentry workshop, gymnasium, or even flat grassland for football and cricket pitches, let alone a tennis court. To swim, we still had to go into the middle of Derby, which we did by bus, combining this with a visit to the old building for physics and chemistry lessons, thus questioning the wisdom of being evacuated in the first place. On the other hand, Bemrose School was a new building, close to where we lived, and with all the facilities one could have wished for, but then I would not have had that bike!

My uncle Horace decided that when I passed the scholarship I should go to a qualified organ teacher. My parents took his advice and, wanting the best for me, took me to Derby Cathedral for an audition with the organist Heath Gracey. He told them he was impressed with my playing and would give me a thorough musical training in church music, lessons on the organ and voice training. This meant singing in the choir and he recommended that I immediately become a chorister, adding that he thought I would be capable of becoming his assistant organist. This of course meant very little to me at the age of 11 except perhaps a bit of pride, but my parents were horrified at the thought of me wearing a cassock and surplice in a choir in the Church of England, albeit a cathedral. In retrospect, there was at that time a deep gulf between the free churches and the Church of England, and no more so than with the Baptists. I was of course conscious of this divide and remember my parents discussing their dilemma, but of course was in no position to influence things.

The organ in Derby Cathedral was a four manual instrument on a gallery at the west end. John Compton had completely rebuilt it two or three years earlier with the console detached and put in the choir. Compton is of course well known for his cinema organs so had the expertise to produce the electronics necessary to abandon the old tracker action and need to withdraw hand stops. It fascinated me, particularly since it was unnecessary to pull out stops, you just touched them and they lit up. The pipe work remained in the original case and was revoiced.

My father would frequently compare the then organist at the parish church with his predecessor Norman Hibbert, about whom he spoke with bated breath because he was a fellow of the Royal College of Organists. He was also well known as a recitalist. I knew my father was of the opinion that the present organist Stanley Mayes was not in the same class, but decided I should now have an audition with him. I must be fair to Stan Mayes, he was an amateur, but so were my uncles, and in fairness to Mayes, he played very well. I had the audition with Stan Mayes on the four manual Willis organ in the church and was overawed by the instrument, Willis of course being the leading organ builder in the UK. Mayes was just as impressed by my playing but said he would not recommend me having organ lessons until I had achieved Grade V on the piano. He added he would also give me theory lessons. My parents were convinced by this, as here there was no question of me having to join the choir. I passed grade 5 on the piano by the end of the first term and immediately began organ lessons with Stan Mayes who was also a town councillor, although I regret to say not in the same class as Heath Gracey at the cathedral. A nice man but it was a mistake, (another one) but it was not long before I started asserting myself and I think about twelve months later he realised my ability and by the age of 12 or 13 he had me accompanying the choir rehearsals. Soon after I decided to join the choir as I was spending my Friday evenings playing for the rehearsals so I might as well put on a robe and sing. I had a bit of an argument with my parents but I did join the choir and at a very early age he appointed me as his assistant, which is exactly what Heath Gracey had said but the standard of music was nothing like as good, which was a great pity. There you go, such is life!

My father, having been a victim of the Depression, never for one moment thought of me making my career in music. Later I discovered he did not even want me to think about a musical career. I should at this point say that my parents, like their parents before them, were staunch Baptists and my father was in fact a deacon. Going to church on a Sunday evening was an absolute ritual and there was no escape until I became assistant at St Werburgs and by 14 I was completely absent from the Baptist Church. My father's eldest brother Horace was organist at Junction Street Baptist Church and Eric, his younger brother, also played there but was not a frequent member of the congregation. He would play and accompany his older brother when needed for special occasions. I think he would have said that he was an agnostic; he never admitted to being an atheist.

Grammar school

My life at grammar school was rather interesting. There was a three form entry to the school and I was put in 1B for the first term. At the end of this term I came in the top five and was immediately put in 1A where I stayed for the rest of that year. I did the whole of the second year in 2A then managed to drop down to 3B. It was the shock of my life. I realised the need to do something about this and after a term of hard work was moved back to the A stream, phew! Once back in the A stream I started doing well, so well that I think the school made a terrible mistake (another one – not of my doing) as the top five, including me were advanced to 5A thus missing out year four completely – not a good decision. This was before the time of sixth forms as we now know them. We were put together with pupils who had already taken and passed the school certificate in a number of subjects, so inevitably we found ourselves well behind the others and had to try to catch up.

The school certificate in those days was a pass in general subjects, English, maths, chemistry and a foreign language. We only had a choice of one language during the war years as the school was short staffed, I had hoped it was German, but only because we had a French mistress who was a real tyrant, Polly Wood, and everybody feared her, a real battle-axe. She seemed as old as the school, and in sharp contrast to my maths teacher who was very attractive. I have already mentioned I suffered from a stutter and this certainly did not help my French. Miss Hepworth, the maths teacher came to the school the same time as me, straight from university so she was young and as already mentioned attractive and I fell in love with her. Of course I was not the only one! We enjoyed her sitting on her table at the front of the class with one leg on the floor which did rather expose her inside thigh, which we discovered when sitting near the front was even more revealing if you dropped your pencil or ruler on the floor and stooped to pick it up. We would also ask for unnecessary help over a problem as she would come and sit by us. This must have been quite a trial for her as I was particularly demanding! The attention soon stopped but when she applied it elsewhere I remarked to my neighbour Dick Townsend that this was favouritism. The theme was taken up by him, and others, and an audible voice would ask 'What did you say Dilkes?' to which I would reply just with the one word 'favouritism' – I never stuttered.

Anyway, I did not manage to matriculate. If you were a high flyer and you scored over a certain pass mark then you qualified to matriculate. There was also an exam called higher school certificate but that was not offered at the Central School and I am not sure at that time it was possible at any school in Derby except perhaps the Derby School. Matriculation was the normal entrance to university, but there were very few places in those days, as there were few universities – Oxford, Cambridge, Durham, London and a few others like Reading. My school days finished in the summer of 1946 when I was about to be 16 years' old. School leaving ages were 14 in state schools and 16 in grammar schools depending on when your birthday fell.

My dream of owning a motorbike came true just after my sixteenth birthday when I got a New Imperial 250cc – although the name was 'New' the bike was second hand. My father had a 500cc BSA but he was never very good on it I and used it more than I used the Imperial. However, I did go back to the Imperial when my father put a side car on his BSA for my mother because she was not very keen on riding pillion. I tried driving it with the side car on and found it impossible to handle. You instinctively heel over but with the sidecar on you have just got to steer it. When turning left you can feel the inertia that is trying to take you in the opposite direction and you desperately want to lean over but you cannot. It is a most peculiar experience.

After leaving school

As mentioned earlier, my father's brothers both had secretarial jobs – they were white-collar workers as opposed to my father who was an engineer. My parents had prepared me for office work. My father did not think that a musical career was an option, for it could only lead to me ending up on the London Thames Embankment. He had of course witnessed the Great Depression.

On the advice of Stanley Mayes, my organ teacher, I took a job as a clerk at the Manor Hospital in Derby. I believe I got this job on three counts – (i) the head of the hospital, Don Whelan, was an amateur violinist whom I would be available to accompany; (ii) I could play for the hospital review entertainment; and (iii) Stan Mayes was a town councillor on the hospital management committee. I was also asked to be organist at the hospital chapel for which I received additional remuneration.

I had no problems getting to know office routine at the Manor Hospital and found myself becoming a proficient typist, albeit not touch typing but reasonably relaxed on the telephone in spite of my stutter. The staff at the hospital put on a Christmas show and there was a surprising degree of talent.

As mentioned earlier, Don Whelan, administrative director and master (there was a workhouse block in the grounds), played the violin, Ivor Gilbert in the office, who we all knew to be gay – not a term used at the time, was completely at home on the stage in drag and, believe me, a challenge to even the most attractive female. There was also a physiotherapist who was a conjurer, and myself in the pit playing the piano. We assembled a chorus both to sing and dance, and a great time was had by all.

The grounds of the hospital provided tennis courts for the staff and I would return some evenings to play with my friend Denis Evans. As mentioned earlier, I met Denis when he had visited his aunt close to us in Findern Street. We had met again when his parents bought a house on St Albans Road. This was some time after we had moved as building work continued until finally joining up with the arterial road (ring road), which I am told was a credit to Derby Town Council as it was among the earliest developments of this idea of circling a town. I must add, however, they did not complete the circular until after the end of the Second World War. As a matter of interest, the northern part of the circular finished at Darley, the stop to which I travelled in my school days. To continue at the time would have meant going through Darley Park and then crossing the River Derwent. Returning to Denis, we were the greatest of friends sharing on equal terms his love of music with my love of science. He was a member of the boy scout movement, which I was not allowed to join, as, in the opinion of my mother it was simply a way of training boys to become soldiers. Baptist upbringing – am I being unfair? It was not that important, however, as the group I would have joined was in the village of Littleover and met on Friday nights. I was, of course, committed to attending choir practice at the parish church in Derby at the same time. I should mention at this point that the head boy was Michael Rayner, about five years my junior. He had a wonderful treble voice and was the idol of the congregation. In later years, as will be revealed, he became a lifelong friend. Returning to Friday nights and boy scouts, there was a great attraction for me to dash out of choir practices and cycle at top speed to Littleover. It was Denis's routine to leave scouts and meet his girlfriend at the village chip shop. Her name was Ruth Hydes and she had a friend, Joan Beresford, so my motives were clear. I have to say the fish and chips were good! However, I was less interested in Joan than Denis was in Ruth, but continued the Friday night rendezvous. In fact, I had become interested in a nurse at the hospital. I had always had an interest in older girls and now in relative maturity it stretched even to married women – this was not the case later in my life! This nurse was not married, but I believe was engaged, though I never saw a ring. My father knew about this relationship having been stopped in the street where she lived by her father who reported my interest in his daughter and had said she was already engaged.

Meeting Pamela

The problem solved itself a short time later when I met Pamela. My meeting with her was in some way contrived. Although I was assistant organist at the parish church I occasionally played at the Baptist church for my Uncle Horace, usually when he did the anniversary or a concert. It was on one of these occasions (a concert) that Pamela was in the audience or should I say congregation; anyway, she spotted me. Apparently, her parents had lived in Derby at one time and had been members of the church. Curiously, Tom, Pam's father had a brother who lived in the same street as my grandmother. Anyway, Pamela told her mother that she would like to meet me. 'Like to meet Neville Dilkes,' said Dolly, 'I know the Dilkeses,' so she planned to visit Tom's brother in Jackson Street and arrange a meeting. When I turned up at my grandmother's house, I was told that someone wanted to meet me. At six o'clock I went outside and saw Pamela walking towards me, we chattered briefly but long enough for me to forget any intrigue and make the most of an opportunity to invite her to join me that Saturday evening so I could take her to the pictures. I met her off the bus outside the council offices in Derby and we walked to the cinema (The Picture House) in Babington Lane to see the film *Bachelor Knight*. For the purpose of this book, it took some time to trace the film as the film was made under another title in America (1947) *The Bachelor and the Bobby-Soxer* starring Cary Grant, Myrna Loy and Shirley Temple.

Although I had left school by this time, Pamela was still a pupil at Homelands Grammar School for girls as she stayed on until she was 18. I think I was a bit bowled over by her and she suddenly took over my life. She was great, grown up right from the start, light years ahead of me.

At this time I was still suffering from my terrible stammer, but it did not stop me from talking to her. It never affected me talking to friends or people I knew well, but as I have already mentioned, when I had to buy a fare on a bus, I could not start the word. I tried all sorts of things like talking rhythmically, stamping my foot, or changing the first word in a sentence at the very last moment. This latter ploy got me into real trouble one morning when I was at school. The register was alphabetical and, on this occasion, instead of the teacher calling out our names we had to concentrate and call out our surnames. The register started with 'Anderson Sir' and followed on until reaching 'Cook Sir'. D is always a difficult starter so I reversed at the last moment and called out 'Sir Dilkes'. The rest of the class enjoyed my brilliant unintended wit, but not our form master who rewarded it with a caning on the hands, which, being a pianist, was disturbing.

Back to Pamela. She lived at the opposite end of Derby on Morley Road, a suburb of Derby called Chaddesden and it was a walk of a good four miles if I missed the last bus. I could do it in about an hour, but I was fit in those days so more like a jog. The only thing was it was all downhill from Chaddesden into Derby and uphill to my home in St Albans Road. I was reluctant for some reason to tell Pam I had a motorbike but I soon tired of this secret and later would pick her up from home and school.

I was becoming more and more absorbed in music. Getting a place at university for academic studies was one thing, but to go to a music college was virtually impossible due to the lack of grant aid at that time. At the age of 15, having passed Grade 8 with the highest marks in the Midlands there was a vague mention that I would be entitled to tuition at Trinity College, but sadly nothing followed. This in more recent times gives such pupils the opportunity to attend the college and have Saturday tuition before being admitted full time at the age of 18. I did, however, continue with Stanley Mayes at the parish church and later went on to take my Associate Diploma at Trinity College. This was before doing my National Service and I was given a short deferment in order to do so.

Chapter 3

National Service and Beyond

1949–1955

Making up for lost time, freedom, Repton

1949

The dreaded letter came early in 1949 with a train timetable saying I had to report for duty in the RAMC on 17 March at Fleet, Hampshire. I remember going to the Midland railway station in Derby with a pass to take me there. The instructions made everything clear – change from King's Cross to Waterloo in London and details of the next leg of the journey. On arrival at Fleet there was an army lorry to pick up all the recruits, not only for Fleet but also for other regiments in Aldershot. There were several of us on the train from Derby, but no one I knew.

The first fortnight was a sorting out period. There were more than two hundred recruits and I have to compliment the army at this point for its organization. The very first thing was to issue us with army clothing, followed by packing our civilian clothing to be sent home. I think we were all affected by this feeling of separation. The next thing I recall was a trip to the barber for a haircut. I had long hair before this but it was all taken off, short back and sides, really short back and sides and not much on top either and then we stripped off and were literally hosed down. We had two weeks of examinations, medicals, fitness, general knowledge, colour recognition, and lecture after lecture about everything, but particularly hygiene.

The results of these tests were of course not made known to us, but the coding was set out on our identity cards. Later, working as a company office clerk I came to know what the coding given to each recruit meant. At the end of the fortnight we were re-sorted when we went on parade, and separated into groups of about twenty in each group being named as a 'squad', in my case E1 squad.

We were marched down to our new hut in which we each had a bed with blankets and, having been previously randomly mixed up, I found myself confronted with a new set of faces. It was a totally different environment; there were at least three if not four ex-public school boys and the general feeling somehow was better. I met a recruit, Donald Hunt, who was musical and an organist. He turned out to be an articled pupil to the then organist at Gloucester Cathedral, Herbert Sumsion, and through contacts he had been given permission to play the organ in Fleet parish church. We had not been allowed out of barracks for the first fortnight, but now if not on duty we were allowed to leave the camp until 11 p.m. He kindly took me with him to the church to play the organ and it had a profound effect. I thought I was pretty good until I heard Donald play. The term these days is 'gobsmacked' and I certainly was! I think at that moment I realized that this is how I would be playing if I had gone to Derby Cathedral. The friendship I had in that squad was rewarding. There were potential dental students and potential doctors. It was made known to our squad that, if interested, we could go on a course to become a commissioned officer. A few of us did successfully qualify, but the best offer was a second lieutenant in the Pioneer core, the labouring unit of the army – they dug trenches – I am not saying we would have been digging trenches as even that would have been better than being a private, but the thing they kept up their sleeve, and never told us until the last moment, was that we would have had to sign on for a minimum of, at the very least, five years, another three years. Nobody did so; we all remained privates.

I hated every minute of the army, but it taught me a lot for which I must be grateful. Not least, it cured the terrible stutter I had suffered from an early age. Being an only child I suppose I had also lived a somewhat protected life and was perhaps a bit spoilt. In addition, I am certain that my Baptist upbringing made my life even more sheltered. My parents were probably a little narrow minded regarding things like alcohol. There were talks about signing the pledge, but I do not believe my parents actually took that step. However, in the army I really saw life and came to meet people from a variety of backgrounds, which enabled me to see the world very differently once I left the service. I certainly learnt how to skive, a word much used in the army to describe avoiding an unwelcome chore. When told to scrub the corridor outside the office in which I worked, I would limit access at both ends of the passage and literally throw a bucket of water onto the floor. When inspected, it was assumed to have been done because it was wet. In our sleeping quarters we had a coal scuttle to fuel the heating stove in the middle of the Nissan hut which, to my recollection, was never used. The coal, incidentally, was painted white! Another skive was to have a duplicate set of belts and brass buckles, which could be purchased from the Army and Navy Stores, and used only for the daily inspections at our morning parade, thus avoiding having to polish daily. For the remainder of the day we would resort to the duplicate set, which was dealt with only when absolutely necessary. I never understood the army's logic here as the state of some equipment was painfully obvious but conveniently ignored by the authorities for the remainder of the day. More difficult to avoid was the question of haircuts. If on inspection, the parade sergeant said you needed a haircut you were ordered to step forward and were put on what we called 'jankers' for the day. This meant doing menial work such as washing dirty dishes in the cookhouse, to shovelling rubbish and emptying dustbins.

After the initial training period we could get a 36-hour pass every weekend. However, this was dependent on not being required for guard duty. The pass was valid from Saturday noon until parade on Monday morning, which meant travelling back Sunday but you could travel overnight. This was possible from Fleet to Derby and back, but in those days it took quite a long time. However, I did go home quite frequently, often getting back in the early hours of the Monday morning. The attraction of course was my girlfriend Pamela.

Having completed the 12-week training period, we were posted to either a hospital, field station, or perhaps regimental medical station. For this, we were assembled into a queue and took it in turn to receive our details. On reflection, it would seem logical to suppose that the decisions had already been taken and all we had to do was give our rank and number; however, the order in which we were being taken was random and all the personnel emerging from one queue were being given overseas postings, at that time mainly in Korea. I dreaded the prospect of having to 'see the world', so was relieved to learn that my posting was to York military hospital. I knew my duties were to be in administration and, on eventually arriving at the hospital in York, I found I was to be a company clerk. The company office was in the grounds of the hospital administering to the needs of personnel, which included company orders, leave decisions, postings, supplies and general company management. The officer in charge was not a medical man, neither was his staff sergeant. I was one of three clerks in the office and due to army regulations the office had to be guarded overnight, which meant seven nights a week sleeping in our day environment. The army has a real thing about 'guarding', and we had been made very conscious of this throughout our initial training.

Pamela started her college training in Leeds that September and I was able to travel by bus from time to time in the evening to meet her. There was, of course, nowhere to go – there were no facilities in her college in those pre-historic days, so on cold nights we had to resort to holding hands in the cinema. For weekends, we arranged for one person to do the overnight surveillances, which released the other two to take the weekend off from Saturday lunch until Monday morning reveille. I do not think I spent a single weekend in York when free! However, a trip to Derby had its drawbacks, although self-imposed. I would sometimes arrive before lunch – occasionally even getting away on the Friday night, there was a return train to York at midnight on Sundays so predictably this had to be the one I caught. My father would drive me to the Midland station in Derby for this and I would arrive in the early hours of Monday morning. Being unable to afford a taxi I would walk from the station to the Fulford Road, vowing I would catch an earlier train the next time. I never did!

I was ordered to go to Nocton Hall, an RAF hospital in Lincolnshire in October, which sadly deprived me of visiting Pam in Leeds. This journey took me by train from York to Lincoln, then by bus to Nocton and after a short walk I arrived at the entrance and walked down a long drive to the hall under the weight of my full army kit and personal possessions. Approaching the first newly constructed buildings built by the RAF to house personnel, I was greeted with the sight of scantily dressed WAFs (Women's Royal Air Force) swimming in a static water tank built for fire hydrants in case of an emergency. This was my first impression of (and I thought spoke well of) the RAF, which I now rated as the senior service. I never understood why it was necessary to have an army detachment on an RAF station, and confess never to have been interested enough in military matters to bother to find out. The mystery remains.

Here the weekend routine remained the same, except for departing from and arriving at the station in Lincoln. When I arrived at Lincoln station in the early hours of the morning I had to wait for a bus to take me to Nocton. I did this by 'kipping down' in the Salvation Army hostel in company with RAF boys making the same journey. They were a friendly group – we were all in this together so to speak. My work at the medical reception station mainly involved writing up clinical notes for the captain (a medical officer), in the office he and I shared with a lance corporal. The three of us were National Service conscripts and on Christian name terms (except in the presence of a higher authority). In general, I preferred the company of these people (perhaps because they were mixed) to that of those in the army. The food was definitely better and the dining facilities more comfortable. Early in the new year I was posted back to York and, after a very short time in the company office there, again found myself dealing with postings both in and out of York. One that caught my notice was the request for a clerk at the medical reception station at Normanton Barracks in Derby. Given that there was a move afoot at that time to post conscripts nearer to their home towns – I think that the regular army was now sick to death of them – I asked my boss, who had always been friendly, if I could put myself forward for the post, since Derby was my home town. He immediately agreed and I duly arranged my own tickets and passes, and swiftly changed places. The medical reception station at Normanton Barracks (well known to me from the outside) was captained by a conscript captain medical officer who lived in Bakewell, Derbyshire. I knew Bakewell and we became good friends. He had no objection to me living at home, so I only stayed in the barracks when I needed to be on overnight watch. Several other RAMC personnel with nursing duties did the same. On detachment we had a cook from the Royal Army Catering Corps and there was always work to do during this round of duty, such as peeling potatoes for our lunch the following day. The medical officer in charge was, if I remember correctly, Captain John Cowie and he too was a conscript, which means that on leaving school he had opted to read medicine and delay conscription with the promise of an officer rank if he qualified; this would follow a short spell working in general practice. This he had done as he still had a place in Bakewell after leaving National Service. In addition to his duties within, he was also involved in duties outside the barracks, requiring him periodically to examine war office invalids on injury pensions from the First World War. One involved him driving to Corfe Castle near Derby. On these occasions, he would take me with him and, knowing I had passed my motorcycle test, he sometimes allowed me to drive his army Morris commercial van in the castle grounds, possibly so that I could drive it if there were an emergency. This particular visit was to a now elderly woman, the daughter of the family stationed there during the First World War, who had been injured by a horse belonging to the Household Cavalry while assisting in the stables as part of the war effort.

Freedom

I remained in Derby until I was demobbed in September 1951. Pamela still had one more year at college so we had to remain apart until the summer of 1952. Terms were short but it was now her turn to make weekend trips to Derby.

Derby Borough Council was obliged to take me back on leaving National Service, but things had changed and there was now a National Health Service. I was given a job in the No. 1 Midland area finance office in the centre of Derby, and sent on a day release course to Derby Technical College during the week to take a qualification in accountancy. This took me back to the time when I left school and the frustration of seeing no future for me in music. My two friends, Bernard Lucas and Denis Evans had both chosen chemistry and were able to find work in their chosen subject, Bernard in a laboratory for a company making paint and Denis, specializing in metallurgy in the laboratories for a company making aeroplane engines, 'Rolls-Royce'. As a result of the 1944 Education Act both had continued their studies under the 'Day release' scheme at Derby Technical College, (now Derby University) and were by this time in their final years. I found myself re-united with my old friends and immediately joined the student union and able to enjoy an even wider friendship, however, I didn't envy Denis, as he still had to do his National Service. Bernard Lucas, due to an eye problem, was relieved of the upheaval. I renewed my position as assistant organist at the parish church and immediately set to work practising for my LTCL piano performer's diploma. I became a member of the Derby Music Club and was invited to take part in a recital for young artists in their venue in Derby art gallery. I was programmed to play a classical piano sonata but in the meantime took ill with jaundice so at the last moment played from memory Chopin's Polonaise No. 6 in A-flat Op. 53, a real show-off piece, ending with a frown from the secretary who had invited me to play but tumultuous applause from the audience. I met Thelma Marion, oboist who played at the same concert and who I later accompanied in recitals. She was in fact my first soloist with the

Kettering Symphony Orchestra after its formation. I later went on to pass the FTCL performers examination and was more than ever determined to advance my career. The question was – exactly how? I had a clearer idea but realized simply getting diplomas was not going to solve whatever the main problem was.

I had sold my motorbike and now turned my attention to owning a car. The first thing was to pass my driving test. There was a rapid growth in car ownership and my parents were keen to transfer to something on four wheels so, knowing that I was thinking of buying a car, my father suggested contributing towards me having driving lessons. I was well taught by the British School of Motoring and, after about four weeks' instruction, passed the test first time. I could now go ahead with my purchase as well as be available as the qualified driver to sit beside my father while he himself was practising.

During my National Service the army had recommended we sent home part of our army pay despite no longer living at home. This I had done, and my mother had very kindly kept the money in a bank account for me for when I was released. I was thus, with the sale of the bike, in a position to look for a car, resulting in the purchase of a 1928 Austin Swallow.

Renewing my links with the parish church in Derby, assisting Stanley Mayes and enjoying the four manual Willis organ was a joy, but I felt my life still fell short of my now wider knowledge of the world. Added to my schedule was a ladies' choir, which Stanley conducted and I accompanied and, as expected, I now took a greater part in services and weddings, but it was all at an amateur level. Because in those days, for tax reasons, it was an advantage to marry before the 4 April, we were so inundated with weddings that Stan and I would literally slide off the organ stool to take over from each other, with the outgoing voluntary becoming the incoming voluntary for the next.

I would never have learnt about the real world without National Service. Through mixing with conscripts from all walks of life, I came to recognise the social differences between people's parental backgrounds due to wealth and education. Looking back, gifts, such as those my father and indeed his brothers possessed, could not easily blossom without some gift from heaven. Until I joined the army, I had never shared a shower with another boy, nor indeed faced such heavy competition. Frankly, I never knew that such a lifestyle existed, but once I did I knew it had to be for me as well. I functioned well in the office and found myself executing important financial work, but music was still my main interest. W. C. Hulin, financial director of the Midland section of the health service was an amateur viola player, and played in the Derby String Orchestra, an orchestra formed by John Pritchard, when due to a lung problem I understand, was evacuated to Derby at the start of the war to work in insurance. He was an accomplished pianist and had lodgings in Bedford Street, which connected with St Albans Road. As a young boy my mother and I had passed the house where he lodged every time we walked to the Baptist church for my organ practices and we had paused on many occasions to listen to him playing his grand piano in the bay window of the house. He was befriended by a Derby man, Arthur Barlow, who brought some culture to Derby during the war years and organized concerts, which, if requiring an accompanist, would use John. I had attended some of those concerts. During his time in Derby, Pritchard formed the Derby String Orchestra and achieved enormous success with this, including the odd broadcast for the BBC Midland region. Having just mentioned Arthur Barlow, I am reminded of a concert in which I played when I was very young, probably nine or ten, and particularly as I was actually paid a fee. (I think it was half a crown.) It was exciting for me on two counts – I was taken by taxi to Ashbourne, and I featured in a concert playing a minuet and trio from memory that had won me the Derby Music Festival award that year. My father insisted on accompanying me in the taxi, later in my adult life I understood why!

After leaving the army I had explored the possibility of trying for a university place, but since I had neither matriculation nor a Higher School Certificate, I thought about doing a degree in music as an external student. This was a possibility through Durham University so I wrote to Arthur Hutchings, then professor of music, for his advice. He replied that I could take the university's entrance examination and, in view of the diplomas I already had, he would offer me a place as an organ student. I could do the entrance examination externally, and did so through a correspondence course.

I passed the examination, so could have taken a place at the university, but by now wanted to marry and not be away from Pam for another three years. After much deliberation I took an alternative route to qualify as a teacher. It was too late to consider my old ambition of being a concert pianist, particularly having by this time recognized that it was a lonely life practising all day on one's own. I therefore decided to compromise and reasoned that there were some excellent grammar schools in the country with well-established musical traditions and that it would be possible to combine such a post with a large church appointment with a good choir and perhaps a local choral society in the town.

Repton School

Events now took another turn when I saw an advertisement for a piano teacher at Repton School, a public school just outside Derby, in the evening *Derby Telegraph*. I gave Hulin's name as a referee, so he knew about my application and came to see me at my desk. Surprisingly, he invited me to visit him at his home, which was close to where we lived. It was a large detached house on the opposite side of Uttoxeter Road, which runs parallel to St Albans Road. He made me very welcome, but said he thought I was making a mistake because (i) I showed great promise in my present role; and (ii) he knew Mervyn Williams, the director of music, and had a low opinion of him, I think perhaps as a man rather than a musician. I do not regret ignoring his advice despite his judgement being correct.

I had an audition-cum-interview for Repton School with Mervyn Williams and was given the job, which I started a year after leaving the army. The journey to Repton, a village near Derby, was possible by bus but I had bought my first car, the 1928 Austin Swallow.

Pam finished college that July and we could now be together full time, both as teachers. The car was immediately put to good use when we drove to Cornwall for a touring holiday. We stayed mainly in B&Bs, but treated ourselves to the odd hotel. It was a fantastic fortnight and I doubt anyone could have seen more of Cornwall than we did. We drove down with several stops for the night, but returned in one day – quite a feat in such cramped conditions with so much luggage, plus the formidable challenge of the engine being unable to cope with powering the windscreen wiper when it rained heavily, especially on an incline; it needed assistance from a hand lever thoughtfully provided for such an emergency. We arrived home very late, but to an empty house as my parents had just left for their holiday.

At Repton, I enjoyed being surrounded by culture, which I had never known in such abundance. That I fitted in well was apparent, I think, from my social life there. I dined at the Mitre, in the bachelor staff quarters and attended social events that were part of public school life. This included dinner parties invitations to me and Pam from members of staff, particularly those interested in music.

Towards the end of my time at the school I left the music school late one evening, sat in the car and started the engine. Noticing a light under the bonnet I stepped out, lifted the hood and saw that the engine was on fire. The petrol tank 'gravity fed' the engine below and it was in serious danger. I ran back to the music school, but fortunately one of my colleagues had seen my plight and was already on his way with a fire extinguisher, which immediately extinguished the blaze. I had to resort to the bus service that evening but not before I had arranged for the garage to take over. The car was repaired and the bonnet repainted but I resolved to find an alternative vehicle. It turned out that Ken Fitzhugh (of Bennet & Sayers) was upgrading his car, an Austin 10 (Cambridge) – the name was also given to later cars – and the company would be selling it. In short I bought it and well in time for our scheduled marriage.

Pamela and I were married in April 1953 in St Werburgh's Church with my friend Denis Evans as our best man. We had the full choir and a full church, followed by a reception at the Friary Hotel, where I had spent so many of my Friday nights in the past with colleagues and old school friends – a short walk, or in our case taxi ride, away from the church. Knowing the ways of my friends, which of course had included me in the past, I took the precaution of not having my car parked in the hotel car park. There was a garage opposite with a car showroom so I arranged with the manager to garage my car the night before the wedding and organised a taxi to take us from the hotel after the reception, literally round the block, to pick up our car to drive to Bournemouth for our honeymoon. By the time we were ready to drive away, the guests had already started emerging from the hotel and, much to the disappointment of many, saw us driving away in our 'undecorated' car. When Denis, my best man, married some time later, he took a similar precaution after their wedding reception by catching a train for their honeymoon, but getting off at the next stop where their car awaited them.

On leaving Repton, I went as a student in September to St Peter's, a church college in Birmingham. Now married, we continued living with my parents at their house in St Albans Road sharing the kitchen and bathroom but having our own sitting room and bedroom. Pam changed her teaching position in Normanton to teach at the Practising School within easy walking distance from St Albans Road. Although I was absent during the week we were together every weekend, Birmingham to Derby being a short train journey. Terms were short and holidays long so the strain was bearable!

Although many of my fellow students were in their early twenties, we were not classed as mature students, as we had all suffered delays starting our studies due to National Service. During my time in Birmingham, I took organ lessons from Dr Willis Grant at Birmingham Cathedral, and sang in the City of Birmingham Choir and also the Bach Choir, which Willis conducted. I quickly, very quickly, joined the Donald Hunt class of player under his guidance. During the same period I attended classes in conducting at the Birmingham School of Music under Clarence Raybould, then conductor of the BBC Midland Light Orchestra. I hasten to add at this point, not because I had any thought or desire to conduct, but that it would be an added qualification should I be successful in becoming an organist and choirmaster of a church, possibly in a town with a choral society where I would be required to conduct with an orchestra.

In my early years attending orchestral concerts, I was not in awe of conductors other than perhaps to recognise their necessity. They were not, after all, playing the notes. My uncle Horace conducted the church choir, but I was much more impressed by his ability as an organist. It appeared to me that some people conducted simply because they could not play an instrument. I knew the names of several conductors as they were in the musical news and remember Uncle Eric talking about them and making comparisons, notably the three Bs – Barbirolli, Beecham and Boult, and also a fourth, Sargent. I subsequently met them all personally, apart from Beecham, but I did see him conduct on more than one occasion.

I was later to learn that conducting is a mysterious ability to 'direct', but I also believe it is imperative to be highly competent as an instrumentalist and, would add, one does not work without the other! We know of many very good instrumental players who fail miserably to direct even the smallest ensemble successfully.

During my college days attending concerts by the CBSO (City of Birmingham Symphony Orchestra) I was far more interested in what the players were doing, and even more in the case of the soloist in a concerto. My very first conducting experience came at college when I formed a chapel choir and conducted a setting in three parts (alto, tenor and bass) for choral evensongs. At this point, I was very interested in early music. Barry Grayson, our music lecturer, described all my compositions from then on as very 'churchy, Dilkes'.

I was able to practise on the chapel organ most days during my time at the college and so quickly built up a recital repertoire, which I was able to put to good use during my long vacations, including so-called 'away fixtures' in Mundesley and Trunch in Norfolk, where we spent our holidays.

However, I must not miss out on a brief mention of the continuation of National Service. When we left full-time service, we were immediately transferred to the Territorial Army, which meant continuing our training, one day a week at our local TA centre, in my case Derby. Again the atmosphere was regulars – 'we want to be here' – National Service, 'we do not want to be here,' but in all fairness both sides got on very well. At college I was exempt from the weekly meetings, but for four years had to attend a fortnight at a military base. On one occasion I caused a bit of a problem for our commanding officer. Having a car, I opted to drive myself to the campsite and naturally used the campsite car park. The unit was informed of a special parade to be inspected by some high ranking dignitary and working in the office I was well aware of the event. Our regimental sergeant major came into the tent in a flap because the car park had not been cleared. There was one solitary car, an Austin 10 in the car park – mine. He was curious to know to whom it belonged as the officers using the park had all obediently moved. He did not know it was mine, but I said it would be removed, which to his satisfaction it was as soon as I found where the others had moved to. Discipline was severely lacking among the 'regulars'. It has to be remembered that not only National Servicemen had to continue in the TA, but also older reservists who had actually fought in the war were part of the government scheme to be at the ready in case of further outbreaks. In many cases, soldiers who had been in active service were now serving under regulars, officers and non-commissioned ranks who had never seen action. If they arrived late on parade they would make it quite clear, 'So what?' On one occasion, we witnessed a member of our platoon leisurely walking past the parade to post a letter, totally ignoring the bellowing's of our sergeant major. On the last camp I attended we were assembled by the major in charge (a regular) who gave us a short speech in which he said he completely understood we had no desire to be there, and added, 'Gentlemen, if you play the game, so will I!' He continued, our duties would terminate each day at 16.00 hours and then we would be free until reveille the following day. We were in Yorkshire on the North York Moors National Park, a short journey to Ravenscroft on the coast where we spent most evenings. Earlier camps had been on Salisbury Plain. This was the last camp and proved to be the most interesting. In retrospect, it was more like an adventure holiday. On one occasion we were taken by lorry, confined so we could not see where we were going, given maps and compasses then dropped in small groups at various points on the moors. We were given a map reference for our rendezvous and told to find our way there. I was reminded of this experience many times later when off-shore sailing, first with the help of a radio direction finder and later of course with GPS, which made life much easier.

Another interesting game was when we were put in lorries, this time open, and told we would be attacked with orders to disperse widely to make us more difficult targets. Having no idea from where the attack would come, we sat in the truck and suddenly there was a roar overhead. Looking out the back we saw low flying RAF fighter bombers swooping down dropping bags of flour on the road ahead of the convoy, the spread of flour indicating a crater. Our drivers were skilled and left the road in both directions dispersing to any shelter we could find over open moorland. If readers have visited the North York Moors National Park they will know its history and its connection with the Royal Air Force.

Chapter 4

New Beginnings
1955–1964

Corby Grammar School, formation of the
Midland Sinfonia, conducting course

1955

I was appointed music master at Corby Grammar School, Northamptonshire. Corby, being a new town, made housing readily available to all teaching
staff at this new school, which opened in September 1955. Pamela and I
moved into a newly built semi-detached council house in Ashley Avenue.

Shortly after, and well before term started, we were visited by a Mrs Marie
Brudenell – I had difficulty with the name, which she announced with a pronounced 'county accent', but subsequently discovered she was the wife of
the squire of Deene Hall, a descendant of the 7th Earl of Cardigan who led
the Charge of the Light Brigade. She was also a governor of the grammar
school. I was told, (ordered) to rehearse her village choir weekly on a Tuesday
night in preparation for the village choir's competition at the annual Oundle
Music Festival of which she was president. I mention this in some detail
because it was really the start of my conducting career. The weekly rehearsal
earned me seven shillings and sixpence plus dinner at the hall. Dinner included Pam as she also sang in the choir. There was an interesting routine to
this meal as the pattern rarely changed. Mrs B always went to sleep and often
snored; the squire always pointed the carving knife at Pamela while asking
her if she would like meat or game, whichever was on the menu; and, finally,
as he knew we lived in Corby, did we know the rector there as I gather he
contributed to his stipend. However, before accepting – I doubt I had a
choice – I stipulated that I would like the choir to give an occasional concert,
perhaps in churches, which would not be too demanding as I would play
organ solos in the programmes. Everyone with a semblance of a voice was
required to sing in the choir, including the rector who immediately appointed

me as his organist in Deene village. I was already in contact with the rector of Corby parish church, who was also a school governor. For several years I gave a series of organ recitals in the parish church and the traditional nine lessons and carols with the school chapel choir at the end of the Christmas term.

1956

On one of our drives through local villages we came across a row of three derelict thatched cottages on a plot of ground in Gretton, a village just outside Corby, which we thought had potential if knocked together into one. We spoke to the landlord of the local pub to see if he knew the owner, called on him and asked if they were for sale. He turned out to be a builder who had purchased them with the same objective in mind. We said we were interested subject to viewing the interiors. He made it clear that if we decided to buy them it would be on the understanding that he would be given the work. We explained we would want to make them into a single residence and he kindly took us down to the site to view them along with the surrounding land. We were agreeably impressed and decided to take the matter further. His terms were £300 for the cottages and garden, that we employed him to renovate them and agreed to commission the architect with whom he normally worked. We decided to buy them and I got in touch with a solicitor in Kettering – Lamb & Holmes, to draw up the agreement. The senior partner at the time, Henry Lamb, I subsequently met on frequent occasions as he later became a staunch supporter of the Kettering Symphony Orchestra. Requiring capital for all this resulted in our selling the relatively new Ford Consul purchased when I left college. I replaced it with a second-hand Morris Minor Convertible. I had joined the Kettering Car Club and taken part in several rallies with the Consul, but now it had to be in the Morris Minor. I mention this because I had promised my grammar school colleagues that I would arrange a car mystery tour based on driving to a series of locations before arriving at a final meeting point. This went ahead shortly after we had completed on the cottages and I scheduled the rally to finish in Gretton. Everything went to plan and, since we had started clearing our very overgrown garden, a large amount of garden waste was waiting to be burnt. On our arrival, we lit the bonfire and were tucking into the food and drinks when we suddenly witnessed, at my expense and to everyone's amusement, the thatched roof of the middle cottage suddenly collapse (not on fire). It was of course of no consequence to us as we only ever intended the new roof to be tiled.

1957

From the outset of my arrival at the grammar school, I made it clear to everyone that music was just as important a subject as any other in the school curriculum and that it encompasses all aspects of learning.

First, it is a language, with which you can read, write and communicate. One simply starts with a line representing middle C on the piano keyboard, the space above is one note higher, and this continues with lines alternatively running through notes and notes occupying the spaces. In Britain, we use what we call 'tonic sol fah' – doh, ray, me, fa, so, la, te, doh. In teaching I would never resort to 'tonic sol fah' as it seemed more logical to me that each note has an alphabetical name anyway, so why complicate matters? And, indeed, the notes 'a to g' are clearly identifiable on a piano keyboard. Interestingly, the piano keyboard, along with other comparable keyboards, is the only instrument that displays the pitch of the sounds it makes. A better system than tonic sol fah, which is used on the continent, in the USA and possibly every other country, is 'tonic solfège'. The reader will instantly recognize why it is superior because all the notes on the keyboard, including the black ones, are represented. On this basis C is always 'doh' whereas in Britain the first note of any scale (and there are 15) is always 'doh', which is confusing and should in my opinion be eliminated. Note values can of course be taught later, involving simple maths. Second, it incorporates history because it has probably been part of us since we first existed, as it does geography, in that it includes every country in the world. It is also highly mathematical and, if you include wavelengths and acoustics, it even includes science.

At the first summer term staff meeting called to discuss end of term exams, I surprised my sceptical colleagues by convincing them that music needed to be included in the exam timetable. In fact, they were probably not that surprised because I had already secured my budget for the music department and persuaded the head to order hymn books that contained both the melody line and the words. These were to be given to each pupil and I said it would not be long before all could fully read them. I had also ordered about two dozen four-part hymn books. The assembly choir was four part as I included staff, some of whom as you would expect were musical. This assembly choir was also the chapel choir.

29 March – first grammar school concert

This was a choral concert for which I had established a school choral society. Being a co-ed school I had girls to sing as trebles and altos, and a small number of the older boys who were just out of the breaking voice phase to sing tenor and bass. As mentioned, several members of the staff already sang with me; others came to my rescue to balance what was to be a large chorus with one or two singing for the first time since their own school days. For this concert I needed an orchestra, and I should at this point say I had made a start at the beginning of my time at the school by first appointing a piano teacher to teach the piano in the school after 4 p.m. There were two pianos in the school, one in the hall and one in the music room. Annabel Mitchell lived in Corby and took on the job and, in return for the guaranteed work, she also agreed to accompany for me when I needed an accompanist. At the same time, I advertised for instrumental teachers to come to the school and teach in the evenings, first, a violin teacher, followed by clarinet, flute, and cello teachers. All came from Kettering. The school purchased several violins, clarinets and a cello, which the pupils could take home. It also purchased two timpani. I did not know of any other state school at that time that had what are now known as peripatetic teachers. I spoke to my newly appointed violin teacher Constance Chamberlayne about the possibility of getting together players to form the string section for an orchestra, which she did, and asked my flautist to organise the wind players. Most of the players who formed the orchestra for that first concert were from Kettering, with one or two from Corby, including one very good trumpet player. Thus, I had an orchestra I was going to conduct for the very first time.

After the concert, several of the players who had kindly given me their services said that they had enjoyed playing so much that they wondered if I would conduct them as an ongoing orchestra. Since the majority of the players were from Kettering, they would prefer to rehearse there and were prepared to contribute towards hiring a hall for rehearsals. I thought the matter over, reflecting I could probably use the grammar school for free, but on balance decided that since the bulk of the interested players did not come from Corby it made more sense to rehearse in Kettering. I resolved to investigate hiring a school hall and the County Education Authority suggested talking to the principal of the technical college. I arranged to meet him, and he surprised me by saying that it was a good idea and he thought that I should run the orchestra as an adult education course. He said that the players would need to register to attend, but that he would provide the accommodation and pay my lecturer's fee. The problem was solved in an instant. I contacted Freddie Baxter, one of the interested parties who had played bassoon in the ad hoc orchestra, and he said 'splendid, I will talk to the others and be in touch.' The Kettering Orchestral Society, later known as the Kettering Symphony Orchestra, was duly set up and commenced rehearsals in September 1957. I did not know it, but it was to be the start of an entirely new career. The first public concert took place in Kettering in the autumn of 1958.

Back to our cottages in Gretton

Under the guidance of our Italian architect, Seignor Picozzi, work was progressing well. I had drawn up our plans and we had made our brief very clear. On his valuable advice, we applied for an improvement grant and, following submission of the plans, were promised a generous grant from Northamptonshire County Council. Anticipating the move to Gretton, Pam moved from the school in Corby, where she had taught since our arrival there, to Gretton village school. This meant that for the summer term of 1957, she needed the car to drive to the village each day, whereas I could walk to the grammar school through a pleasant wood. There was, however, an incident when Pam drove into a ditch on her way home from school. A farmer kindly towed her out and there was no damage to the car, but I clearly upset her when, on hearing the news, rushed to see the car before showing any concern for her. I was unconvincing in my defence as I had said she looked in perfect health. The conversion of the cottages had seemed to take a long time but was eventually finished and we were able to move in during the half term to our now single converted detached cottage. That summer I drove her with my mother and father to Cornwall for our annual holiday. During the trip I recall Pamela not feeling well but it was a long journey and I had to make several stops due to the engine overheating, thus necessitating refilling the radiator. Finally, a garage mechanic told me that the thermostat was not functioning properly and, being unable to supply me with a spare, simply took it out. It provided me with a temporary solution. On our return, we decided to release a bit of capital and buy a used MGTC roadster. The autumn term was well under way when Pamela, still teaching at the village school, again felt unwell and this time decided to see our doctor. She made an evening appointment and waited for me to arrive home with the car to drive her back to Corby. I left Pamela at the surgery and walked to the school where I was able to fill in the time by playing tennis. Sometime later, Pam appeared outside the court where I was playing to whisper through the net that she was pregnant – our current sports-car lifestyle was clearly going to be short lived. However, we thought we would be able to put a carry cot behind the two front seats, which we eventually did. I, however, was finding the steering and road holding of the MG unsatisfactory and later replaced it with the newly announced Austin Healey (Frog-eyed) Sprite, still a two-seater.

Since boyhood, for as long as I can remember, I had an interest in boats. I loved our holidays at the seaside as a boy and remember it always being an eternity before the next holiday by the sea. Boats always fascinated me and I was equally excited by liners, fishing boats, even rowing boats. One day, while paging through some boating magazines in a dentist's waiting room, I was amazed to discover that ordinary people like us could own a boat. I knew about rowing boats of course, for I was forever pressing my father to take me on the lake or river, but to discover sailing dinghies and then boats you could actually sleep on was a revelation. It is therefore not surprising that one of the first things I did in my Corby days was to explore that interest further. Pam and I had joined Thrapston Sailing Club, but being unable to afford a new boat, purchased a quarter share in a club dinghy. This was in the days of mainly clinker built boats, but moulded ply and hard chine hulls had appeared. I particularly liked the National 12 (Clinker), but it was well beyond our means.

1958

Clare Vivienne was born on 6 March in Market Harborough Cottage Hospital. Pamela kindly invited her friend from schooldays, Vivienne Keenan (now Thacker), to look after me. I confess I would have been hopeless on my own. I visited Pam in hospital and was soon able to bring both of them home in the MG.

By this time, I was convinced that conducting was going to be my future, but without professional experience it was clearly going to be difficult. I read Sir Adrian Boult was running a master class for conductors in Bromley, Kent, applied and along with five or six others attended his classes for the week he had set aside. We had the daily use of a local amateur orchestra, which had some very good musicians in it and perhaps a few friends of his. We conducted in turn, listened to his advice and freely discussed our musical problems. Summing up at the end of the course, Sir Adrian said that it was a difficult profession to enter because the number of orchestras in the country was so limited, unlike the continent, and that we should content ourselves with doing our best with amateur choirs and orchestras of which there are many in Britain, but added that he knew not all of us would heed his advice, and I believe to this day, he looked at me. Sir Adrian did say to all of us, if we were likely to attend one of his concerts we would be welcome to sit in at his afternoon rehearsal. Just make yourselves known to my secretary who would be somewhere around. Interestingly, Rothwell, a small town close to Corby had occasional orchestral concerts and I remember following up his invitation when I saw that the LPO (London Philharmonic Orchestra) was playing in the church under Sir Adrian's direction. I attended his rehearsal and was inspired by the experience. There was later a second occasion, also in Rothwell, when I was able to repeat it.

1959

Having attended Sir Adrian's conducting class in Bromley, I decided to explore ways and means of getting on the conducting ladder. As far as I could see, there was no accepted route. Unlike all other professions, a qualification in your chosen career simply meant applying or answering an advertisement to the relevant organization. I was familiar with all the music magazines but do not recall ever seeing an advertisement for a conductor. There seemed only one thing to do, write and ask for an appointment. I ruled out the provincial orchestras as I knew that their conductors were fixtures, which left the four major London orchestras, which frequently engaged guest conductors. I wrote to them and received varied replies. One advised me to continue my valuable work at the amateur level; another expounded on the cost of assembling an orchestra for the benefit of an unknown conductor; and two, the London Philharmonic and the London Symphony Orchestra, invited me to meet their managers and I had friendly conversations with both. Since John Cruft of the LSO is going to appear many times in this book, I will provide some details of his interview. I believe that John had once played second oboe in the orchestra, but had opted to move into administration. This coincided with Colin Davies, who played in the orchestra, stepping in just before a concert performance of Mozart's *Don Giovanni* to replace Otto Klemperer who had been taken ill. Colin had fortunately just conducted stage performances with Chelsea Opera and so was familiar with the score. This turned out to be a lucky break for him because he was given more concerts with the orchestra. John Cruft said that this now gave him a hard schedule and why would anyone envy him as sometimes he had to work 12 hours a day to keep up with learning scores. It was a friendly interview and I remember my last words when I left his office, 'If there is ever an opportunity to conduct the orchestra I will work 24 hours a day!' I remember he smiled.

On the leisure front, our sailing experiences continued, but we now had a small baby and relied on bankside babysitters to look after her while we were learning the sailing basics by scooting around stretches of water that had once been gravel pits. From memory, I had only one capsize, but as usual I made a good job of it by sticking the mast in the mud. We sat on the upturned hull and awaited the arrival of the club rescue launch.

I think it was towards the end of 1959 that Stanley Vann's assistant organist was leaving his position at Peterborough Cathedral and Stanley said he would be pleased if I would take his place. He added that the position of director of music at the King's School was also becoming vacant and, although it would be subject to an interview with the school, he thought that I had a good chance of getting that appointment. This was a difficult decision for me to make as the opportunity was a stepping stone to my one time ambition of becoming a cathedral organist. I thought about this very carefully, discussed it with Pamela, but on reflection realize there was never any doubt what my decision would be, and was.

Following this, Pamela and I resolved it would be in my best interests to cut our overheads and move back to Corby. As a result, we put Fugue Cottage on the market and had completed the sale by the summer. However, in spite of it being supposedly safe to have intercourse while breastfeeding, we discovered Pamela was pregnant again. Rachel Maria was born on 7 September, so just before the move I took Pamela and Rachel to Rochdale to stay with her old college friend and husband, dropping Clare off in Derby to be looked after by her grandparents. I supervised the move and arranged to have a maisonette in Corby within easy reach of both the town centre and the grammar school. This was a three bedroom home and we were all reunited ready for the autumn term. With the capital we had secured from the sale of our Gretton cottage, I was able to buy a typewriter (a computer would be the equivalent these days) and a grand piano. The piano was a Bechstein (one size down from a concert grand). It was in London and belonged to Franz Reizenstein, who was born in Germany in 1911 but took refuge in England from 1934. He had formally been a pupil of Hindemith and Vaughan Williams and had contributed to the Hoffnung festival in 1958. The piano virtually filled the sitting/dining room, so we decided to use the largest of the three bedrooms as a TV lounge, leaving a bedroom for Clare and Rachel and the smallest bedroom for Pamela and me. My car by this time was a Jaguar XK 140 hard top, British racing green, which had two small bucket seats in the rear, perfect for our two daughters! It was a successful time for me at the grammar school following an upgrade to my head of department allowance.

1960

During 1960, several new staff joined, including Enid Hastings who came from Durham where she had sung principal roles in the Palatine Opera Group. She persuaded me to start an opera group in Corby, which I did under the name Opera da Camera. Rehearsals started that year with Haydn's 'Apothecary', the text of which Enid translated into English. There are four principals – soprano, mezzo soprano, tenor and baritone – sung by members of the staff with a small male three part chorus for which I used three sixth-form boys. Brian Stokes from Uppingham School produced the opera for us and, having heard there was an interesting new theatre in converted stables at Harpole Hall near Northampton, I approached Jessie Knight to see if she would be interested in our group performing there. She was, and our first performance took place in the stable theatre on 9 May 1960, from then on to become an annual event in May for the first performances of our annual season of opera. I directed and accompanied these performances from the piano in a tiny 'pit' in front of the stage.

In June I read that Hugo Rignold had been invited to take over the City of Birmingham Symphony Orchestra. As a student in Birmingham, I had attended many of the orchestra's concerts in the Town Hall and even sung with them when, as a student I was encouraged to sing in the City Choir – at the time under the direction of David Willcocks, then organist at Worcester Cathedral. I confess to having no interest in conducting at that time, and, when attending concerts, was far more interested in the concerto soloist and the players than in Rudolph Swartz who was the resident conductor at the time.

Reflecting on my time in Birmingham, I resolved to write to Hugo Rignold and ask him if he would mind me sitting in at some of his rehearsals and I received a welcoming invitation to do so. I met him, and his daughter, Jennifer from a first marriage, who was a ballet dancer at the Royal Opera House, but now devoted herself to acting as her father's manager. At the age of 14, then known as Jennifer Gay, she had become an announcer for the BBC's 'Children's Hour' programme. I was introduced to the manager and concert manger of the orchestra and informed of its routine commitments. There was a weekly Friday night symphony concert, which I decided to attend, and generally a full day's rehearsal in a nearby hall on the Wednesday before. This was no problem during school holidays, but what about term time? Although grammar school teachers had a generous number of free periods during the daily timetable, these were of course not generous enough to allow travel to Birmingham. I approached John Kempe with my problem and he kindly offered to have my timetable adjusted so that by lumping the free periods together I could drive to Birmingham at least in time for the afternoon rehearsal on the day of the concert and stay for the performance before returning to Corby. John also took into consideration the amount of 'out of school time' I spent with choirs and instrumental groups, but I never thought this was proportional to his generosity.

1961

On 14 April this year I conducted a concert with the Kettering Orchestra with Sylvia Cleaver as soloist in a Mozart violin concerto. She was chosen to play as she was a local (Northampton) girl who had achieved considerable success as a violinist in London leading the Georgian String Quartet and playing with the English Chamber Orchestra. After the concert she suggested that I conduct a professional orchestra. On explaining that I had already tried to obtain work with a number of orchestras but that I could not persuade any manager to offer me a concert, Sylvia said, 'Form your own. I will lead for you!'

A short time later I followed this up and she added that I could rely on her string quartet to be my principals, and she also knew a handful of free-lance professional players living in Birmingham, some of whom I already knew as they had come to play with the Kettering Symphony orchestra from time to time under a scheme operated by the National Federation of Music Societies, a branch of the Arts Council that supported amateur orchestras to fill gaps for concerts with what we knew as 'professional stiffening'.

Formation of the Midland Sinfonia

On this basis, I went ahead with the idea of forming my own professional orchestra. The Northern Sinfonia formed in 1958 was by this time established and I was able to arrange a meeting with its conductor Michael Hall through Louis Pearson, friend of Enid Hastings whom he visited most weekends in Corby. Louis was a music lecturer at St John's College in Durham and was chorus master of the Palatine Opera Group, of which Enid had been a member. Louis knew Michael Hall and arranged for us to meet. I have no recollection of learning anything from the meeting, but confess to thinking if a 'Northern' Sinfonia why not a 'Midland' Sinfonia?

Having been born in the Midlands it seemed logical to me to have the orchestra outside London and where better than a shared orchestra between Derby, Leicester and Nottingham. I knew the concert manager of the CBSO and he already helped me with musicians from the orchestra to provide 'professional stiffening' for the Kettering Orchestra. I had no problem extending this to include a few more to combine with London players who were 'fixed' by Sylvia. The orchestra's principals were the Georgian String Quartet, plus a bass player. Enid Hastings helped enormously and found friends and others prepared to guarantee the inevitable loss on the first concert to involve fees for the orchestra, hire of a concert hall, and publicity. Already known to the Arts Council through the National Federation of Music Societies, I had successfully engaged the odd important woodwind principal. I now approached the main body of the Arts Council to ask if it would be prepared to support a new orchestra in the Midlands. It expressed interest, stressing that such aid would be subject to required standards being met – first artistic standards, and second reliable administration. To start to meet its demands, I formed two companies – (1) the Midland Sinfonia Concert Society Ltd and (2) the Midland Sinfonia Orchestra Ltd, which had three shareholders, Keith Diggle, manager, David Cound, accountant and myself, music director. Having researched the constitution of London Chamber orchestras I followed the same lines. The society was a charitable company paying the fees of the orchestra. Both companies had directors, in the case of the Concert Society, artistic directors with Sir Max Bemrose, a Derby master printer, as chairman. Other members of the council either had an interest in music, as in the case of Bernard Lucas, an old school friend two years older than me, now successful in business was friendly with Sir Max Bemrose and had suggested he would be a good choice for chairman. He most certainly was. Other board members were all connected with the arts, namely Ivor Keys, professor of music, Nottingham University; Robin Wood, director of music, Uppingham School; Ray Thorpe, music adviser for Derbyshire; Philip Foulds, owner of the music shop in Derby and president of Derby Choral Society; John Neville, director of the Nottingham Playhouse; Bernard Lucas, managing director of Masons Paints and interested in the arts; and Philip Bromley, head of the design centre. At the start I did the administration with the help of a neighbour who had secretarial experience.

I was still making my weekly visits to Birmingham to go to the Friday night concerts in the Town Hall and sit in at the afternoon rehearsal. When free during holidays, I could also attend the mid-week rehearsals and I befriended several orchestral players, the orchestra's concert manager and of course the maestro himself. When the CBSO needed extra players for particularly large scale works it would employ local musicians from a very small number of professional musicians living in the city, some of whom I had met in Kettering. Colin Radcliffe, then concert manager, learning about my plan to form the Midland Sinfonia was more than happy to assist with fixing any extra musicians I needed for the Sinfonia.

This arrangement only later became a problem when the number of engagements increased, but I was helped for a time by the English Chamber Orchestra with which I became friendly during the Watney-Sargent Award year. Its secretary arranged for its 'fixer' to book musicians to fill our gaps.

I must mention at this point that to be a freelance musician in London demands not only the highest standard of playing but also flexibility. The rewards are high, but it is safe to say that they are the best sight-readers with the ability to play as an ensemble in the world, and it was these musicians who played in the Sinfonia. As the number of concerts increased we eventually acquired our own 'fixer' and, as was our tradition, paid London rates. Thus, we were something of an anomaly, basically a London orchestra but doing the bulk of our concerts in the Midlands and the balance in the provinces.

This in many ways replicated the experience of the London orchestras, apart from the contracted ones such as the BBC and Covent Garden. The history of the four symphony orchestras in London is interesting, but that is another story, suffice to say that only the last one, the Philharmonia, was not formed by someone who wanted to conduct. Each in turn became self governing when their founders abandoned them. Writing this in 2020, our wonderful 'kingdom' is becoming increasingly aware that England is more than just London. In the late 1970s there was still a great deal to learn.

When we learnt that Pamela was again 'with child', George Hattersley, our doctor, warned us not to undertake long car journeys but I, some considerable time before, had purchased tickets for Gyndebourne during the summer. We nevertheless chose to go and enjoyed a memorable performance of Beethoven's *Fidelio* with Gré Brouwenstijn, a Dutch singer singing the part of Leonora – hence we gave our third daughter that name. Lucia Gré was born on 29 August shortly after our return home. Pamela had wanted her to be called Lucy, but I disliked the name and we settled for Lucia Gré. Despite this, however, she has always just been known as Gré. I sold the Jaguar at this point and replaced it with a Red Austin Mini Estate, more practical for the addition to the family, now three girls.

The first concert by the Midland Sinfonia was in the King's Hall, Derby on 26 November 1961. Despite a large audience my guarantors had to pay out the total of their guarantees. The concert was a success and the Arts Council agreed to support the orchestra on the basis of matching pound for pound grants made by local authorities. The mathematics – one-third local authority grant, one-third Arts Council and one-third audience receipts. This was a successful formula that was to work well for several years.

However, with regard to the first concert, I confess to one on 17 November that actually preceded the debut as I used the same musicians to accompany a fifth school concert with the Corby Grammar School Choral Society. In addition to choral works, which included a rarely performed work by C. V. Stanford, namely Phaudrig Crohoore, I also encroached a little on the debut repertoire. I was made aware of what professional musicians could achieve with only one rehearsal the afternoon before a concert. Playing the notes was no problem for the musicians, but it was my responsibility to do everything else.

Earlier in the year, having decided to form a professional orchestra, I invited Keith Diggle, who taught maths at the grammar school, to manage the orchestra. Keith had actually been a student at the same college as myself in Birmingham but had arrived there a year or two after I left. Once established in the school he expressed his interest in jazz and demonstrated a real flair for arranging jazz concerts for the school. He formed a jazz club that was an amazing success.

I already had a music club in the school and knew that I now faced a real challenge. From the start, he managed the orchestra with equal gusto and enormous success. The board of the orchestra, as distinct from the Concert Society, comprised me, Keith Diggle, manager and David Cound, accountant.

1962

The orchestra achieved its first booking in Gloucester, on 29 January. Credit for this must go to my old friend Bernard Lucas who drove to Gloucester to meet the town clerk who had responded to our advertisement.

After an eventful 1961, I resigned from the Kettering Symphony Orchestra to concentrate on the Sinfonia, but my trips to Birmingham continued. I carried on with Opera da Camera and commenced preparing for our second opera – Cimarosa's *Il Matrimonio Segreto, The Secret Marriage*. For this opera, following the first performance at Harpole Hall with piano accompaniment, further performances were now with the orchestra for which I used Midland Sinfonia musicians. These were given in Corby and Uppingham School. Apart from Enid Hastings, who was highly competent, knowledgeable and experienced, I had seen the need to have trained singers and found these from Stamford, Derby, Loughborough and Wellingborough. Elizabeth Banks, a very experienced coloratura soprano, Michael (always known as Mike) Rayner, baritone, formerly head chorister at the Derby parish church where I had been assistant organist, David Cound, my accountant, formerly a chorister at Winchester Cathedral and now a director of the Sinfonia, Pauline Huckle, a soprano with considerable experience singing leading roles in light opera and finally Joy Singlehurst who lived just outside Corby and was a RADA trained actress with a good mezzo soprano voice. An impressive array of talent prepared to travel to Corby for a few music ensemble rehearsals, and later for the production rehearsals. Our producer continued to be Brian Stokes.

Music was not neglected at the grammar school and family life continued apace with weekend camping visits to Wells-next-the-Sea. I drove to London from time to time to see opera at Covent Garden and hear concerts at the Royal Festival Hall. I think about this time we had the new M1.

1963 Conducting course

On the advice of Hugo Rignold, I applied to the Netherlands Radio Union to attend its annual conductors' course during the summer term. John Kempe again came to my rescue by allowing me a full term away from school on condition I paid for my replacement. I recall my term's salary was paid in full. Sir Adrian Boult and Hugo Rignold supported my application for the course. About 25 applicants were selected to compete to become a 'working student' of which I was one of five to win a place. The remainder could stay on as auditors, but I do not recall any actually staying more than a week. The American conductor Dean Dixon was our tutor. I took Pam and my three daughters in our Mini estate car and rented a rectory in Bosum close to Hilversum. My fourth daughter was also there but still in her mum's tum. Rebecca Helen was born after our return on 30 August, daughter number four! I am reminded of the comment someone made that, 'It takes a man to have four daughters, but an idiot to have five.'

The course was directed by Dean Dixon, born in the Caribbean in January 1915. He defined his life in three phases – (i) the black American conductor, Dean Dixon; (ii) the American conductor Dean Dixon; and (iii) the conductor Dean Dixon. His instrument was the violin and, frustrated at not being able to conduct, a feeling with which many aspiring conductors are familiar, formed his own orchestra. He had a typical American approach to his work and was a great inspiration to me.

We had to explain all our directions or actions and I found myself having to put into words gestures that hitherto had always come completely naturally, for example my first beat to the orchestra, setting primarily the tempo but also the dynamic and the mood of the work. Time was also spent on how to handle pauses, changes in rhythms, or coping simultaneously with two or more different times. I was later very grateful for this discipline but for a short period after the course found myself nervous about things I had always found very easy like starts. However, he achieved what he wanted and, in a word, that was authority. I believe to this day in the power of the 'stick' and am acutely aware of how any professional orchestra will have got the measure of its conductor within 30 seconds of him mounting the rostrum. This is not to say one conducts every single beat and bar, but there are moments when an orchestra really does need a clear decisive beat. Dixon also proved that a difficult change in tempo needs delicate handling. One student failed to cope with an example of this and, after several attempts, Dixon gently took the student's arms and held them behind his back. With his left hand Dixon gave one clear down beat to the orchestra, which played the passage perfectly in a section of *The Three-Cornered Hat* by Manuel de Falla. I can't remember the bar number! My recollection of Hilversum Radio Union, the complex that housed five radio stations each having its own orchestra. One being a 'light' orchestra left four – symphony, philharmonic, medium, and a chamber orchestra, all of which were available in rotation for the course. Dixon very occasionally would ask the players to slip in the odd wrong note, rhythm or perhaps dynamic, but these were not regular tests. Interestingly, the four who were not conducting frequently found it easier to spot the deliberate mistake. I experienced one such test while conducting Wagner's *Siegfried Idyll*, when I thought something was not quite right. I asked for the passage to be repeated and thankfully it was still wrong as the flute was playing a section with the right notes but at the wrong pitch. It was cleverly chosen as it was not very obvious. Do not imagine that a conductor should be capable of spotting every mistake as this is not always the case. Classical, romantic and some contemporary music is straightforward enough but some modern music can be difficult. I understand that the French composer and conductor Pierre Boulez had an incredible ear even to the point of locating a single musician off pitch. I was told an interesting story later that when Stravinsky conducted his last concert in London in 1965, which included his *Firebird* suite No. 3 (revised in 1945), the principal of the clarinet section of the 'New' Philharmonia, as it was called for a short time following the death of Walter Legge its founder, suspected he had some wrong notes. He asked Stravinsky if he was playing the correct notes and was told he was. Still suspicious he stole a look at the full score during the interval in the rehearsal and discovered that his band part had been given the wrong transposition in one of the movements (a copyist or printer's error). Clarinets are 'transposing' instruments so parts are written to be played using either an A or B♭ instrument. The musician's band part indicates it is to be played on a B♭ or A instrument, so playing 'C' from a band part on a B♭ clarinet C will sound B♭. Written for an A clarinet C will sound 'A'. It was corrected before the concert, but interestingly I don't think had been noticed earlier at the first performance in New York.

As part of the course we were encouraged to attend an aural class on several evenings each week. Anyone who has taken a practical examination will know all about 'ear tests' as we knew them. A simple example of this is being able to recognise the interval between two differently pitched notes. This requires a basic knowledge of harmony, which, in turn, is based on various scales and key signatures. The scale of C major is the simplest to understand as, in the case of a keyboard instrument it does not include any of the back notes. C and E played simultaneously is identifiable as a third and being the first three notes of the 'major' scale the chord is known as a major third. However, if the E is changed to the black note immediately below, the sound changes to a 'minor' third. The test is to identify the chord without seeing it. Another test is to play a tune and identify the 'time signature'. Such tests are usually played by the examiner after a practical performance by the candidate on their chosen instrument. These tests are graded and become more advanced. I was familiar with such tests as I had undergone them at every stage, but I had never experienced being anything of the standard now expected. The first one I experienced was being asked to write a clarinet melody from a recording. First, the test was longer that I was used to and second, we were not told the key signature. I asked what the key signature was and he simply replied 'you decide'. Not having 'perfect pitch' I made a guess and wrote the tune down correctly for what I took to be a B flat clarinet. The tune was correct in both pitch and rhythm, but not surprisingly, it was in the wrong key. However, the other four students, two American, one German and one Dutch, all had them correct in every detail. I thus assumed they had perfect pitch, but none had and, in conversation with them afterwards, I learnt they had all been brought up with tonic solfège. At the first opportunity I purchased a middle C tuning fork, which I still treasure, and frequently during the day would remind myself of the pitch.

Earlier I described 'tonic sol fa' and the realization of this notation suddenly became completely apparent to me. In Britain, as I said earlier, doh is the first note of any scale. In Europe and the United States, and I suspect everywhere else, doh is always C, thus if one learns by this method the memory eventually associates doh with the pitch of middle C. I have since witnessed this as a result of working with French *animatrices* who lead the singing in churches. They frequently have no musical training but nevertheless know from memory all the settings of the mass. From time to time when playing for a service I was not given a score to accompany from, so would listen to what the tune was and hurriedly write it down to play harmonies to accompany them. Alternatively I could sometimes find the music in a folder, but the thing that astonished me in this case was that they were nearly always in the correct key. On reflection, I put this down to the fact that at school they learnt all their music for singing by solfège.

Chapter 5

Crossroads

1964–1967

A hectic year, Watney-Sargent Award, Russia

1964 A hectic year
Gulbenkian Trust

Early in the year I had decided that the Concert Society should apply to the Gulbenkian Trust for financial help. I avoided the usual routes like sponsored concerts or commissioning new works and made the point that, more than anything, we depended on good administration and a proper office from which to work.

The application, which was first made by letter, included full details of location, costs and forecasts. This was followed by Keith, David and me receiving an invitation to attend an interview at the trust's impressive office at 98 Portland Place, London W1. When we rang the bell a very well-dressed doorman admitted us to a spacious hallway, took our coats and, to our surprise, our briefcases containing copies of our application and other relevant information we thought would be needed to justify our cause. We were led into a spacious drawing room, the only evidence of it not being a drawing room was the very large desk behind which sat a distinguished immaculately dressed gentleman. He stood and leaned over to shake our hands. I observed his starched white cuffs with gold cufflinks, his immaculate appearance and completely empty desk top. The meeting was friendly, short and to the point. We shook hands, left, and subsequently heard that the trust would pay our full-time administration costs for the first three years. This was truly a gift from heaven.

Our decision to work from Nottingham had already been made on the grounds that we could best serve the East Midlands area of the country from there without treading on the toes of either the Hallé or City of Birmingham Symphony Orchestra. Other contenders were Derby, at the time still a town, and Leicester, then the most organized of the three in that it had a purpose-built concert hall, along with an entertainments manager who was already promoting regular concerts there. There were also several other factors that influenced our choice, not least the new Nottingham Playhouse, which had emerged as a very successful venture under its joint directors John Neville and Peter Ustinov. John Neville was invited to serve on our board of artistic directors and had joined Professor Ivor Keys, head of the university music faculty, Philip Bromley, head of the design centre in Nottingham, Philip Foulds, chairman of the Derby Choral Union who was also the proprietor of a successful music shop in Derby and had connections with Derby Education committee, and Raymond Thorpe, county music adviser for Derbyshire.

It was now left to Keith and me to terminate our contracts at Corby Grammar School. We decided that Keith would leave first in order to organize the Nottingham office, which was covered under the terms of the grant. My income could only be determined by the number of concerts we were successful enough to achieve.

On the home front

At the beginning of the year I must confess to arriving in the kitchen one morning to the spectacle of Clare and Rachel sitting at the table getting on with their breakfasts, Gré in her high chair banging a spoon heavily and not very musically on the board that prevented her escape, and baby Rebecca crying in her carry cot. The spectacle filled me with horror and made me wonder 'what have I done?' I realized that six of us in an apartment in Cromarty House was becoming uncivilized. We decided to move and, having got to know Stamford through Elizabeth Banks, my lead soprano in Opera da Camera, mentioned we might try to buy there. She immediately said that Freddie, her husband and the director of Williams & Cliff in Stamford, was trying to sell a Georgian house that the factory owned in St Mary's Street. The house had been used as a hospital during the war and subsequently as a hostel for some of its workers. We investigated it, saw its potential, and Pamela adored it, but it was in need of extensive improvement. We then established with Stamford Borough Council that we would qualify for a grant, so I successfully applied for a mortgage, still being in work at the time, did my own drawings for the improvements we wanted to make, and agreed to the purchase. My drawings, much to the amusement of the county architect, were to the wrong scale, which apparently confused him but they were passed and certified for a generous grant from the borough council.

The Watney-Sargent Award

Early in the year I remember being breathlessly interrupted by the school secretary during a music lesson in the grammar school to answer a telephone call from Sir Malcolm Sargent. The call was in response to my application to enter for the Watney-Sargent Award. He asked me to visit him at his residence in the Royal Albert Hall mansions, adjacent to the hall, at 10 a.m. the following Saturday. I drove to London a few days later and duly arrived on time. It was a relaxed and friendly meeting, our conversation being in general terms particularly since I was busy improving the house we had bought in Stamford earlier in the year and Sargent was born in Stamford and had been a pupil at Stamford School for Boys. His international fame had earlier secured him a freeman status of the town, which I gather allowed him to graze cows freely on the town meadow. Then followed the interview. We moved to his music room, which contained two Steinway concert grands interlocking so that two pianists could face each other (useful for rehearsing a piano concerto with the soloist playing the concerto, and in Sargent's case the conductor playing the orchestral accompaniment realized for the keyboard). He played me intervals on the piano, the first I said was a fourth – E to A. He said, 'Oh you have perfect pitch.' 'No,' I replied, and related my experience in Holland. This was followed by several other ear tests, one a four part chord. He asked me to identify the four notes adding which horn would play each note? This was a clever trap question as the score shows the four notes in the order of 1,3,2,4. The reason for this goes back to the time when horns did not have valves, so it was necessary to change the length of tubing according to the key signature. The advance of four horns frequently meant using both pitches, which resulted in 'dovetailing' them; however, even with the advent of valve horns, the tradition continued. I was not caught out! He finally handed me a baton and asked me to conduct, as if I were in the Royal Albert Hall, the national anthem with the 120-strong Royal Choral Society accompanied by a full orchestra. I think I included all the gestures he was looking for, first pointing to the timpani for the roll and then an indication with both hands (baton inverted) for the choir to stand, and finally the down beat with the baton conducting the picture rail in the room as if it were the choir, and not the orchestra. (A tradition we no longer afford to our Royal family!) This audition, if you can call it that, left me feeling he could not be convinced by it, but now after many years of experience myself, I would know immediately if I gave a similar test to an aspiring conductor. I left with the instructions to arrange Chopin's famous A major polonaise for full orchestra and send it to him by first post on Monday morning. I drove back to Stamford deciding how I would arrange the polonaise, and, realizing I would need orchestra size manuscript paper, deviated to the centre of Bedford to find a music shop and, with a sigh of relief, was able to purchase exactly what I needed. I stayed up most of the Saturday night and drove to Kettering on the Sunday night to post the finished arrangement.

There followed several meetings with Trevor Russell-Cobb of Public Relations Consultations in Bond Street, which were managing the award for the Watney Mann Group. Trevor was a very interesting person. He was born in 1918, educated privately and later became a piano student at the Royal College of Music. He had worked at the British Council and enrolled at London University as an external student taking two degrees – a BA in English in 1952 and then a B.Sc. (Econ) in 1956. This was followed by a job in Geneva for the United Nations, but he did not find international diplomacy a sufficient challenge so returned to London, his favourite city, finally setting up his own PR consultancy Russell-Cobb Ltd. He was a lieutenant-colonel in the Welsh Guards during the Second World War, a leading supporter of industry and author of *Paying the Piper: The Theory and Practice of Industrial Patronage* (1968). I remember several meetings with him and finally lunch in a London Hotel to which my wife Pamela was also invited. It is also possible that someone came to one of my concerts.

On 19 June, it was announced at a concert in Northampton that I had received the first Watney-Sargent Award. Guy Phipps Walker, chairman of Phipps Brewery, part of the Watney group, was also on the Watney board of directors and furthermore the chairman and owner of Walker Organs. At his request, I had played a Handel organ concerto with the Sinfonia at that concert and his company had provided the chamber organ for the occasion. The award was in the form of a bursary to enable me to travel and attend rehearsals and concerts with any orchestra at the BBC, as well as all the provincial and freelance ones – London Symphony, London Philharmonic, Royal Philharmonic and the Philharmonia. Trevor Russell-Cobb, personnel manager for Watneys, was also on the board of the English Chamber Orchestra where I was made particularly welcome. It was, however, too much to hope that I would replace its conductor, Raymond Leppard who at that time was shortly to leave, in competition with Daniel Barenboim, who had been associated with the orchestra for some time before. He will be remembered for marrying the cellist Jacqueline du Pré.

The award was subsequently presented to me by Edgar Palmer the chairman of the company in the presence of Sir Malcolm Sargent. This was on the top floor of a high-rise building from which we had a view of the gardens of Buckingham Palace, which I confess I found rather amusing.

A brief note on the short history of the award

Unfortunately, there does not appear to be a clear record of the candidates and selection process. As the first recipient, I recall an advertisement in the national press to which I applied. There is no record of my immediate successor, possibly due to Sargent's deteriorating health – he died on 3 October 1967. However, there was a winner in 1967, Leonard Atherton. I cannot say if Sir Malcolm chose him, but I understand that Sargent suggested he should be succeeded by Sir John Barbirolli, who certainly made the choice in 1969. This was Oliver Knussen. In 1970, the award went to Barry Wordsworth, formerly conductor of the BBC Concert Orchestra and subsequently the Royal Ballet. I spoke to Barry and he told me that he was first recommended for the award by the principal of the Royal College of Music, where he was a student and was subsequently interviewed by Barbirolli. However, before the award was actually made, Barbirolli died and it was left to his widow Lady Barbirolli, better known in the music world as Evelyn Rothwell, a solo oboist. She called Barry on the telephone and said there had been two candidates, but she thought Barry may have been his first choice. However, would he be happy if they shared the prize? This turned out to be the result. My impression was, talking to Barry, that they did not share the same grilling that I suffered.

27 June

John Kempe, chairman of the appeals committee for a youth centre in Corby, organized a pageant at Rockingham Castle. He invited Michael Fraser, a gifted actor and producer and member of the grammar school staff, to provide the script. The setting was superb and success seemed certain, unless it rained. A fortnight before, the script writer declared his inability to provide the script in time so a new plan was called for. I stepped into the breach with my Opera da Camera group and we staged our latest opera, Bizet's *Dr Miracle* with orchestra, which we had recently performed in May in a double bill with Weber's opera *Abu Hassan*.

Leaving teaching

It was sad to leave Corby Grammar School. The situation was that, because of the Gulbenkian grant, Keith had handed in his notice and moved to Nottingham. I had decided not to leave teaching until there were enough concerts to support us, but now, as a result of the award, I gave notice to leave at the end of the year. Corby Grammar School was a great success under the superb leadership of John Kempe who, in my opinion, with a public school background, bridged the gap between the commoner and the aristocracy. The school, which was anything but public in the class sense, was nevertheless run on public school lines. To illustrate this point, I remember following a theft in the school when John failed to punish a pupil after taking his word that he was not guilty. I did not share the opinion of several members of staff who saw this as a weakness and not a strength. I had spent a short time teaching the piano at Repton School and had already decided that there are two ways of living our lives – (i) as a lord, or (ii) as a tramp. Needless to say, I preferred the 'lord' option! I benefited a great deal from my time in Corby as it was a NEW TOWN and populated by young people. With so little social history, Corby did not appeal to already established professional elites, but it offered opportunities to the younger generation of doctors, dentists, town clerks, and architects who, in established towns, and particularly in later life, were usually fixed in their ways, which certainly did not apply to Corby. There was, in fact, little to do in the town, so we resorted to being friendly. We were in it, so to speak, together. Bridge was a popular pastime and friendly dinner parties took place frequently with the new young elite.

It is worth noting that several of my colleagues at the school went on to achieve great success after their time in Corby, some with headships, others like Keith Diggle, first to manage the Sinfonia, and later in publishing and an international authority on arts marketing. Colin Dexter, a classics scholar became a well-known crime writer renowned for his *Inspector Morse* detective novels, which were also extensively filmed on television. John Kempe finally left in 1967 at the invitation of the Royal Household to become headmaster of Gordonstoun School in Scotland and responsible for the education of our royal princes.

John kindly wrote this of me in his book *Memory's Truth*:

Neville Dilkes had built up a remarkable school music tradition and had founded orchestras in Corby and Kettering with his wife's help. He was ambitious and had presence and ability to conduct a professional orchestra. When he stepped up to the conductor's stand aside a long (cultivated) lock of hair with an airy gesture, he exuded the confidence of a professional of long experience who knew what he was doing. A habit of swallowing when he was about to make an announcement might have given the impression of nervousness, but a volley of words starting like a hiccough and exploding like a load of shrapnel, belched forth and the music started. When he told me he was leaving I thought he would be irreplaceable.

Looking back, my biggest regret, and I cannot for the life of me account for it, is that I did not thank Hugo Rignold in the way I should have done. I had the greatest respect for him as a conductor and, perhaps more importantly, also as a man. I learnt a tremendous amount about conducting technique watching and listening to him during rehearsals and many happy hours talking with him between rehearsals and concerts, sometimes over a light meal. There was an occasion when he invited me to his afternoon rehearsal and concert at the Royal Festival Hall with the LSO. There was a considerable reverence surrounding this orchestra and I remember Hugo Rignold, when engaged to conduct them, was surprisingly excited at the prospect. My learning curve shot up steeply that day. Hugo seemed to have very little feedback from the orchestra, for which I was later to be given the reason during the break. He was rehearsing a concert they had played many times under its resident conductor during a tour in Europe from which they had only just returned. The concert was a great success, but I knew he was frustrated. He himself was a string player and taught me how to achieve certain nuances with strings, which I was to use for the rest of my life. He had appointed a new leader to the CBSO – John Georgiardis – who at the time I think came straight from college. Hugo knew that he was a brilliant violinist and leader, which became evident to the profession in due course. John has since crossed my path on several occasions, especially when he stood in as leader of the Sinfonia, a notable occasion when he led for Schoenberg's *Verkläte Nacht* with just the afternoon rehearsal.

I would occasionally park Hugo's car for him – it was a Jenson. But, most importantly, I had an opportunity to conduct the CBSO. The orchestra was large enough to be split into two, which was perfect for giving concerts on the same night in neighbouring suburbs such as Edgbaston, Moseley and others. This was a joy as quite a few of the players had already worked with me in the early days of the Sinfonia. Harold Grey, Hugo's assistant, conducted the other half of the orchestra on these occasions, and had experienced seeing CBSO players in the Midland Sinfonia in the early days as he conducted the Derby Choral Union, which, thanks to Philip Foulds, the choir's president and member of the Sinfonia's Artistic Council, engaged the Sinfonia to accompany its concerts.

My route to any success may have been changed had I retained my interest in the CBSO, but there is a faint mitigating factor that goes back to the time I spent in Bournemouth during my award year. Shortly before I stopped my visits to Birmingham, the general manger of the orchestra had died. He was replaced by Arthur Baker, formerly the concert manager of the Bournemouth Symphony Orchestra. The orchestra's general manager, Kenneth Matchett knew of my connection with Birmingham through his former concert manager, Arthur Baker, and was horrified to learn from him that I had used CBSO players in the early days of the Sinfonia. I was happy to argue with Ken about this, pointing out that we also used players from the BBC Midland Light Orchestra when it existed. I think that Ken took the matter much more seriously than I ever imagined at the time and he vowed he would never allow this to happen in Bournemouth. He proved this shortly after by forming the Bournemouth Sinfonietta, using his own players to give other concerts in the region and thus avoiding the likelihood of potential competition. I realized the essential difference between orchestral music in London and orchestral music in the provinces. My affinities were decidedly London but I had lived, and continued to live, in the provinces.

Arthur Baker's management, along with Hugo Rignold's replacement of the French conductor Louis Frémaux, finally came to a precipitous end.

The award was a crossroads for me, a chance to move freely in the world of orchestras, but with a bursary worth only half my teaching income, most of which would be spent on travel and expenses. Also, I had the impending move to the house in Stamford currently being renovated. Regarding this I should mention about this time we had a visit from Bernard Lucas, an old 'centaur' and member of our artistic council. Knowing he would be interested, we showed him the Stamford house. Bernard started work in the laboratory at Masons paint making company in Derby and in a very short space of time had moved up to become the company's managing director. It supplied Rolls Royce with the paint for its cars and had a reputation for producing the best range of black paint in the country. This was always a joke but apparently true. Bernard told me he had recently appointed a colour consultant and, provided we agreed to buy their paint, would send her to Stamford to advise us on a colour scheme. She spent a day in the house and sent us a folder with everything down to the last detail. The ground-floor room with its bay window visible in the photograph, had wood panelling to the chair rail. The wall above to the ceiling was a stretched fabric, which I confess I had not realized. Every wall, door and wooden feature was itemized with full instructions and, in the case of the panelled doors, the moulding was to be picked out. The book also contained examples of wallpaper to match the paintwork and suggestions about furniture, which I mention because it provided me with an interest that has remained to this day. She suggested visually breaking the chair rail by standing a longcase clock against the wall. The Stamford decorators were very generous in their praise for the paint with which they found themselves working, but confessed they had never heard of it. The sequel to this was that the next time we visited Derby it was to go into an antique shop and purchase a longcase clock made by Whitehurst Derby, which I later discovered has the reputation of being one of Britain's leading clockmakers. The purchase excited my mother as it transpired that her father had worked for the company in Derby following his apprenticeship in Coventry. Furthermore, she had been left bits and pieces from his workshop that she gave to me. When we eventually moved to Stamford we started to visit the local salerooms and was surprised to witness several longcase clocks selling for next to nothing. I bought one, joined the Antiquarian Horological Society, read its magazines, and learnt about famous clock makers and their values. With the help of a local clock maker, I restored the one I had bought at the sale, polished its case and returned it to the saleroom to sell at a profit in order to buy an even better one next time. Later, when passing through a nearby village, Folkingham near Bourne, Pamela and I saw a notice outside the manor house announcing that its contents were for sale and on view that day. There was a longcase clock in the hall, which I observed was a Knibb. The sale was due to take place a few days later and we went. I said, to Pam's horror, that we should bid up to £700. The bank allowed me an overdraft of £800 at that time, but to my surprise the clock finally sold for more than £1,000. Several months later, I am certain that the same clock was advertised in the Horological Society's magazine for £1,750.

Returning to our change of location, Pamela came to the rescue without hesitation and took the decision to return to teaching. With the kind help of Heather Diggle, Keith's wife, who was able to recommend a former pupil of hers, Rosemary Pheasant became our resident child minder.

Move to Stamford: 1965

We moved to Stamford before the work was completely finished and, to make ends meet, Pamela returned to teaching, this time at Uffington primary school just outside Stamford. Being out of work, I tried for the dole and was asked to go before a committee in Grantham to asses my case. I placed before it all the facts, the award and my likely expenditure, and it granted me benefits for the year.

At this time I changed the Mini estate car for a new Mini, it being the fashion at that time to keep a high mileage car only for a short time and sell for the least depreciation. It was, however, some time before I was able to afford a second car. This occurred later, shortly after the orchestra purchased a Morley single manual harpsichord, which I was able to transport and keep at home. After another year the Mini saloon was replaced with an MG Healey 'Sprite', a more up-to-date version of the original having wind-up windows, proper boot and moulded-in headlamps. Continuing the car saga, my next two cars were larger front bench seat Ford Estates with the gear change on the steering wheel, thus allowing us to seat six comfortably.

Having moved to Stamford we left the sailing club, but my interest in sailing never flagged. I continued to read the yachting press and kept up with developments in the yachting world. There was a trickle of concerts for the Midland Sinfonia, with, as previously mentioned, the first outside engagement being with the Gloucester City Council. The orchestra had also been engaged to play at the Anglesey Festival conducted by Sir Charles Groves. I attended the concert and remember a wonderful performance of *Il maestro di Capella* with Sir Geraint Evans as the maestro, which Charles directed from a harpsichord. The orchestra is reversed on the platform so the soloist – the maestro – faces the audience, which can see all his grimaces and gestures.

With regard to my award, I was required to give a monthly account of my visits and meetings with conductors. Somewhere copies may exist, but

I very much regret I did not keep a record myself. I reserved the final weeks to attend Sargent's rehearsals at the BBC Maida Vale Studios and the Royal Albert Hall for the promenade concerts. Before this, however, I spent a month with the Bournemouth Symphony Orchestra under the baton of Alan Sylvestri and later had the pleasure of conducting the orchestra at the end of the award year. While in London, I had decided to find my own accommodation and rented a house in the north of the city from four university students who were happy to be relieved of the responsibility during the summer vacation. Having my own accommodation, I was able to take my family there from time to time and, on one occasion, remember meeting Sargent at a bus stop in Kensington – he was just about to cross the road – but saw me, and met Clare and Rachel. He gave them each half a crown, 2/6d. 'Who was that nice man?' they asked. For his concerts, I had a seat reserved for all those I wished to attend and was always welcome in the green room before and after the performance. There I met soloists and many of the maestro's distinguished friends and guests, including royalty, MPs, eminent writers and broadcasters. It was absolutely mind boggling! I especially remember Lord Boothby who was frequently in the news over his politics, affairs with prime ministers' wives and, though clearly heterosexual, staunch support for the rights of homosexuals in parliamentary debates. Looking back, I acknowledge my own shortcomings with regard to the subject of homosexuality and now fully recognise how naïve my working-class upbringing, not to mention Baptist influence, had left me. I can recall countless instances during my professional career when I failed to overcome my inability to befriend homosexuals, despite our differences. This topic could take up considerable space.

At that time, the Proms series was shorter than at present and nearly all the concerts were played by the BBC Symphony Orchestra under Sargent, who resurrected the series after its founder, Sir Henry Wood died. He closely followed Wood's arrangement of the sea shanties, which still conclude the last concert.

This was also an action packed year with Sinfonia concerts interspersed throughout. The particular climax of the year was when Watneys arranged with Phipps Brewery to sponsor a concert with the Bournemouth Symphony Orchestra for me to mark the end of my year. This was given in Franklin's Gardens, Northampton on 22 June.

1966

The year 1966 marked the opening of the Midland Sinfonia's Nottingham office at 66 St James's Street on 19 July. Keith had successfully increased grants to provide concerts for the orchestra. Nottingham City Council generously supported the orchestra in return for a monthly series of concerts and this was followed by Keith's County Plan, which involved even small local authorities contributing by way of a grant for which, in return, the orchestra would give a concert in a local venue such as a town or village hall or parish church. The concert could be tailored to fit the size of the grant. This would range from as few as 11 strings, sometimes plus wind players, to a chamber orchestra of some 35 musicians. We made full use of the Gulbenkian grant for the three years to cover administrative costs and office accommodation.

During this period I recall receiving an unexpected visit from Eric Thompson of the Arts Council at the house we had quite recently moved into in Stamford. I was out at the time but our child minder confirmed that I would be home any time. I understood he was suitably entertained by three of my daughters with a ballet dance demonstration. He told me that the council was very impressed with my programmes for our first season of concerts in Nottingham since opening the office and went on to inform me that the newly formed Ulster orchestra was looking for a conductor and asked if I would be interested. I was, but knew it would involve toing and froing between Belfast and Nottingham, but was aware that many conductors lived this sort of life. Hugo Rignold, after all, lived in London and commuted to Birmingham not to mention a whirlwind of other destinations. I subsequently learnt that Maurice Miles had taken the position.

We were made very welcome in Nottingham, with the exception of the Nottingham Harmonic Society, which I know Keith Diggle had approached in the hope that it would engage the Sinfonia to accompany the choir in its concerts, but it never did. The orchestra had already been hired to accompany the Derby Choral Union and we had hoped for a similar relationship with Noel Cox, the conductor of the Harmonic Society Choir, which was well established in the city when we arrived there. That there was a clash of interests, I believe, was reinforced later when the choir refused to partake in the Beethoven choral symphony under my direction at a later festival concert.

The Nottingham Playhouse had previously opened under the direction of John Neville, whom we had invited onto our board and with whom we subsequently worked closely. Performances needed to be outside the theatre's timetable, so were mostly held on Sunday nights. The Playhouse was very good with its publicity and John had a good relationship with Heather and Keith, who were both keen and knowledgeable about the theatre. Nottingham is well known for its annual Goose Fair and the Playhouse always took a stand there. John asked me if I would play the piano for any musical items they decided to stage, which I was happy to do. He and his players were incredibly versatile and I happily watched some of the funniest slapstick comedy I had ever seen. There was indeed no shortage of publicity either for the Playhouse or the Sinfonia.

Success breeds success, this time in the form of 'sponsorship', which Keith successfully negotiated with John Player, the Nottingham-based cigarette manufacturers. I subsequently met the chairman, Tony Garrett, together with his wife Marie, and we became close friends. Tony became a staunch supporter of the orchestra and this sponsorship continued for many years, indeed until a short time after his departure to become chairman of Imperial Tobacco. The sponsorship included London concerts and our first liaison with EMI to make our first recording.

Russia

Before this, however, I was invited to conduct the Byelorussian State Orchestra in Minsk. Nottingham was associated (twinned I suppose in modern terms) with Minsk, the capital of Byelorussia (now Belarus), through the British–Soviet Friendship Society. I spent two interesting weeks in Minsk for the rehearsals and concerts, then for the middle weekend went to Moscow as a cultural guest. The Friendship Society paid my fare on condition I travelled over land rather than by air. My first experience of the division between East and West was on reaching Berlin and being struck by the blaze of lights to the west of the wall and the total blackness to the east. The train was boarded by Russian guards doing their routine checks before we were allowed to continue. We travelled across Poland, passing through Warsaw to the border town of Brest (Belarus.) This stop was necessary to change the carriages to fit the different railway line gauge. We were ordered to leave our baggage as the coaches were just craned from one set of wheels to the next. We were moved into a very cold reception hut and again had to verify our identity and reason for travel. I had been advised by the Friendship Society to send my main luggage ahead, so I was travelling with just an overnight bag. This was viewed with suspicion and I was made to go into an adjoining room for further questioning. When I explained that I was a cultural guest of their country and was conducting one of their orchestras, I found myself suddenly a very important visitor. I was taken to a warm comfortable room with full hospitality. Back on the train, I went to bed until we finally arrived in Minsk in the early hours of the morning. The station was deserted and I emerged onto an empty snowy street. I had expected someone from the orchestra to have been there to meet me, but the town was deserted save for a solitary young woman waiting for a bus with a cello case at her side. I spoke to her in English and was staggered that she was able to reply in kind. I had assumed she was probably a member of the Minx orchestra, but she was not. She was a cellist in the Moscow Chamber Orchestra, of which I have recordings under its conductor Rudolph Barshai, whom she said I would meet in a few minutes as he was due to join her. They had played a concert the previous night and were returning to Moscow that day. When he arrived we talked, again in English, and, knowing the orchestra and manager, he accompanied me in a taxi to the orchestra's office where I met an apologetic manager who had not been informed of my ETA. They certainly made up for the inconvenience they had caused me. I was curious to know if my suitcase had arrived with everything I needed, including evening dress, but I was to be deprived of this for several days. It eventually turned up and had clearly been emptied and thoroughly examined. It was not long before I met the orchestra and had the luxury of several days of rehearsals – unknown in England – they were so incredibly friendly and wanted only to please me. A measure of their keenness was that, at the end of my rehearsals they would to go off to the practice rooms and work on their sections – so intent were they to please the maestro.

My schedule gave me an extended weekend in Moscow as a cultural guest. I recall being met off the train by a young man associated with the Friendship Society. He took me via a very large, impressive looking hotel, which he referred to as 'the American', before crossing the square to the equally impressive but more traditional Hotel National where I was to stay. He arranged for me to see my bedroom and, walking up the very grand staircase, I was struck by the similarity of everything to my hotel in Minsk. The same carpets, the same landing between floors with a concierge seated at a table where I had to reveal my identity. He said he would meet me in 30 minutes in the reception area which, after unpacking, I did. Feeling like a celebrity, I eventually descended this magnificent stairway with an aerial view of every-one and could not fail to notice a beautiful looking female standing and talking to my friend – or should I say 'comrade'? Oh to have her as my guide thought I, and she *was*! She spoke perfect English with an American accent, of course, and I was told that she would be at my side all day. She had an itinerary to which I could agree or not, and I could eat and drink anything at anytime I chose. I was somewhat overawed by this treatment and asked for suggestions. I took her advice and we visited sculptures, an artist's colony and the composers' union where, among others, I met the composer Shostakovich, this actually in the subway as I was leaving. It was action packed and a relief to enjoy the calm of an art gallery or museum. However, there were two highlights. One was attending a special performance based on the original Stanislevsky production of Tchaikovsky's opera *Eugene Onegin* in the Bolshoi Theatre featuring the original scenery, production notes and costumes. The other was a performance of the opera *Carmen* in the magnifi-cent concert hall/theatre. Champagne in the interval failed to convince me that the performance was very 'Spanish!' Russian hospitality was good and, despite the obvious vigilance, I must say friendly. I think that I successfully convinced my interpreter that we did not live in Dickensian times in Britain, contrary to what she had been led to believe. On my return to Minsk I renewed my rehearsals with the orchestra and must relate an interesting story with regard to the programme, which incidentally included a 'first' perfor-mance of the Second Symphony by the Russian composer Glebov, the full score of which I only saw for the first time on my arrival. Before leaving England, I had taken advice from Sargent about working with a foreign orchestra, and he advised me, if possible, to take my own band parts as they could be edited with any special requirements I might need. I already knew Sargent kept his own library of band parts as they were bowed and marked exactly as he wanted them performed. I also knew that John Barbirolli insisted on the Hallé library containing all the parts for the orchestra in duplicate – one set for his use only. This saves rehearsal time and facilitates 'repertoire' concerts on just one three-hour session (or sometimes not even that). I was asked to conduct Britten's *Young Person's Guide to the Orchestra* while in Minsk, so knowing the orchestra would not have this work in its repertoire, I spoke to the librarian at Boosey & Hawkes with regard to hiring the parts. It is normal to state the venue of the performance for royalty purposes. When I did he could not authorize this as a performance of this work was still under copyright and the Russians refused to pay the West any royalties. I mistakenly thought there would be a change of programme; but no, the orchestral librarian in Minsk had all the parts hand copied, presumably from a miniature score. Good thinking? No! It is easy to make mistakes, and hand written music is never easy on the eye. I spent a considerable amount of time having to stop the orchestra to correct wrong notes.

The members of the orchestra were very warm to my presence and there was a wonderful atmosphere of friendship through the music. To show their appreciation, and to my embarrassment, they presented me with a generous cash gift, in roubles of course. At that time it was a serious offence to use any other currency in the Soviet Union. There was no way I could convert this to sterling, so I purchased a handsome amber necklace for Pamela and treated myself to a gold wristwatch. The necklace is now in the possession of one of my daughters. The wristwatch functioned for about two years and was deemed by our watchmaker at the time in Stamford to be rubbishy, but he acknowledged the gold was worth its weight, so credited me with its value and sold me a replacement that I still wear to this day.

I enjoyed the experience of Russia in every way but was glad to escape. I was faced with the return overland to England and duly boarded the train from Minsk to Calais. The train was very crowded and the compartment I occupied was mainly of women. I slept in a middle bunk which was smelly and airless so, on the final day of the journey, I walked to the front of the train where there was no overnight accommodation and found myself in the company of young Americans returning from the Far East. To my surprise, the train arrived at the Hook of Holland and, on questioning a porter, I learnt that the front coaches had been detached at some point for precisely that purpose. I decided that my best move would be to leave the train and buy a ticket for the Hook to Harwich crossing, which I did, but had no time to ring Pamela who had arranged to meet me at Waterloo in London. I explained my plight at the reception desk on the ferry and was taken to the bridge where I was given a line from the North Sea to home to explain the change of plan. Pamela duly met me at Liverpool Street station and we stayed the night in London before driving home the following day.

On 22 April, Vitaly Katae, the conductor of the orchestra with which I had worked in Minsk, came to Nottingham to repay the compliment I had made by going to Russia. He stayed with us as our guest in Stamford, but with no language in common we had to converse through drawings and sign language. This particularly fascinated our children and they quickly made a friend of him. As he was taking the baton for our monthly Nottingham concert on 22 April, I had both hands free to accept a generous cheque from the Arts Council, coming on top of Nottingham's corporation grant, substantial aid from John Player & Sons and the Musicians' Union. We were beginning to feel very welcome in Nottingham.

I was soon to learn that my move to Stamford had not gone unnoticed as I received an invitation to take over the musical direction of the Stamford Gilbert & Sullivan Society, which I gladly accepted. Mark Hooson was at the time chairman of the society and I knew him through his wife who had sung small parts with Opera da Camera. The society employed a professional producer who had been, for many years, with the D'Oyly Carte Opera Company and it was agreed I should receive a similar fee and contract as his. It was, of course, well known that Sir Malcolm Sargent had conducted the company in his early days in Stamford.

1967 Concerts and relaxation during this time

In 1967, relaxation took the form of the purchase the previous year of a caravan we kept at Blakeney in Norfolk. This is a magic spot and we spent many family weekends there, not to mention extended periods when time permitted during school holidays. We had at this time an estate car and Healey Sprite, with which I was able to commute to Nottingham, concerts and meetings, leaving the family basking in the sun in Norfolk. Rosemary left us in the summer, so we took on a Portuguese au pair in the autumn. She was to remain with us for several years and we are still friends today.

There was a very sad ending to the Promenade concerts this year. Sir Malcolm Sargent, due to an illness of which I was aware both from a meeting and a postcard, could not conduct the last night. Colin Davies took his place, but to everyone's surprise Sargent came onto the platform, mounted the podium and gave his, by this time traditional, final speech. His doctors had authorized a blood transfusion to give him enough energy to walk on in full evening dress to the immense applause of the audience, but sadly he died on 3 October 1967.

By the end of 1967 our Stamford house was bothering me on two counts; (1) there were three levels above the ground floor with no fire escape; and (2) there was no parking for our cars. We decided to move to a house with a garden and parking. This resulted in us looking at houses in the Stamford area and would have bought one in Empingham had we found a buyer for our house in St Mary's Street. We looked further afield and, when our house eventually sold, decided to buy in Oxfordshire and agreed on a very fine period house in the village of Adderbury. The same evening on our arrival back home we had a phone call from a local estate agent, Sam Scorer, whom we knew well, asking us if we were still interested in Tixover Hall just outside Stamford, which we had previously looked at, but was well outside our budget. I explained we had agreed that afternoon to buy in Oxfordshire. Sam said the owner of Tixover was prepared to lower his asking price and wanted to know what I was paying for the other house. I told him and received a telephone call very early the following morning saying we could have Tixover for another £500. We were to move there the following May, 'I Bought a Hall!

Meanwhile, the chorus master of the Ceramic City Choir in Stoke on Trent had asked me to take over from Sargent, who for many years had been conducting the choir's two annual concerts. I accepted, took over in 1968 and continued the work for several years.

By the autumn I decided to form a Sinfonia Chorale to work in conjunction with the orchestra and I also replaced our leader, Sylvia Cleaver, with Ronald Thomas. I had earlier met a soprano who lived in Nottingham and had done some work in the past with Opera da Camera, arranged a meeting and asked if she knew of other singers of similar calibre – good voices and good readers – whom I could invite to sing along with my Opera da Camera members. I quickly formed a very select group of voices to sing as a chamber choir ready for a Christmas concert. Keith immediately got on to publicise the event, which he did in his usual dramatic style with the result that within 24 hours of its first rehearsal we were whisked off to Birmingham to televise the newly formed chorale singing carols for ITV. We broadcast from there live and subsequently recorded a concert for Radio Nottingham entirely of Sargent's arrangements of carols with due reference to my association with him following the Watney-Sargent Award.

Chapter 6

The Glory Years
1968–1971
First QEH concert, home and family,
challenges and success

First QEH concert 1968

While still living in Stamford, on 21 February 1968, the Midland Sinfonia Orchestra made its London debut at the Queen Elizabeth Hall. The concert was sponsored by John Player the Nottingham based cigarette company, with the added attraction of 'Player Girls' carrying trays and distributing packets of cigarettes to the audience. Perhaps not entirely in harmony with a symphony concert, but fashions and traditions do change as we came to realize by the twenty-first century.

Following our debut at the Queen Elizabeth Hall, the London agent Wilfrid Van Wyck offered to represent the Midland Sinfonia exclusively. His agency already representing such eminent artists as Arthur Rubinstein, Victoria de los Ángeles, Henryk Szeryng, and José Iturbi. He was extremely impressed by the standard of the orchestra and felt it had an exciting future. He would handle all the London concerts and the planned Wigmore Hall series.

Unsurprisingly, I decided to change the name of the orchestra to the English Sinfonia. The quality of our musicians plus the response we were getting from knowledgeable members of the music world led me to the conclusion that we were ready to take the orchestra abroad and make recordings. Not least, however, was my passion for English music. I duly registered the name about two days after the QEH concert and discussed my proposal with the concert society, which met with board approval. We little knew what was in store for us a short time later.

The new name was officially adopted at the final concert of the season in July. By this time, it had become an annual event called the Summer Serenade

Concert, which included a formal dinner in the university dining hall during the interval and lavish sponsorship from John Player.

Our chairman Sir Max Bemrose announced in a speech after the interval that, from now on, the orchestra would be called the English Sinfonia. He went on to say that 'this name gives a far clearer picture of the scope and composition of the orchestra, as it was not composed exclusively of Midland musicians nor did it play in this area alone.'

The press reported that I intended to extend our work to include more London appearances and a more comprehensive coverage of the Midlands region. We had indeed planned our following season with a monthly series of concerts in Nottingham, which were to include John Ogden, Paul Tortelier with his family from France, Alfredo Campoli, and Owen Brannigan, plus a series of 'gold leaf' concerts in the Wigmore Hall in London.

In the meantime, however, I had invited Dean Dixon who had directed the conducting course in Hilversum to guest conduct the Midland Sinfonia in Nottingham on 31 May. He rehearsed the orchestra for a full day in London and I have to say was very impressed with the standard of playing. They were equally impressed by him! We drove to Tixover, having only just moved there, after the rehearsal where he stayed with us before travelling to Nottingham the following day for the concert. It was a programme of his own choice:

Mendelssohn	Fingal's Cave overture
Wallingford Riegger	Sonority for ten violins
Frank Martin	Concerto for seven wind instruments, timpani, percussion and strings
Dvořák	Nocturne
Haydn	'Oxford' Symphony

On 28 September we commenced the series of four Wigmore Hall concerts in London. Sponsored by John Player, these four gold leaf concerts featured all six Bach Brandenburg concertos, two choral works with the Sinfonia Chorale, Purcell's Welcome to All the Pleasures and Bach's Cantata No. 51 with Sheila Armstrong soprano and David Mason trumpet. Other works included Vivaldi's Four Seasons, Bach's C major suite and E major violin concerto.

Early in November the Czechoslovakian Brno Philharmonic had played in Nottingham for the first time in England since the Russian invasion and, on hearing that the Sinfonia was based in the city, invited the orchestra to play in their country. Knowing that the British Council subsidized visits of this kind, an application was immediately made and, unknown to me at the time, three musicians had attended our final Wigmore concert on 28 November to assess the orchestra.

Our request, to my amazement, was turned down and I immediately rang Barry Iliffe in charge of these decisions to know why? He kindly invited me to meet him at his office in London, which I did, and he showed me the actual written reports of each. I knew two of them, Denis Matthews, the pianist and John Manduell, at that time controller of music for the BBC Midland region. I had played Brandenburg No. 5 at this concert and Denis was very complimentary about my playing and direction, together with the playing standard of the orchestra, the second whose name I do not recall was also complimentary. Two of these people were clearly in no doubt about our ability to undertake this tour, which prompted me to ask why, despite what I perceived to be the majority vote, we could not have the support of the British Council. He replied that its decision was based on the conclusion of the person appointed to lead the auditors. I do not recall any criticism in John's report other than that in his opinion our string playing did not reach the standard expected in the country we had been invited to visit. I found this very hard to believe.

Well before we were due to announce the name change, Keith, our orchestra manager, rang to say that, to his surprise, he had heard from the Arts Council that the Northern Sinfonia, now a permanently contracted orchestra based in Newcastle upon Tyne, had decided to change its name to English Sinfonia but could not do so because it was already registered. I took legal advice and was assured that my registered name was indisputably mine. A bitter struggle between the Arts Council and Sinfonia followed and, sad to say, our relationship with John Cruft, the director of music there at the time, became stressful. In the event, the Arts Council firmly took the side of the Northern Sinfonia on the basis of its permanency. Since the change was registered in my name, I was seen as the perpetrator, so there was a lot of antagonism directed against me and manifested through dotting every 'i' and monitoring all our moves, whether artistic or from a business point of view. Without doubt, John was doing his job, but then so was I. Grants were occasionally withheld, but never cut or withdrawn, as it causes great embarrassment when musicians cannot be paid on time. However, the Arts

Council never terminated its subsidy to the orchestra while I remained musical director. So, in spite of everything and against all odds, we survived with the new name and continued to grow with the help of foreign tours and recordings, factors that I suppose kept the wound open. Later the Arts Council set up regional Arts Associations to be responsible for financing 'the arts' in the provinces, leaving them to encourage their local authorities to provide the necessary funding. This took some of the strain off the Arts Council as they now only had to balance their books, so to speak, leaving the administration to a local level. The provincial symphony orchestras were not affected by this, but it was suggested by John Cruft that the Sinfonia should become dependent on the newly formed East Midlands Arts Association, rather than directly funded by the Arts Council for future grants. Not wishing to be under a local thumb so to speak, I opposed the idea and met John Cruft in London to state our case. The threat was thankfully withdrawn, but in common with the other provincial orchestras in the country, we had to agree then to have a representative from our Derby based local arts association on the concert societies' board of directors in return for any aid they would give us. Their financial support continued to come our way in full.

Home and family

Moving back to home and family events, earlier in May 1968, against the advice of many friends, including our accountant and doctor, we had moved to the grandeur of Tixover Hall. I said it was for my pension and could have been proved correct had we stayed the course, but that is the story I am now writing.

The hall stands in three acres of ground with the River Welland marking the southern boundary. The east wing was a later addition to what was already a manor house with two floors and the staircase remaining to serve both wings. This provided the basis for five bedrooms on the first floor and the same number on the second floor. On the first floor there were two bathrooms, the larger over the original kitchen, which on the second floor was occupied mainly by the water tanks. The east wing had similarly sized dining and drawing rooms with a hallway between them, as clearly seen on the photograph. It was originally owned by the O'Brien family, which still lives in Ireland. It was donated freehold to a descendant of the family who married Michael Goddard Jackson. The surrounding countryside still belongs to the O'Brien Trust. Michael and his wife Eileen moved to Beaumont House in

Duddington after the sale of the hall. To complete the picture, I should add that the owner of the manor in Duddington was also a Goddard, and it was not long before we all became friends, with Faith, at the manor, letting us share her housekeeper.

While still in Stamford, Clare my eldest daughter had won a scholarship to Stamford High School. This was when we were still resident in Stamford and that entitled her to a free place there. She was allowed to retain her place after our move to Tixover, despite now being in Rutland, which was outside the catchment area. All four daughters continued their schooling at Ketton Primary School, and were transported there and back daily by taxi – in those days at the expense of the local education authority. Clare was, of course, only there for one term before transferring to Stamford High School, but in the meantime was honoured by being made May Queen in the village. On the day of our arrival at Tixover, we received a visit from an Elizabeth Thompson bearing a welcome casserole to celebrate our move. This proved the start of a lasting friendship that found us moving in a social circle hitherto outside our previous measure.

We had planned for my parents to move into the cottage adjoining Tixover Hall when my father retired early the following year, and work started soon after we moved. I employed a local building partnership, Gregory & Sauntson, which had a barn workshop on the corner to the Tixover hamlet, to update the cottage with a new stone fireplace in the sitting room, French windows onto the garden, a spacious dormer window in the principal bedroom, a new bathroom and a wood burner in the newly fitted kitchen, which also provided central heating. This was ready in time for their move which took place early the following year. They were very happy and of course pleased to be near their grandchildren. This also meant that Pam could now accompany me to concerts, which pleased my agent who regarded Pam as an asset when it came to meeting promoters, other agents and sponsors. Indeed, he thought I should never be without her, as on one weekend visit to our home he secretly said to her, 'Neville is good with orchestras but not so good with people, but you will make up for that!' This curiously reminded me of Dean Dixon saying a similar thing to her, his face is good with the orchestra but his back needs to be improved with the audiences. I know what he meant!

It seemed rare for a Sunday to go by without an invitation to lunch-time drinks, perhaps an exaggeration but they were quite frequent. We met many new faces and found ourselves with lots of new friends, including Michael Jackson, the previous owner of Tixover Hall and, as mentioned earlier, now living in Duddington, a pretty village a mile down the road from Tixover. His predecessor at the hall had been an MP in the British government who frequently travelled to and from the House of Commons and, I understand, had figured prominently in the Corn Law debates. The O'Brien Trust, of which I became a trustee and which owns most of the land in the area, is a charity that supports the hamlet of Tixover and sometimes donates money at Christmas to individuals in need.

We discovered the King's Head public house in Wing, up the A47 but about a mile off the main road where the publican had once been chauffeur to Sir Max Aitkin, who on the death of his father in 1964 took his title, but disclaimed it three days later on the grounds that 'there shall be only one Lord Beaverbrook in my lifetime.' It was of interest to me that, with sponsorship from the *Daily Express*, he founded the London Boat Show in 1954 and that his maritime interest centred on power boats. He had a residence in Cowes and kept his motor cruiser there. On his death in 1985, his son (also Max Aitkin) did assume the full title. Such was the popularity of this pub that a short time later I was to meet a dear friend from Derby who knew of it and I should add there were others.

At this time, the idea of flying fascinated me. We knew that Victor Wood, the owner of a garage and salesroom in Oakham, flew light aircraft and was an instructor at Leicester Aero Club, so one night over a pint in the King's Arms in Wing I decided to take flying lessons with him. It had been a boozy evening because a group captain from RAF Luffenham had invited us to the mess for a night cap and, as we were leaving, Victor said 'see you tomorrow 2.30 at the airfield.' I turned up but, no surprise to me, there was no sign of Victor. In fact, the airfield was deserted apart from someone in the control tower. I climbed the steps and spoke to the controller who said that Victor Wood was flying with a pupil and would be landing any minute. I thought he must be mad after the previous night, but down he came, turned the aircraft round and I had my first lesson. I spent some fascinating weeks afterwards buying books on air navigation and making comparisons with sailing, but finally decided that the expense of a six-seater plane for the family would prove too much and flying was less rewarding than sailing. Just one correction at this point – buying and maintaining a light aircraft can be cheaper than buying, maintaining and berthing a yacht.

Sailing cruisers with three or four berths were becoming cheaper and I read a revue of a build by Offshore Yachts based in Royston. It was a Debutante 21 footer with a hard chine ply hull. The price new was about £660 in 1965, which was comparable with the Ford Consul I had bought new ten years earlier. Out of interest, I resolved to visit Offshore Yachts to see the boats and took the opportunity to do so by deviating from the A1 on our way back from London. We saw a boat nearing completion, but I resisted the temptation to buy one as we really needed six berths. I then started searching the yachting press, getting myself hooked on the second-hand market and researching the various builders. By this time we had discovered that Elizabeth (who had brought us the casserole) and her husband Rex, a leading consultant surgeon at Peterborough Hospital, already had a boat (*Lady be Good*) berthed on the river at Oundle. The boat was a motor cruiser, but it emerged that Rex's father, a GP in Cornwall, was a sailor and had owned a large sailing yacht for which he had had a skipper. Rex, as a boy and young man naturally spent a great deal of his spare time on the sea and had sailed from Cornwall to Norway, I think at least on one occasion without his father. Rex was clearly experienced, this common interest bringing us closer together. GRP (glass reinforced plastic) was now the 'in thing' for boat building and, having been left a large sum of money by an aunt, Rex decided to sell the motor cruiser and buy a sailing boat. *Lady be Good* was sold at Oundle marina and replaced by *Shorelark*, which he berthed in Woolverstone Marina on the River Orwell between Ipswich and Harwich. She was a 35-foot GRP hull (one of the earliest) with teak decks and superstructure in varnished mahogany – a handsome boat designed by Alan Buchanan and built by Seamaster Ltd and Stebbings in Burnham on Crouch, Essex.

Challenges and success

Returning to music, things were difficult following our ongoing conflict with the Arts Council, but made worse by what I sensed was Keith's declining interest in his work. He mentions this in his book, referred to shortly, as an imbalance between the fees of conductors and those who promote them. I suspect this coincided with the start of the conflict with the Arts Council, which he may have seen as a threat to his future. However, his final decision to resign followed a disastrous mistake of failing to publicise one of our promotions in Nottinghamshire. It was an expensive programme in terms of players and of hiring a concert grand from Steinway for the Ibert

Divertissement, which was in the programme. Unfortunately, no more than a handful of people attended the concert. I called a meeting with David and Keith and was sorry he did not discuss his declining interest in the orchestra and the question of fees. Indeed, my first knowledge of his intended departure was on receiving a telephone call from Sir Max Bemrose from his home in Derbyshire after a successful series of autumn concerts at the Wigmore Hall, saying he had just bid farewell to Keith who had rung him earlier in the day to discuss a matter concerning the orchestra. Max said Keith had strong feelings about what he felt were the high fees paid to conductors and citing as an example the fee that Sir John Barbirolli had been paid for just one Hallé concert he had recently conducted in Nottingham. From our earliest days together, I had foreseen the possibility of this problem arising. At the beginning, the three of us did not receive a fee or even expenses for our work, and indeed following the support of the Gulbenkian Trust, Keith was the first to receive any remuneration. Indeed, going back in time, my first fee to conduct the orchestra was £25, which was for a concert at Nottingham University, which Ivor Keys, then professor of music, organized and said I should be paid. (It went on a speeding offence on my way to the rehearsal.) After this and as the number of concerts started to increase, I anticipated possible problems occurring in the future based on the simple knowledge that whatever my fee at any time, my income would be governed by the number of concerts I conducted. Anticipating the possibility of future unrest in this area, I asked the Royal Society of Musicians, of which I was a member and which recommended fees for all sections of the music profession, for advice. I presented its findings to the board of the Concert Society, which suggested I be paid an annual retainer and a fee for each concert, plus a half fee for a full day's prerehearsal. The precise amounts were specified and had been unanimously agreed. For the record, I never took the prerehearsal fee or charged any travel expenses to the orchestra. Furthermore, all my travel on behalf of the orchestra, including talks with agents, meetings and piano rehearsals with soloists, I did at my own expense. Any suggestion of me living in an 'ivory tower' could not have been further from the truth. At the time it seemed this was acceptable to my two colleagues, and I recall there were increases to Keith's salary, while David simply invoiced the orchestra for his work at a favourable rate, but he was of course part-time and running his own successful accountancy business in Loughborough, so not dependent on the Sinfonia. I have to say thanks to Keith, however, as the number of my concerts was growing at an enviable rate. In retrospect, I think some of the unrest was the result of our move to Tixover Hall, which was not the most sensitive thing I could have done. Keith's view of this can be read, as I have just done at the time of writing this in his book *Not Heavy Enough to Win a Prize*, published in 1997 by Greenfield House, London. Keith and I have never lost our friendship and we still keep in contact. He achieved wonders for the orchestra that gave me the break I needed. My admiration for him as a person and leader has never waned.

1969

In 1969 I was now commuting to our Nottingham office sometimes several times a week when there was a lull in concerts. Keith had formed a Sinfonia Association – Friends of the Orchestra – and had volunteered help from several members who came to the office to assist with advertising and mailing. The orchestra had become a member of the Association of British Orchestras and thus fully accepted as an integral part of the nation's music. In addition to my travel to Nottingham, I found myself more and more in London. I had a regular meeting with my agent, piano rehearsals with soloists who were due to appear with the orchestra and frequently attended concerts at the Royal Festival Hall before driving home.

More concerts and for me personal success were to follow. After the first Queen Elizabeth Hall concert, I was approached by Wilfrid Van Wyck who ran a concert agency listing some of the world's most famous musicians, soloists and conductors. The Sinfonia made good use of his best known international soloists, and later he frequently found work for me guest conducting foreign orchestras. I had, of course, experienced my first guest conducting engagement in Russia.

While on the subject of soloists, I should mention that Keith engaged the winner to be of the world famous Tchaikovsky piano competition in Moscow. He was John Lill, who not only became a frequent soloist with the Sinfonia, but also a friend and later president of the orchestra. Other distinguished soloists such as Victoria de los Ángeles, soprano, Zabaleta, harp, Ruggierio Ricci and Henryk Szeryng, violin to name a handful, also appeared often and looked forward to the next. Around this time the orchestra also agreed to give ongoing engagements to winners of the BBC Young Musician of the Year competition.

I must relate an amusing story about a concert at the Llandaff Festival on 2 June in which Wilfrid had booked Henryk Szeryng to play Vivaldi's *The*

Four Seasons, with my permission under his direction and not mine – a reasonable request to which I was more than happy to agree. As this was a baroque programme, the harpsichord was positioned in the place of the rostrum. At the rehearsal, though not intentional on my part, the orchestra happily followed me. After several stops Szeryng appealed to me, with a smile, to stop 'directing'. I realized what was happening and solved the problem by having the harpsichord moved to the back of the orchestra just for the Vivaldi. He could then direct without competition.

At the end of 1969 I was booked to conduct the Ulster Orchestra for two concerts on 30 and 31 December. They were the inevitable *A Night in Vienna* with soloist Marion Studholme. This was my first meeting with James Allaway who was much later to take over the management of the Sinfonia.

Following Keith's resignation, I had hoped to appoint the concert manager of the Bournemouth Symphony Orchestra, whom I had got to know during my Watney-Sargent year. Unfortunately, the present general manager Ken Machett was approaching retirement age and he thought he was in a strong position to replace him. He would certainly have been my first choice! However, we were helped by the Arts Council to find a replacement. I think this was a shrewd move. The Arts Council ran a training scheme for arts administrators and suggested a suitable candidate for the position. They put me in touch with Alan Rodford, who spent a weekend with us as a family guest to discuss all aspects of the work involved. After a visit to see the office in Nottingham, I was satisfied with his knowledge and personality and offered him the position, which he was pleased to accept. Alan turned out to be well versed in the affairs of the Arts Council and, from the orchestra's point of view, the outcome pleased me and gave me hope it would ease the conflict we were having with it at the time. Alan was certainly qualified to administer the orchestra but was probably over ambitious. He saw a need for a concert manager, which I accepted, but on reflection it would have been more prudent to have found a member of the orchestra who was prepared to act as librarian and fixer rather than the route we took in appointing Richard Toeman who was salaried. In terms of the management, Alan was a success in that he had good ideas and was a friendly negotiator. However, he came to an orchestra that by this stage had its roots firmly in the ground thanks to the work of his predecessor, Keith. Alan was heavily involved in the Nottingham Festival, which an independent group funded by Nottingham City Council had just set up. They had engaged Richard Gregson

Williams to manage the festival and it was a huge success. The festival boasted nothing but the best, and the English Sinfonia, along with other major orchestras, shared its limelight. We were accepted as the resident orchestra, so to speak, and appeared several times under my baton and the ones of guest conductors. Richard's main interest was in music, and in spite of small outside events, the festival was primarily one of music, choral and orchestral works. Sponsorship was generous, mainly from Nottingham based companies, and the impact of the festival became nationwide.

1970

Alan Rodford was beginning to prove his worth both with ideas and his ability to liaise with promoters, in particular at this point with the new festival director in Nottingham. It was Alan's idea to appoint a composer in association with the orchestra and it was my responsibility to choose a suitable candidate. Alan approached the Arts Council for support, which in turn was to provide a grant for the chosen candidate and extra support for the first performances of several works written during the association. Colleges of music were alerted to the proposal and I received recommendations and scores to help select a candidate. I chose Paul Patterson, now professor of composition at the Royal Academy of Music. I introduced him to the orchestra and explained he would sit in at rehearsals and hoped players in all sections would offer advice on his music for their sections. He quickly became a familiar part of our work and was able to hear his compositions and edit what he had written with the help of the players. The first work he composed was a Concertante, a composition with plenty of work for all sections of the orchestra, a small but compact ensemble consisting of strings, one wind instrument representing each wind and brass part, and a substantial percussion section. The work was Webern in style and dry and staccato in utterance. It was performed in Derby and Nottingham. His second work was especially written for children, so we toured many Lincolnshire schools during March.

Around this time, Sir Michael and Lady Faith Culme-Seymour invited Pamela and me for sherry at Rockingham Castle. I had earlier, on 27 June 1964, given a performance with Opera da Camera of *Doctor Miracle* by Berlioz on a stage specially erected for the occasion on the castle battlements. The opera was one of a double bill in the repertoire for that season. It was a beautiful setting and a very memorable occasion. Sir Michael was soon to give the castle to his less wealthy nephew Michael Saunders Watson, a naval officer commander with whom we later became great friends. The story of his becoming the new owner of the castle is superbly dealt with in Michael's book *I Am Given a Castle* published by Quiller Press in 2008. The castle is now in the care of his son James.

I remember Pamela and I joined them on their first evening there. We sat in the library surrounded by packing cases still to be emptied, evidence of work still being done by an independent team of workers who were drawing up a complete inventory of the castle. In order to enjoy a celebratory drink Michael and I had first to drive down to the village pub in Rockingham to buy the gin and tonics! More of our friendship later.

On 26 February, we had the monthly concert in Nottingham which was to feature Gillian Weir playing two organ concertos with the orchestra. However, earlier in the week she was taken ill with appendicitis, thus prompting us to act swiftly for a replacement. Francis Jackson, organist and master of the choristers at York Minster took her place, which required him to play two organ concertos:

BRITTEN	Frank Bridge Variations
HANDEL	Organ Concerto No 14. in A
MOZART	Divertimento (K 136)
POULENC	Organ Concerto in G minor

Francis Jackson rang me at home the following week about a letter he had received from a local member of the Musicians' Union to say that he had performed with the orchestra and was not a member of its union branch. I was able to assure him this was not necessary for soloists or conductors unless by choice, it also gave me the opportunity to acknowledge the success of his performances at such short notice.

On 23 March this year Pamela and I attended the showing of a film at the National Film Theatre that John Player & Co had commissioned to publicise their role in sponsorship. Our contribution to the event was a filmed performance of Prokofiev's Classical Symphony, and this included an interview with me on the rostrum. This was followed by a buffet lunch during which I had an interesting chat with the then sports minister Denis Howell. He sympathized with me over the government needing an Arts Council to advise it on how to distribute its funds to support the arts as opposed to sports, which answered directly to the government. This was of particular interest to me at the time as we were still involved in the battle over the name change.

Sponsoring an orchestra, of course was only one of John Player's interests and a departure from their usual sponsorship, which mainly covered sporting events such as motor racing, tennis and the Henley Regatta.

During the summer the Sinfonia also played at the Hintlesham Festival in Suffolk, which ran from 10 to 26 July. This was an annual event for a number of years and featured a wide range of concerts, including lieder recitals and talks, but had for its central attraction the Kent Opera formed by its producer Norman Platt with Roger Norrington as music director. Several years earlier, Roger had approached the Sinfonia (then the Midland) to accompany the company's first production. This we did and the relationship flourished, later requiring larger orchestras for its more ambitious repertoires. The Arts Council at this point agreed to support the company and asked the Sinfonia's Concert Society to channel its subsidy through our charitable company, which we were happy to do. This continued for some time until the company finally established its own orchestra and was on a sound footing.

The Nottingham Festival, under the direction of Richard Gregson Williams, invited Jascha Horenstein to be its artistic director. He conducted the Royal Philharmonic Orchestra in a festival concert and also the English Sinfonia in a concert that included Mahler's Fourth Symphony. This was especially memorable to me as I had previously thought Mahler to be outside the scope of the orchestra, but subsequently became more adventurous, as I shall later show.

I was surprised that Jascha Horenstein came to my performance of Beethoven's Ninth Symphony, which featured the Stoke Ceramic City Choir. As previously mentioned, I was the choir's permanent guest conductor. I hasten to add that I thought he only came because I had included in the first half of the programme a work he had not known, a lesser-known choral work by Beethoven, 'Der glorreiche Augenblick', which only the English Sinfonia Chorale sang, though it was also singing in the Beethoven. I was gratified to learn that, rather than leave at the interval, he chose to stay for my Ninth Symphony. I subsequently learnt that Richard Gregson Williams was more than impressed with my performance and that he had a high regard for my ability as a conductor. Pamela had been sitting with Richard Gregson Williams and his wife. The concert was sponsored for the festival by Boots, the Nottingham-based chemist. A London critic referred to me as 'a conductor of statue excelling in large scale works'.

83

It befalls conductors from time to time to conduct first performances, usually (but not always) during the composer's lifetime. Nottingham Festival this year featured an organ concerto played by the composer. Arthur Wills, organist and master of the choristers at Ely Cathedral, played the organ. This was a programme of twentieth-century music at which the second performance of Paul Patterson's trumpet concerto was played in association with the English Sinfonia.

Tippet	Concerto for double string orchestra
Wills	Organ concerto (first performance)
Patterson	Concerto for trumpet, timpani and strings
Poulenc	Concerto for organ, timpani and strings

Richard Gregson Williams had a flair for publicity and could capture people's imaginations, for the following year the Sinfonia was to give a midnight fireworks concert in Wollaton Park, Nottingham. For this event he had dramatic coverage in all the national newspapers as he had invited a South African witch doctor to cast a spell to guarantee us a warm and a rain free night with no wind. With respect to the concert, I have to give credit for this idea to Alan who sold it to the festival director saying it would be more than special as we would use the original scoring, augmented in this case as it was not being performed on a barge, to a wind orchestra of 24 oboes, 12 bassoons and contra, 9 trumpets, 9 horns, 3 pairs of kettle drums, and side drums. This formidable wind band was led by the eminent oboist Leon Goosens. The massive fireworks display had suitable staging and was fronted by the orchestra. The park had a natural slope on which the audience could sit, stand or wander around. The director of the fireworks company and I worked out the timings for the music to fit in with the fireworks display, making allowances for the inevitable bangs, which worked perfectly. We had timings and traffic light controls to ensure that the orchestra could be heard at all times and to avoid the bangs. The main work was of course Handel's 'Music for the Royal Fireworks', but I started the concert with an arrangement I made of Handel's D minor Overture. No amplification was used for the band, but I am told it could be heard throughout the park. It was the largest visually 'live' audience to which I had ever played. To assemble this number of musicians we drew professional players from London, Birmingham and Manchester and the concert was played without a rehearsal.

Parents, Nellie and Arthur (above).

About two years of age
(above left).

Paternal grandparents with
youngest son, Eric (right).

Maternal grandparents with
three daughters, Jennie, Nellie
and Evelyn (below).

Central School,
Darley Park.

School days (above).

On holiday at Butlins (right).

With Denis at Butlins (above).

Pamela (right).

On holiday
with Pamela.

Fleet, National
Service Training.

Austin
Swallow.

Our Wedding at St Wurburgh's.

Gretton before renovation.

Corby Grammar School Choir and Orchestra.

Gretton after renovation.

Kettering Symphony
Orchestra (above).

Thrapston dingy
sailing (above).

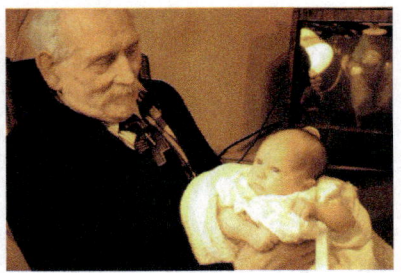

Clare with
Albert (great
grandfather)
(above).

Opera da
Camera.

Midland Sinfonia Orchestra at Nottingham (above)
and Queen Elisabeth Hall concert poster (below).

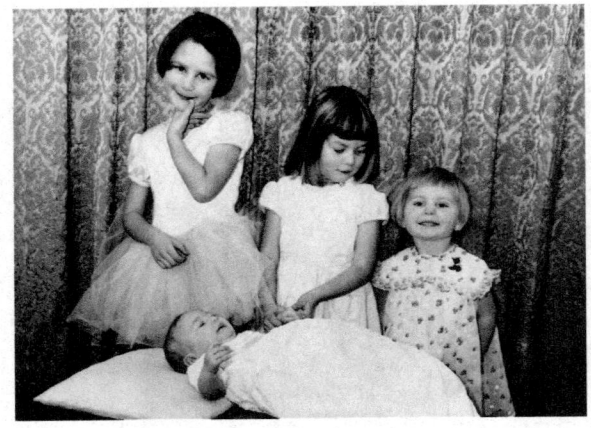

My four
daughters!

Left to right: Edgar Palmer, Malcolm Sargent and me.

Before a
concert
1964.

St Mary's Street (top left). Family at St Mary's St. (top right).
Nottingham rehearsal (above left). Rehearsing, 1967
(above right). Tixover Hall (below).

Parents'
cottage,
Tixover (left).

Gina (au pair) and my
daughters (right).

Beethoven's Ninth
Symphony,
Nottingham
(below).

Leaving for the Royal Garden Party.

American tour with John Solum (below).

Maestro.

At the Bechstein in Tixover Hall (above).

Maestro in
London.

Rex and Elizabeth
on the Channel
Islands.

Easton Hall (above). In front of Easton Hall (below).

Michael Saunders
Watson, Scotland.

Rachel and Gré
in Scotland.

In Rome with Resphi's wife
and Patricia Chiti.

Philomusica
meeting with
David Littaur.

Clacton Music School with Anna Rendall.

Neil and Clare's wedding.

Richard and Rachel's wedding (above).

Seacure, Italy, 1984 (left).

Family holiday in Italy (below).

In September I spent several days in Dublin where I had been invited to conduct the Radio Teilisis Éireann orchestra in a public concert, which was also broadcast live and included Elgar's First Symphony.

I flew to Brussels on 12 October to work with the Belgian radio orchestra. This concert was broadcast before an invited audience. I have fond memories of my time there as I had previously been introduced to Baroness Marie Thérèse Ullens de Schooten, wife of the late baron associated with the Belgian Raffinerie Tirlemontoise, which I understood to have been connected with the Lyle family who owned a sugar refinery on the Thames, later merging with Tate (founder of the Tate Gallery) to become well known for their golden syrup.

I had met the baroness at a reception organized by the local music society after a Sinfonia concert in Tonbridge Wells and, on learning that she lived in Belgium, I naturally told her that I would shortly be conducting in Brussels, whereupon she insisted I stay with her at her home in the nearby countryside. I think she may have had some connection with the radio, although now on reflection and knowing more about the family and their friends imagine her interest in the arts went much further. I accepted her kind invitation and a chauffeur met me at the airport and drove me to her residence – the dowager house conveniently hidden by a large laurel hedge and close to the château where her son now lives. She had a resident butler who served all our meals and I was driven daily to Brussels to rehearse and later conduct the orchestra for the concert. I remember her house being full of works of art, magnificent oil and watercolour paintings, which I admired and which never ceased to slow my progress up and down the impressive stairway. If we met I could be sure of a word or two about certain ones and also how different they looked when viewed under day or artificial light.

1971

Following these successful years it was sad to experience Arts Council grants being continually pruned, or at the very least not keeping up with inflation. This was of course happening to all grant aided organisations – playhouses, opera companies and the provincial contracted orchestras. Survival at this point in history was difficult for us all. Even in London the four major symphony orchestras, London Philharmonic Orchestra, London Symphony Orchestra, Royal Philharmonic Orchestra and the Philharmonia, were under threat, and even prompted John Cruft to go as far as suggesting that four major orchestras in London were three too many. He correctly made comparisons with Berlin and other major European cities with not one boasting four. He was right of course, but it must be borne in mind those same countries were not short of professional provincial subsidized orchestras, not to mention opera houses also with orchestras.

However, the four self governing London orchestras stood their ground and survived due mainly to not being funded directly by the Arts Council but through the London Orchestral Concert Board. To sum up matters at this point, the 'going' was tough, but was going to be even more tough. As the Americans would say 'You've got a problem? that's good!' – which amounts to knowing you have a problem in the first place suggests you are half way to solving it!

The Sinfonia faced financial problems that could only be circumnavigated by cuts to the orchestra's administration and we had to forego the luxury of a concert manager, so Richard had left and we were about to lose Alan. Denis Arnold, the then professor of music at Nottingham University who replaced Ivor Keys in 1969 when he moved to Birmingham, had suggested we appoint Rex Lawson. Rex had just graduated but sensibly agreed to act as concert manager only if he could avoid making decisions that required considerable experience and knowledge. I agreed and spent several days of each week at the Nottingham office to support him, frequently taking Pamela with me to help. Pam had a good telephone manner and I think made a good impression on callers. Further help came from the Friends of the Sinfonia, which Keith thoughtfully set up in his early days and which had experience of duplicators and mailing lists.

Looking back I am reminded of lunches with Denis Arnold while giving ten lectures on modern music and one on baroque music at the Adult Education Centre at Nottingham University. For the lecture on baroque music I had arranged to have both a piano and a harpsichord on the platform and was overjoyed when the piano turned out to be a concert grand and the harpsichord a Goble with 16-foot, 8-foot, and 4-foot stops. These coupled give three octave sounds from one 'played' note.

I remember seeing a poster advertising the lecture as I entered the hall. It was illustrated with the opening bars of 'Fur Elise' (not baroque) and it occurred to me to start the lecture by asking members of the audience if they knew the piece of music on the poster. I of course was not surprised that many did, but it gave me an excuse to play the piece on the harpsichord followed by the piano, thus emphasizing the difference between the two instruments and the added dimension of the sustaining pedal in the case of the piano. Another particular highlight of the lecture was the cadenza from Bach's Fifth Brandenburg Concerto also played on each instrument. Though never one for the sound of my own voice, both the audience and I enjoyed our time together.

In retrospect, I had other connections with the university. During the period when I was spending time at the office in the absence of a manager, I had a room at my disposal in one of the students' (female) residential blocks. I remember idly looking at the notice board in the entrance hall one morning while waiting for the rain to subside and was amused to read that all male visitors were asked to leave the building before dawn! I reflected that in my day we were not allowed visitors at all, though I had heard about one college that was a little more generous regarding visitors, but stipulating that if they were of the opposite sex, the beds had to be moved into the corridor.

In March 1971 I was invited to conduct the Orchestre des Concerts de Saint-Germain-des-Prés in Paris. I remember arriving for the first rehearsal; the full orchestra was assembled but there was no leader. I sat in the church waiting for his arrival to the embarrassment of the orchestra's manager. The first half of the programme included Bach's Cantata No. 106, Actus Tragicus, and the choir and soloists were assembled ready for action. The leader finally arrived, apologized to everyone, and the rehearsal got under way. There were no hard feelings, but at the interval the tenor soloist, Schuyler Hamilton, an American singing with the Paris Opera, introduced himself to me and said he admired the way I handled the situation, adding that no French conductor would have dared to have done it. He had a flat in Paris and entertained Pam and me for supper after the concert – spaghetti bolognaise.

In June the orchestra made its first recording with EMI in its Abbey Road Studio with an album of English works. I recall my first down beat in Studio 1 was the start of Warlock's 'Capriol Suite'. There were further works by Hamilton Harty, George Butterworth and Arnold Bax.

There is an interesting story to 'Dance in the Sunlight' by Arnold Bax, as this short piece was needed to fill the space on the record. I recall visiting Novello's music shop library in London to look at English orchestral works and selecting the Bax. Unfortunately, there were no band parts, just the full score. Rex Lawson, our concert manager, came to the rescue by photocopying the full score and then painstakingly cutting out each part, sticking it on separate sheets of paper and then photocopying them, in the case of the strings, duplicate parts for each desk. This was completed just in time for us to sight-read the work and record.

While in the shop, the manager said I might be interested in listening to a tape by a young up-and-coming composer, with whom I had just shaken hands as he was leaving the shop with his friend. I briefly listened, but was unimpressed. How wrong can one be? It was Andrew Lloyd Webber and the piece, I think, was *Jesus Christ Superstar* with lyrics by Tim Rice.

16–23 August: Olaf Krogh-Jenson, Esberg Denmark

I was invited to conduct two concerts in Denmark with the By-Orkester-Jydsk Symfonisk Orkester. There were rehearsals for both concerts and, following the first performance on the Thursday, I took the train to Esberg to spend the Friday and Saturday nights with Olaf Krogh-Jensen and his wife. I had met Olaf through our doctor, George Hattersley, who had invited him to a medical conference that Mike Saunders Watson was hosting at Rockingham Castle. Knowing that Olaf was interested in music and that I was scheduled to conduct in Denmark, he thought we should meet and it was through that introduction that he invited me to his home in Esberg. After the first concert on the Thursday, which featured Ifor James playing Strauss No. 2 horn concerto, Beethoven's Sixth Symphony and the Prokofiev 'Classical' symphony, I travelled to Esberg to face an action packed weekend involving a long drive on the Saturday up the east coast, round the top of Denmark and then down part of the west coast before returning to Esberg. I was also to experience the effects of drinking Schnapps, but was able to recover in time to return on the Sunday for the second concert on the Monday. The Monday concert started with Walton's 'Façade' suite, which was a sharp contrast from the previous concert as it centred on works by Hoffnung. The soloist in 'the concerto to end all concertos' was Niels Viggo Bentzon. This concerto, known as 'Concerto popolare', was written for Hoffnung by Franz Reizenstein, who sold me his Bechstein grand piano in my Corby days. The concerto begins with the orchestra playing Tchaikovsky's Piano Concerto No. 1, while the pianist believes he is playing the Grieg. Other themes appear, including 'Rhapsody in Blue', the 'Warsaw Concerto' and the song, 'Roll out the Barrel'. My soloist fortunately had a great sense of humour, which kept me on my toes throughout his performance, which started with him reclining on a chaise longue close to the rostrum leisurely reading a newspaper. When I finished the introduction he hastily abandoned his reading and rushed to the piano. He had asked me to have my revenge during his cadenza by yawning and dropping asleep on the rostrum. I did and he kept trilling waiting for me to wake up until transferring the trill to his left hand at the top of the keyboard so that he could reach over to poke me into action and be back at the piano in time for the end. The programme also included Hoffnung's Beethoven Leonora No. 4 overture featuring an offstage trumpet.

I later thought of including a Hoffnung concert in our Nottingham series but, in spite of several attempts, could not persuade Dudley Moore to undertake the solo piano part.

Worth a mention is 6 October as Clive Lythgoe was our piano soloist in a performance of the piano concerto by Howard Ferguson, rarely heard. This took place in the Guildhall, Northampton.

Later in the month there were several concerts with the clarinettist Jack Brymer, including one in Ilkeston Town Hall. At the end of the concert, I was chatting with Jack and noticed a couple standing by who seemed to want a word with me, but it appeared they were close friends of Jack's and I was duly introduced. This was my first meeting with Ken and Noni Gurling, who, it transpired, lived in Allestree just outside Derby, my home town of course. This was the beginning of a long friendship and his name will inevitably reappear. I said we would shortly be giving a concert in Derby and on this occasion he came alone, but invited Pamela and me to their house for drinks and supper afterwards.

An important landmark in my career came during this year when I had a call from my agent who also represented an American flautist by the name of John Solum. John had moved to London with his family – a wife and two boys – wishing to establish and further his career in Europe. He was keen to develop a relationship with a freelance orchestra and Wilfrid Van Wyck advised him to hear a concert by the English Sinfonia. We had first met briefly in the green room after a concert and then, later on 1 October, when John invited me to lunch at the Saville Club, which, as a member of the New York branch, he was able to use. He was familiar with my first recordings of English music, which I had made with EMI earlier in the year. He thought that perhaps we could develop a working relationship together for the purpose of concerts and possibly recordings. At that time, I was a member of a club in Curzon Street, which I found useful for taking colleagues to lunch, but I quickly realized that the Saville Club was closer to the arts than most others I had encountered. John put my name forward for membership and I immediately became a member. I enjoyed working with him as both a person and a musician. He became a very close friend and I have to say a tremendous influence on my attitude towards forwarding my own career. For me, he epitomised 'do it now' and 'respect for detail'. He never waited to be asked, he volunteered. It was a partnership that worked.

We regularly toured Europe visiting concert agents to obtain work. It is by no means unusual for artists to make themselves known to concert agencies for this purpose and we met agents in Germany, Italy and Switzerland, with some success. Interestingly, one country we did not visit was Spain, but due to a happy coincidence as a result of meeting René Klopfenstein, the artistic director of the Montreux Festival, we soon heard from an agent in Madrid who, being friendly with him in Montreux booked the orchestra for a week's tour in Spain. This later became an annual event for several years.

I introduced John to EMI and we recorded a large repertoire of flute music with both the English Sinfonia and eventually the Philharmonia. Our first concert together was in the Queen Elizabeth Hall, but was followed by concerts in the Midlands and several tours in Europe.

* * *

Just a brief update on the family to end the year. Clare was by now well established and making some good friends at Stamford High School. Alas, living outside the Stamford catchment area now prevented any of my daughters having a 'scholarship' place there. Though opposed to fee paying in terms of education, regarding it as buying a place in the world, so to speak, I nevertheless swallowed my ideals and gave all my daughters the same start. I said that if Rachel, followed by Gré and Rebecca, passed the entrance examination to Stamford High School, we would pay the fees. Rachel took the examination, passed and followed in Clare's footsteps. I am glad to relate that both Gré and Rebecca also passed in turn and, for a short period, all four were pupils there at the same time. They had a ten-minute walk to Duddington from where they travelled by bus into Stamford. They were sometimes relieved of a return bus journey as their grandparents would time their shopping to pick the girls up at the school bus stop. Also Mum and Dad came to their rescue, particularly if the weather was bad.

Chapter 7

Tours and More
1972–1975
Tours, boating diversion, more concerts

1972

In February 1972, I was invited to Bochum in Germany to conduct the Bochumer Symphonica in a programme of English music that would include Elgar's First Symphony and Britten's Cello Symphony with Anja Thauer as the soloist. There is an interesting story surrounding this concert, about which I am writing today on 2 October 2020 (48 years later), having recently received a telephone call from BBC's Radio 3 Philip Hebblethwaite asking if I remembered working with the German cellist, Anja Thauer. I said that I did, but that it was a long time ago. I was very impressed with her playing and with her as an attractive and vivacious person. In fact, I suggested that if she would like to come to England I would programme the Cello Symphony for her and, on her agreement, duly arranged four concerts for March 1973. The day before the first concert in the King's Hall Derby we had our customary prerehearsal in London after which I drove her to Tixover to spend the night with us. Not surprisingly, she greatly impressed all my daughters. At the time of writing this, I telephoned my second daughter Rachel in England to ask if she remembered Anja. 'Vividly,' she said, 'I remember her visit well. I recall her arriving at Tixover Hall and resting her cello by a chair, and then putting her hat on the top of the neck part of the case, then made some comment about her cello being like a best friend to her.' Anja retired early that night because she was not feeling well, but I have no recollection of any mention of that the next day. We drove to Derby and the concert successfully took place. The members of the orchestra were booked to stay in a hotel as there were three more concerts to go, but I drove back to Tixover. The following day, I was told that Anja had taken ill and was being flown back to Germany. Her place was taken in Loughborough at short notice, by our

91

principal cellist Anna Shuttleworth playing the Haydn Cello Concerto, which was programmed for the second and third concerts with the Britten again in the fourth. There was enough time before the third and fourth concerts to fly Thomas Oglio, the Hungarian cellist, to England from Switzerland to deputize for the remaining two concerts. I already knew something of the story that was of interest to the BBC after 48 years, but had to wait until 22 November to hear it in full.

In April of this year I featured the Moeran G minor Symphony at the Queen Elizabeth Hall in a programme devoted to English music. EMI showed interest and I was invited to record the symphony. I remember a discussion at the time about the possibility of recording it in the Albert Hall Nottingham, which had an agreeable acoustic, but after making sound tests they decided on our usual venue in the famous No. 1 studio in Abbey Road.

During this year I also visited New York with John Solum to meet Nancy Tuttle, who was director of promotions with Columbia Artists. She already had recordings of the Sinfonia and was interested in discussing an American tour for the orchestra. It was suggested I submitted three programmes to them so that each included John as soloist, and a contract was eventually drawn up for a six-week tour to include concerts in America, Canada and two in Bermuda. The tour was scheduled to begin in November 1973. Each of the three programmes on offer contained works from the classical, romantic and modern periods. For the record, tours of this magnitude can involve the need for a subsidy. Predictably, the press and Arts Council questioned us on this matter, but our defence was secure. First, we were not interfering with any of our commitments in the UK and, second, we had already arranged four recitals featuring members of the orchestra who had agreed to give their services free for the cause in the event of a deficit. On the business side of things, our contract with Columbia Artists was drawn up on the basis of the exchange rate being agreed on the day of the first concert. By the end of the tour this rate was very much in our favour and any loss was inconsequential. However, having prepared three harpsichord quartet concerts to take place on our return, these went ahead to the orchestra's advantage.

* * *

Two important social events took place in the summer. The first was on 28 June when Pamela and I were invited for the second time to the Henley-on-

Thames regatta, which, as in the previous year, John Player was sponsoring. As before, this was a leisurely trip up and down the river in a comfortable launch to observe the racing and enjoy cocktails. We were later wined and dined in a hotel where we spent the night. Among Player's guests was Bill Kallaway, who later became a self-employed consultant. Part of the conversation round the table was spent discussing what the Sinfonia might have in mind for the following season and I remember suggesting the possibility of a conductor's competition in association with the English Sinfonia. This actually went ahead in 1974 when Players sponsored an international conducting competition – please note, using the Bournemouth Symphony Orchestra, not the English Sinfonia as I had suggested. (I should have kept the idea to myself at the time!) This was won by Simon Rattle who then became assistant conductor of the Bournemouth Symphony Orchestra.

The second event was on 21 July when Pamela and I attended the Royal Garden Party at Buckingham Palace. Our invitation was in connection with my work with the Sinfonia in Nottingham. Philip Vine, chief executive of the City Council and a strong supporter of the Sinfonia, had put our names forward. This was another occasion on which Pamela and I met Sir Adrian and Lady Boult. He was interested in what I was doing and remembered meeting us in Blakeney; and was curious to know if we still had the caravan there.

Just before this I had undertaken a short tour for the Eastern Authorities Orchestral Association. The performances were, as usual, in churches and featured Malcolm Williamson (the then Queen's musician) as the soloist with the English Sinfonia to play Haydn and Handel organ concertos. During the tour, he mentioned that he had an annual commitment to nominate musicians to attend the annual Royal Garden Party and would be pleased to recommend Pamela and me at any time. I told him that we were already invited for that year, but he said that his offer would be open for the future if we were so minded.

* * *

Back to my interest in boats. I had already started taking *Yachting Monthly* to dream about one day realizing my ambition to sail the high seas, but that was still a long way off. I did, however, learn that New Parks College in Leicester ran evening classes to prepare candidates for the Royal Yachting Association's many sailing qualifications. They had a good team of instructors and were proud of being one of the best schools in the country and the furthest from the sea! I met the principal, Bill Hudson and enrolled as a student on the first course 'Competent Crew', which was due to start in September and run through until the following Easter.

Bill Hudson then charted boats on the south coast and those of us wishing to qualify shared the charter cost and spent a week of practical experience. New Parks had by this time trained several of its former pupils to the rank of instructor and they were registered with the RYA (Royal Yachting Association) to instruct and assess crew members. I took the first course and found myself on a 35-foot sailing boat with Bill Hudson as skipper. This was my first time on a sailing boat on which I could live for a week and go to sea. It was an exciting time. Five crew and skipper – six berths, each person contributing to the provision of food and one day each being chef for the day. Four of us were there for 'Competent Crew' and the fifth for 'Day Skipper'. We visited most of the Solent ports, staying in some, and circumnavigated the Isle of Wight. We took turns in helming, sail management, sail trimming and tying up, and learnt to do exactly as told. Bill was everybody's friend and had our respect. He was a good sailor and we later became close friends, frequently sailing 'in company' when we later had our own boats.

However, in August I was determined to have a well-earned break and take the family for a holiday on the Isle of Anglesey. Earlier in the year Pam and I had looked at several boats for sale second-hand at various marinas both on the south coast and in East Anglia. Several I took to sea for a trial sail, but we found it difficult to find a boat with six berths. However, Anglesey was to be a holiday and not a boat search. It was a wonderful fortnight, I raised the family every morning at 6 a.m. followed by breakfast before exploring the island, swimming in the sea and making occasional trips to the mainland. On 29 August, Gré's birthday, we climbed Snowdonia. The time we spent at the peak coincided with the time of her birth, midday, so she remembers being ten on the way up and eleven on the descent! We also visited several historic houses and castles, and of special interest Portmeirion, a tourist attraction in Gwynedd, designed and built by Sir Clough Williams-Ellis between 1925 and 1975 in the style of an Italian village, and now owned by a charitable trust. It has served as the location for numerous films and TV shows, most famously in the 1960 TV series *The Prisoner*. We even found time for the girls to go pony trekking. The day before driving home I bought a *Yachting Monthly*, read about a second-hand Debutante for sale in Conway and just could not miss the opportunity to arrange a viewing. To cut a long story short, we met the owners (a father and son), threw caution to the wind and bought *Booster*. (NB: I had resolved to have an alcohol-free holiday and until that moment we had done so.) Purchase price £700 including trailer. In those days you could expect to sell for at least the price you paid for a boat new – later you could profit from it!

On returning home, I had a tow bar fitted to my VX 490 and drove to Conway with my father in the October to tow the boat back to Tixover. The trailer was parked at Deganwy, on the opposite side of the estuary to Conway. I drove directly to Deganwy and in a dinghy I had borrowed from Peter Baker, who had bought our St Mary's Street house in Stamford and was also a keen sailor, rowed across to *Booster*, which was on a buoy on the opposite side of the estuary. We motored *Booster* back to Deganwy and tied up to the harbour wall, fortunately next to a vertical steel wall ladder, which was a long way down from the quayside.

We climbed the wall several times and made certain the crane would be available, as arranged, to lift us the following morning. My first night on my own boat was memorable. We dined on board, slept and I was woken early, with movement round the boat arranging a sling for the crane. I dressed quickly, went on deck to help. Father was still in his bunk but finally got up and was sitting on the 'bucket and chuck it' when he looked out of the port-hole and saw the harbour wall dropping down as if by magic. Just imagine his surprise at being airborne! The boat was safely put on its trailer and I drove back cautiously to Tixover where we jacked the trailer and boat up onto sleepers to preserve the tyres. It remained there for the winter just outside the kitchen door. I worked on it during that time adding a fourth berth, repainting the hull and deck and adding guard rails for the sake of the children. There was a famous chandlery in London (Kelvin Hughes) which Pam and I frequently visited to buy oilskins, charts, hand bearing compass and hosts of other 'boaty' things. This was really 'BOATING'.

Earlier in October I went to Finland. This was to conduct the Oulu Symphony Orchestra, which I understood to be the most northern orchestra in the world. We were just a short distance from Lapland, which I was able to see briefly. Now, since coming to live in France I have come to understand my laziness in not mastering the language. I did French at school so can stumble by here but it does not amount to what I would call 'conversational French', which in any case is difficult in company, especially when several

95

people are having different discussions at the same time, and made more difficult with the noise factor. I think I can now ascribe my linguistic laziness to the fact that there is always someone, usually several people, who can speak English in whatever country I visit. There was and still are other factors – (i) there is a limit to the number of languages anyone can be expected to speak; (ii) rehearsing an orchestra is possible using just Italian musical terms; (iii) in Europe there are a surprisingly large number of English players who have chosen to live abroad; and (iv) English is a second language not only in Europe but all over the world, as evidenced by the vast number of immigrants landing on our shores at the time of writing. The main reason English is so widely spoken I suppose, is because it is also spoken in the United States, the world's largest economy. On casting my mind back to my first interpreter in Minsk, I came to realise that rehearsing an orchestra involves first talking to them. Interpreters can manage introductions, but rehearsing is different. One can be descriptive, poetic, amusing, or describe what one is looking for in conversational terms, but all this is totally confusing to an interpreter. I tried and quickly realized that she was translating as much as she could, but it clearly was not being understood. I thought I would make better progress without her and from that moment decided that my most important 'weapon' was my baton, my magic wand, so to speak, which I then waved and believe in to this day. (It does not work at French dinner parties though.)

Rex Lawson's interest in ancient pianos went much deeper than the 'honky tonk'. All categories of mechanical music, from a small music box to a fairground roundabout, held a fascination for him. I remember once when we were together in London in November, Rex suggested we visit the Piano Museum in Chiswick to meet his friend Frank Holland, who I believe owned the collection. The museum was in an old church with all the seating removed and filled with pianos and a multitude of other exhibits, including fairground machinery and every type of automaton. Rex was particularly interested in pianolas and the piano rolls on which the museum had a very large library. I discovered performances, I cannot say recordings, by many famous pianists such as Paderewski. Many of these rolls in the museum had been punctured years before the earliest gramophones. Of particular interest to me was a performance of the Grieg Piano Concerto by Percy Grainger. The performance was complete in that it included all the orchestral tuttis. A discussion inevitably followed when Rex suggested, perhaps jokingly, that we should accompany a performance of this roll with the Sinfonia. I pointed out the problem would be with the tuttis (orchestral interludes), which Rex said he could edit out. He finally settled my doubts about whether all this was possible and we decided to go ahead with the project. Not only was Rex able to cut out the tuttis, but in the process of editing the roll he also corrected several wrong notes! It was necessary for Rex to sit away from the piano with a remote control to stop and start the piano roll, which now rotated electrically, while the orchestra played the tuttis. To the best of my knowledge, this was the first time such a performance had ever been attempted and it became a feature of one of our John Player concerts in the Queen Elizabeth Hall on 13 December. Looking Rex up on Google, I discovered that he later repeated it at the QEH, kindly mentioning that it was first done with the English Sinfonia. Rex had a great sense of humour, which added to the drama. I recall no publicity for the concert other than that it was the Grieg Piano Concert with Percy Grainger as soloist, but there was more to it. Picture the event, normal start to the programme, overture, conductor walks off, the piano is placed in position for the second item – Grieg Piano Concerto. When the piano is ready – lid opened – but no pianist, before my appearance, Rex had put several As on the roll to which the orchestra dutifully tuned. Critics described it as 'ghostly'. I came on, took the bow and the performance went through without a hitch – the Grieg Piano Concerto played by Percy Grainger. The Piano Museum remained a principal interest for Rex and he eventually took it over.

1973

The main event of the year was certainly going to be the American tour, but we followed our pattern in the Viennese tradition and gave a concert on the last and first days of each year. The main concert season in Nottingham started in September and ran through to July, so we had a pattern that soon became familiar with our audiences. This sequence of concerts was always preceded by a full day's rehearsal in London and was frequently repeated in other locations such as Derby and Leicester, but also further afield as we were able to offer a symphonic programme, usually with soloists of international repute.

In January, Ephram Kurtz and Elaine (Shaffer) invited John Solum and me to visit them in London during their stay at the Strand Palace Hotel. He frequently visited England to work with the BBC Symphony Orchestra and the Hallé in Manchester. On the occasion of our meeting, he reiterated his interest in my career. He said, 'Your lack of success is not to do with your ability to conduct, it must be your name.' (I had previously had a similar conversation with a musician who thought I should be better known and suggested it was because my name had 13 letters in it.) Ephram thought that combining Neville with Dilkes was the culprit, and asked me what my grandfather's name was. Thinking of my father's father I said 'Albert', which amused him. What about your maternal grandfather he asked? And I replied, 'Charles. Yes, yes', he said, 'that is better – Charles Dilkes – STRONG! And then added, as a matter of interest what was your mother's maiden name? I replied 'Aston', 'Even better,' said Ephram 'ASTON DILKES – could not be better! On a sad note, John told me just as we were leaving that Ephram's wife Elaine (flautist) had throat cancer and she died on 13 February.

Following on from this sad news, John Solum was our soloist later in the month and thoughtfully dedicated his performances of the Mozart G major flute concerto to Elaine Shaffer's memory. He had been a close friend of hers in his earlier years in America. This was while touring in Spain. At this time I will mention Ken Gurling (referred to earlier) as he was as excited as I was about the orchestra being invited to do a week's tour of Spain and said he would very much like to come with us at his own expense. I could not hear of this, but suggested we could find him things to do – I was thinking, we did not have a concert manager and he could probably help with travel subsidy payments that had to be made to the members of the orchestra. These were daily cash allowances insisted on by the Musicians' Union. So not only did we have the luxury of a travelling doctor to look after us, but also a paymaster. It did not stop there either as many of the concerts were paid in cash to the orchestra after the performance, presumably from members of the audience who had not purchased tickets in advance. Ken was happy to take over the accounting, he had travelled with the rugby team when a student at Kings College, London performing exactly the same task. On top of this he also took over the job of orchestra librarian, which entailed putting up music stands and distributing the music before the seating rehearsal, sometimes behind a cinema screen while a film was showing if that was our venue. Ken clearly took great delight in giving us his services and came with the orchestra on several occasions afterwards, including two trips to the Montreux Festival.

I worked for a second time as a guest conductor with the Ulster Orchestra, followed by some broadcasts with the RTE orchestra in Dublin.

While in Ulster, I was approached by its general manager, James Allaway, whom I had already met on my previous visit. He knew the Sinfonia was without a general manager and, wanting to return to the UK, James kindly offered me his services. Things had settled somewhat and it was on my mind to start looking for a suitable person for the position, so I appointed him. James kept the orchestra going, though frequently offered programmes to promoters without consulting me about their content. However, this did not interfere with the orchestra's repertoire insofar as our own promoted grant-aided concerts were concerned and, furthermore, the timing was good because we now had someone with experience to hold the fort during the impending absence of the orchestra in America for six weeks.

Writing about James is difficult for me. I believe that his main problem was not understanding the sophistication of a fine chamber orchestra compared with a concert orchestra. I use this term when referring to the performance of 'light music'. He certainly found work for the orchestra, but this often involved augmenting the number of players to the large symphonic range of works. He had no control over the concerts we promoted in Nottingham and the Midlands. Those promotions had local government and Arts Council aid and it was my duty to programme them. Hitherto, for bookings outside our region, we would try to repeat these programmes. James, however, took a different line and suddenly I found myself conducting programmes normally in the repertoire of a full symphony orchestra. This was no challenge to me personally, as most of my guest conducting was with symphony orchestras, but was less appealing to a few of my chamber music players. However, I will add, they would not turn down work of this sort as they themselves frequently took on work involving 'light' music, not to mention 'film music'. James could of course sell programmes of this nature, and did, and I hate to remember the number of times we suffered the 1812 Overture. I do not think a single string player ever tolerated it without ear plugs! Another favourite of his were concerts featuring film and television themes, including one we did at the Victor Hockhauser weekly Sunday night concerts at the Royal Albert Hall with Moura Lympany, piano and Steve Race acting as compère!

The forthcoming American tour had a downside following a decision I had to make sometime before leaving. Ron Thomas, my leader and I could not have had a better one, said at the last minute that he was not prepared to go on the tour if it meant leading the orchestra for a flute concerto at every concert, but would if I gave him a violin concerto to play from time to time.

Three things influenced the decision I made: (1) it was a late decision; (2) the fee he would expect had not been included in our agreement with Columbia Artists; and (3) John had arranged the tour. My response was that he would not be the orchestra's leader when we came back if he chose to desert us. John Ludlow, our subleader and a close friend of Marilyn Taylor who also subled in John's absence, agreed to lead the orchestra for the tour. John had formally led the Royal Opera Orchestra at Covent Garden and I was grateful to him for his interest in the music we were performing, which went beyond just leading. I stood by what I said to Ron and he ceased to lead the orchestra after our return to England. I was worried that the members of the Sinfonia would take sides on this decision, but there was not even a ripple of discontent. The concert tour covered a total of nearly 15,000 miles (including air flights), with events that could half fill this book but just a few will suffice. Landing in the early evening, American time, we stayed in a hotel and the following morning flew to Bermuda. Here we stayed at the palatial (five-star) Princess Hotel in Hamilton, my first experience of air conditioning in such sumptuous accommodation. We were scheduled to play two concerts on consecutive nights but with different programmes, John Solum playing a Mozart flute concerto on the first night and John Ludlow playing a Mozart violin concerto on the second. Before the second concert we were all invited to a buffet lunch at Fen Kranenburg's mansion in a park overlooking the estuary to the harbour. Fen, an expatriate from the Netherlands, moved to Bermuda after the Second World War as a safe haven. Wine importer, amateur flautist and a good friend of John's made sure that music was not bypassed on the island of Bermuda. This was very much an open-air gathering and we enjoyed walking in the grounds with our cocktails. Being undecided in my choice, an attractive waitress encouraged me to have a Bloody Mary on the assurance that it was not too alcoholic. However, feeling it was having some effect on me I enquired what it was, only to be told VODKA and tomato juice. I recalled on a previous occasion back in my Corby days, when being showed how to make an authentic Spaghetti Bolognaise my American tutor who had served me 7 Ups throughout his instruction, learnt too late it was vodka and 7 Up and I vowed never to touch vodka again. Until this moment I hadn't but thankfully stopped on this occasion in good time.

We arrived back in New York on the Monday morning ready for the tour to commence in earnest. For the most part we travelled by coach, but there were exceptions, one being the need to get to St John's Newfoundland. For this we flew from Halifax, which included two stops. It seemed evident that there was some problem at the time of the first landing, but following passengers leaving and others boarding, we took off to continue the flight. The second landing, however, seemed more problematic and we were asked to disembark and go to the restaurant where we would be served refreshments before our next departure. As time passed, I decided to investigate. The runway was visible from the windows and, to my horror, I saw a forklift with one of the engines of our plane in its claws, and an engineer perched on the top of a stepladder busily working on it. I refrained from reporting my findings and felt grateful that the others had been less inquisitive. However, there was unrest later on arrival at St John's airport when some members of the orchestra asked for the plane to be replaced. Our tour manager enquired about this possibility but was assured that the fault would be looked into overnight and the flight would almost certainly take off as planned. Everything was now behind schedule. The coach to take us to the hall for our usual seating rehearsal had moved on to its next assignment, thus barely leaving us time to locate our rooms and change. The entire orchestra was transported to the concert hall by a fleet of overcrowded taxis doing return trips, and leaving me (the least important one) until last. The return was as scheduled and the hotel laid on a memorable meal. There was a little unrest the following day when boarding the same plane but the flight was uneventful at each of the landings. Arriving in Halifax, the next stage of the tour took us to Quebec, which meant an overnight train journey. For this I remember my cabin – a single, with a toilet, washbasin, comfortable seat, and open-ended tunnel bed. The bed linen and towels were impeccable, and I slept like a log. This was followed by Vermont and two days later we arrived on the north side of the Niagara Falls, where we gave two concerts. This was followed by appearances in Michigan, and the states of Ohio, Pennsylvania, Virginia and Delaware. Another memorable moment was when the coach driver got lost in Detroit in the enormous Ford Motor company complex, and the highlight was Billy, our Columbia Artists tour manager who was on hand 24/7 for the entire tour.

Probably my fondest memory of the tour was the turning point in my conducting career, as I now found repeatedly conducting one of the same three programmes every day somewhat boring. In the past, for all the practical piano examinations and the odd recitals I had given, I had always played from memory. I had made a serious study of how to do this from a book that made it clear that, although there was some merit in rote learning, it was unreliable. Rote implies repetition, so by repeatedly playing a piece of music the fingers will, without thinking, automatically select the notes to play. A more reliable method is to memorize the score away from the instrument and hear the sounds in one's mind. Thus, as a boy, I remember setting myself the task of learning and memorising a Mozart minuet and trio that I had never heard or played before, and finally sitting down and playing it for the first time from memory. I had played all my practical piano examinations from memory and I resolved to do the same now with the full scores of the present series of concerts – first reading and memorizing the score while travelling on the coach, then closing my eyes and hearing it in my mind. I eventually prepared all three programmes in this way, cautiously checking the result on the concert platform with the score there but not looking at it, and finally dispensing with them without the music desk. The one exception is the concerto, which is usually played just before the interval, so the conductor leaves the platform to reappear with the soloist, with the music desk being brought on before their appearance and of course removed during the interval.

There was a memorable concert with a marvellous audience of over 2,300 in New York.

HAYDN	Symphony No 44
DEBUSSY	Danse Sacrée and Danse Profane
RAVEL	Introduction and Allegro
BRITTEN	Variations on a theme of Frank Bridge
MOZART	Concerto in C for Flute and Harp
	John Solum Flute
	Nicanor Zabaleta Harp

The tour concluded with a further two concerts in Kingston (Rhode Island) and Princeton. On our return from the American tour, I from then on, conducted from memory.

After we returned, as promised we gave three harpsichord quartet concerts, two in Rutland (Tixover and Ketton churches) and one in London in a private residence. Tixover church is remote from the village and without electricity so was performed entirely by candlelight. Ketton was without problems. We hosted the Tixover audience at the hall after the concert, and Freddie, a dear friend of ours and also our solicitor, and Eileen Stevens, hosted the Ketton concert afterwards in Ketton Hall. Thanks go to John Solum, Tamara Coates, and Nicola Anderson. I played harpsichord at the first two, and piano at the third. Donations were generous. James Allaway had not been inactive during our absence, and I was pleased I had left someone in charge with experience of orchestral management. We returned to England on 6 November and having earlier spoken to James on a transatlantic telephone call was aware of several new booking for concerts for which I had been able to alert musicians to for their diaries.

Our first concert was in Repton exactly one week after our return. This was followed by our monthly Nottingham concert with the Schuman Piano Concerto in A minor with Belgian soloist Abel Matthys. The concert ended with Beethoven's 'Eroica' Symphony. The concert was repeated the following evening in Derby. On the 3 December we were booked to play for the Maidenhead Music Society followed on the fifth with a different programme in Melton Mowbray, Leicestershire which was 'home ground' for the Sinfonia.

The following day we travelled to Lancaster for a concert at the university which featured the soloist Jana Frenklová in Mozart's piano concerto (K 271) The programme also included the 'Variations on a theme of Frank Bridge' by Britten and I had arranged for John Ludlow to lead for this concert and the following night in Kendal in the Lake District as we had played this difficult work many times during the American tour. After the concert John and I were talking in the green room when I received a surprised visit from my organ tutor during my Birmingham days as a student, Dr Willis Grant. He said 'this is indeed a memorable occasion for me as I can shake hands with two of my former pupils'. I felt this needed some explanation as I was not aware John had ever played the organ. It transpired John had been a pupil at the King Edward's school in Edgbaston at the time when Willis had been Director of Music at the school and Cathedral organist. He was now Professor of Music at Bristol University.

Following this burst of activity my need to replace Ron Thomas was now very evident. Amongst the several musicians who had replaced Ron during this period I learnt Ray Cohen was interested. I had met Ray during my Watney Sargent year when he led the R.P.O. and asked James to see if he was interested. He was but wanted at the same time the promise of being able to conduct the orchestra. I felt this would need a contractual agreement which would be difficult as we were a free-lance orchestra not sharing the luxury of guaranteed concerts, and in any case were already inviting guest conductors on an engagement basis as we would for soloists. However, it is a sad reflection that opportunities to conduct are rare in Britain, particularly compared with Europe where permanent professional orchestras are to be found in all principal cities and towns. Furthermore the number of opera houses there adds to the opportunities for many aspiring conductors to emerge from the ranks and being taken on, first as a répétiteur and then followed by the experience of being a chorus master. I'm glad to say Ray understood and we worked together many times afterwards.

There was also at this time in Britain a tradition that once a player always a player. I understand the BBC would not offer Daniel Barenboim a conducting contract with the English Chamber orchestra because he was listed and categorized as a 'pianist' on their books. Colin Davies was one of the very few who was able to rise from the ranks. John Georgiadis another, but he could only find acceptance abroad.

Around this time I remember being offered work in South Africa but the Musicians' Union advised against it. Shortly after that I was also offered a contract with the Australian Broadcasting Company, but with a young family to consider, I declined because it entailed a minimum stay of six months. The year ended on 31 December in Nottingham with 'A night in old Vienna'.

The boating diversion

In the spring we had trailed the boat back to Deganwy, and slept aboard for a couple of nights during the antifouling and provisioning. The evening before launching we drove into Llandudno to find a restaurant or 'chippy', but the only sign of life in this sleepy town was the main hotel. I spoke to the receptionist, apologising for our jeans and tramp like appearance, to which he replied, 'We never judge bananas by their skins' and then seated us behind a screen in the dining room. I think there was only one other resident couple. The boat was launched the following morning and we motored over to our mooring, finally organized the boat, and returned to Tixover. We made several visits to the boat for weekends before taking a longer break in the summer. Two daughters took it in turns to accompany us, the remaining two being looked after by my mother and father, who were of course resident at the hall in their cottage. For the last visit of the season we took Rebecca and

Gré and sailed the boat over to Puffin Island, which is just clear of the channel between the mainland and the Isle of Anglesey. We circumnavigated the island, misjudged the tide on our return and ran aground. Being a bilge keeler the boat sat upright, but as the tide dropped even further I leant over the side to look at the water; this caused the boat to dig one of its keels into the sand, so we were left at an acute angle. Pam came to the rescue with afternoon tea, which was more than welcome and had a calming effect on Gré who was convinced she would not now be home in time to be able to start Stamford High School in just a few days' time. The tide started to rise and the buoyancy of the boat freed the offending keel without difficulty and floated us upright. We sailed back to Conway and finished the break in excellent health. I resolved to know my exact position in a channel in the future, though to be fair there were very few buoys at that time.

We had sailed *Booster* throughout the summer, at weekends and for our main holiday, but with only four berths we were limited with crew. As one might imagine, not all our daughters wanted to go to sea, but I was convinced we should have a boat with six berths. We decided to take the plunge, so to speak, and buy a larger one. Offshore Yachts by this time were well into GRP boats and were producing a Halcyon 23, 27 and a 32 foot Nantucket Clipper. We decided on the Halcyon 27 to meet out budget, but exceeded it when we saw the 32 footer and immediately signed the contract for the Nantucket Clipper later to be named *Maestro*. *Booster* immediately went on the market and, in Pam's capable hands while I was in America, sold for our asking price of £750, which was £50 more than we had paid for her.

1974

A condition for buying the new boat was that it had to go to the London Boat Show to be exhibited at Earl's Court in January. For this, Offshore Yachts generously threw in several 'goodies' – cockpit cushions and other gear on exhibit at the same time. Extras for the boat that we had paid for included electronics, furling genoa, spray hood, and mizzen staysail. The basic boat cost £7,500 and was registered with Lloyds during the build and included in its register. This was the year the IRA decided to plant a bomb in Earl's Court, which to our horror, exploded somewhere in the roof. We experienced no real damage but the decks were covered in soot, which meant they had to be repainted with the usual non-slip deck paint. The boat was delivered to its new home in Tollesbury Marina, Essex at the end of January and it was a proud family that spent the first of many weekends there. We joined the Yacht Club, a short walk from our berth at the marina. During that summer, through sailing on the Deben, Orwell and Walton Backwaters, we became very familiar with the Essex coast. Looking back in my logbook I am reminded of a quick dash back to base after a lunchtime shipping forecast and increasing wind strength. We heard that Ted Heath, with members of his racing crew, had been sailing the same waters from Burnham on Crouch and that he left the boat in view of the forecast to get back to the House of Commons, with instructions to his crew to return it to the south coast when conditions improved. It transpired that, despite the forecast, the crew decided to make an overnight passage and the following morning the press reported that *Morning Cloud II* had sunk off the Sussex coast with the loss of two lives, which included his godson Christopher Cadd, whose body was never recovered.

As a member of the Royal Hawich Yacht Club, I was proudly able to fly a Blue Ensign, which I did. An elderly woman looking down on *Maestro* from the quayside once asked one of my crew why our flag was blue? He replied, 'because Her Majesty the Queen had granted the skipper her permission to do so.'

At New Parks College I had by now moved on from day skipper to coastal skipper. Like me, a number of students had their own boats. Bill Hudson was able to dispense with some the charter boats and use suitable ones belonging to the club. With the coastal skipper qualification I was able to benefit from this arrangement as I could assess a crew member's ability with regard to the lower grades, which Bill as a fully qualified instructor could later ratify. For this we were able to receive a small charter fee, which helped a little towards berthing and insurance costs.

1974 More concerts

The year began with a Queen Elizabeth Hall concert on 9 January. This featured Gayle Smith in the Shostakovich cello concerto, Britten's Variations on a theme of Frank Bridge, and Mozart's 'Jupiter' Symphony. Still without my former leader Ron Thomas, and searching for a replacement, I invited John Georgiardis to fill the chair, which he did for me on this and several other occasions.

March saw another tour to Spain, which started in Valencia but was extended to Portugal where we played in Oporto and Lisbon. We flew from

Madrid to Lisbon and then went by train to Oporto. The final concert was in Lisbon, after which I was the British ambassador's guest for dinner. We flew back to London the following day.

Following the Spanish tour, still without a permanent leader for the orchestra, I was now conscious of the urgent need to find a replacement. John Georgiardis would have hardly surprisingly been my first choice, but I was beginning to learn that his interest lay more in the 'baton' than the 'bow'. Now, writing in January 2021, I have read that he has just died, but that he did have some measure of success with the 'baton'.

I eventually appointed John Glickman, better known to us all as Jack. Jack had led the London Mozart Players and seemed happy to consider a change. I gather he was not fond of Jane Glover one of the earliest of this new breed of conductors who was now working with the orchestra. Earlier, Jack had been principal viola (not leader) in the Bath Chamber Orchestra conducted by Yehudi Menhuin. He took over as leader at the end of March, but in all sincerity I cannot say this was a wise choice for me.

Looking back to concerts and all the many programmes I conducted, I cannot avoid mentioning the one at the QEH on 6 November. This included William Walton's *Façade*, with well-known broadcaster Robin Ray reading the narrative. I should mention here that there are two different versions of the accompaniment and for this performance I used the version with flute, clarinet, saxophone, trumpet, percussion and cello. The first half of the programme was for wind ensemble only, and included the Mozart 'Wind Serenade' in E-flat and Dvořák's Serenade in D minor Op. 44.

1975

Need I mention it? The year started as usual with the traditional Viennese concerts. Early in February, Tony and Marie Garrett invited me and Pam to a Royal Opera House performance of Verdi's *Un Ballo in Maschera*. It will be remembered from earlier that Tony was chairman of the cigarette manufacturers John Player in Nottingham, but on leaving Nottingham, took over the chairmanship of Imperial Tobacco, which was sponsoring this opera. We met in the foyer followed by a reception and attended the performance as a small party in the comfort of a box. Tony remarked with a smile that they could not afford to be the only sponsor, as for the Sinfonia, but had to share this one with the National Westminster Bank. We had sat in many different places in the opera house, but never with this degree of comfort! I recall following the performance with an evening meal in an up-market Indian restaurant, after which we were given hot towels. Tony promptly placed his over his face, and slid down in his chair to recover from the effects of the curry – an amusing end to a memorable evening.

There was a QEH concert on 7 May followed by more recordings in Abbey Road for EMI (French music including Ibert and Honegger), thus making May a busy month for me in London. To save hotel expenses, I sailed *Maestro* down from our permanent berth on the east coast to St Katharine's dock by Tower Bridge in London. My management had alerted the London press to the voyage and they were there to welcome me. The result of the meeting was rather a 'put up job' as they wanted to photograph me getting off the boat to conduct a concert. I obliged by putting on my full evening dress, climbed out of the hatch and was duly photographed, but not following it with a concert! I used the boat as a base in which to stay and was even able to take all my family during a school holiday. Thus, my children had an opportunity to visit places of interest in the capital, a pleasure that had only been afforded to Clare and Rachel during my Watney-Sargent Award year. This was in the early days of VAT and I remember the following year being visited by a VAT inspector who spotted a claim for the reimbursement of VAT on my mooring fees at St Katharine's Dock and was curious to know how I could conceivably justify it. On producing evidence of the article and photograph in the *Daily Telegraph* of me emerging from the hatch in evening dress, he eventually smiled and left.

The summer saw a break from music and I decided to spend our family holiday in Holland to enjoy the sheltered waters of the Dutch canals. To do this, and to spare my family the ordeal of having to cross the North Sea, I undertook the 12-hour open water passage without them. Remembering Rex Thompson's earlier trip from Harwich to Cornwall and his family later joining him there, I chose to take *Maestro* over in June – my first open sea crossing – from our now permanent berth in Woolverstone, and leave her in a marina there in readiness for the family holiday in July. For moral support, I asked Mike Saunders Watson, who had the advantage of a naval past, to crew for me and he accepted. Mike had a Westerly ketch, which he kept in Scotland, so I knew he was totally at home with our sort of sailing. We left Woolverstone at 20.15 and sailed overnight direct to Flushing arriving at 08.15 the following morning. Rex had sailed to Holland several times and kindly lent me a complete set of charts of the Dutch inland waterways. He had told me what a charming marina there was in Goes (pronounced 'Hoose') and so we sailed there. A very pretty harbour with a welcoming lighthouse, which on closer examination revealed a toilet.

A beautiful 38-foot Nelson motorsailer with an equally beautiful sunbather on the aft deck was moored just inside the entrance. Its owner, who came to the rail, guided me in and said he would wait for me around the corner to help me into a berth. He did so and for his help I invited him, and the woman I took to be his wife, for drinks that evening. Disappointingly, he came on his own – it transpired that the woman on his boat was only crew and not his wife – and after a couple of G&Ts with Tony Simmonds, as we now knew him, suggested we all visit the clubhouse. It has no bar, simply a trapdoor in the floor with steps down to shelves of drinks and a large 'honesty' box in which to leave your money to pay for whatever you take. Apparently, this is still the case today. While there, we discovered that Tony was in property. I confessed to being a musician and awaited Mike's answer. I expected him to mention Rockingham Castle, but he just said he was a farmer, which was true but it amused me. It was a disappointment to find, when speaking to the harbour master the following day that we could not leave *Maestro* there until July so, after a couple of nights, we returned to Veere where we were more successful. We were to meet Tony again during our summer cruise and we all became good friends. We returned by the overnight ferry from Ostende to Felixstowe, took a taxi to Woolverstone, and returned to Rutland in my car, which was conveniently parked at the yacht club.

In July, the whole family returned to Holland on the ferry and we had an enjoyable four weeks on *Maestro*. At Veere, we found that our boat had been given another berth and was now lying with another Nantucket moored astern of her. We immediately recognized the Wakefield family who had bought one of the three Clippers being built at the same time as *Maestro*. From this moment on, our paths were to cross many times and still do at the time of writing this book. At the end of our holiday we sailed to Ostende, where we put Rachel, Gré and Rebecca on the ferry to Felixstowe where my parents would meet them. They had given our friend Rex a lift to the ferry as we had arranged with him to accompany us on the return passage. Clare had decided to stay on board and sail back with us to Woolverstone. Sailing continued into autumn and, being members of the Offshore Yacht Owners' Association, we were able to take part in its rallies, which continued during the winter months with meetings in London.

By this time, the Sinfonia was under secure management and I was able to concentrate solely on the music. I could learn scores just as easily on a boat as I could in an armchair at home. Interestingly, one of the first people I met as a member of the Tollesbury Yacht Club was Alberto Semprini, a well-known and loved pianist, and frequent broadcaster with the BBC, both in his own programme series and as a guest artist with other promoters. He had a motor cruiser in the marina at Tollesbury and lived permanently on a houseboat on the mud flats at West Mersea. Needless to say, it was not long before we worked together. I could not imagine a better choice of soloist for our concert to celebrate the new concert hall in Corby new town than Alberto. At that stage in my career my repertoire was rather limited to the classics, so I took it upon myself to convince him to learn the Schumann piano concerto, which he did for this occasion. I was very interested to listen to his next broadcast on the BBC, which not surprisingly included a movement from the Schuman piano concerto! Later in my career I conducted the Gershwin 'Rhapsody in Blue' several times and have to say none was better than Semprini's.

In the September, we made the first of our visits to the Montreux festival. For this, I conducted two concerts, one in Montreux, which included the Mozart flute and harp concerto, with John Solum, flute and Marilyn Costello, harp. There was also the Vivaldi Concerto in D for guitar and orchestra, soloist Alexandre Lagoya, repeated at the second concert in Fribourg.

On 1 December, I recorded the Constant Lambert piano concerto with soloist Richard Rodney Bennett for Deutsche Grammophon, subsequently made available by EMI. I followed this, shortly after with another visit to Germany for concerts with the Göttingen Symphony Orchestra. One programme included Elgar's cello concerto with the German cellist, Klaus Storch, Britten's variations on a theme of Frank Bridge and Beethoven's 'Eroica' symphony. We also travelled to Buckeburg where, in the concert hall they had a historic purpose built grand piano with two sets of interlocking piano strings played from keyboards at both ends, thus enabling the two pianists to sit facing each other. This concert featured Mozart's double piano concerto.

Chapter 8

All is Not What it Seems

1976–1978

Unrest, family and boats, relocation

1976 Unrest

A troubled period was to follow after Sir Max Bemrose retired from his chairmanship of the board because it was followed by pressure to recruit a more (so-called) democratic board with new members mainly representing local authorities. His replacement was Geoffrey Moore, a lecturer at Trent College in Nottingham, who turned out to be a disaster. Geoff Moor epitomized the gulf which can sometimes be detected between the academia and the practical. That some academic musicians are practical goes without saying as in the case of Professor Ivor Keys, an academic and very fine keyboard player, and includes many instrumentalists of considerable repute who also teach, but importantly thoroughly understand the difference between the class room and the concert platform.

I frankly despaired at this new board of directors, none of whom, with the exception of the chairman, had any musical knowledge or even an interest in music. Strong words I know, but true! The chairman should have made it clear to the board that its only job was to ensure that aid from individual authorities was being used as intended and to satisfy the charitable status laws. The Arts Council could look after itself. Most importantly, it should have been made clear that the direct management of the orchestra was first and foremost the responsibility of the orchestra's manager and his team. Following a small audience turn out to one of my concerts I later heard there was a suggestion by one new board member they should invite the Austrian conductor Herbert von Karajan to permanently take my place. After my departure this same person succeeded in ridding the company of its obviously weak chairman, only to get himself appointed in his place. Still not satisfied he finally sacked and replaced James Allaway. This proved to be the final demise of the orchestra in Nottingham. On the other hand, there was no doubt in my mind that it could not be ignored, and it had been evident to me for some time that the Arts Council basically wanted to rid itself of its liability to what was now the only freelance orchestra operating in the provinces with direct Arts Council funding. I thought its aid might stop at any time, but reasoned that it could be controlled (i) by making the orchestra permanent, or (ii) by re-establishing a competent concert board.

Establishing the orchestra on a permanent basis was discussed and I tried to help by producing a paper recording our musicians' views on the subject. A few indicated their willingness to consider moving to the Midlands, while others said they would continue to travel or commute to Nottingham on a 'first call' agreement to the Sinfonia and combine this with other freelance work in London. In any event, I never thought the Arts Council would support this move, which proved correct. I had to sit through board meetings listening to a considerable amount of rubbish being discussed without any intervention by the chairman.

After my Watney Sargent year I had talked with Sir Malcolm Sargent about the Midland Sinfonia as it was then called, and he, having been brought up in Stamford in the East Midlands, thought like me there was indeed a case for such an orchestra in that area. From my point of view his death later was untimely as I am certain he would now have been a very strong ally in my cause to continue the work of the orchestra in the Midlands.

Since the concert board controlled the purse strings, I decided to find an escape route, which I did by registering the name 'English Sinfonietta'. This afforded me some breathing space in which to work independently from the Concert Society if it were ultimately to prove necessary. From its outset, I saw the Sinfonietta as a self-governing orchestra and invited members of the Sinfonia to be shareholders. Harry Legge a member of the orchestra, well versed in orchestral politics took the chair. In this way, we could escape the interference of the Concert Society, although clearly we could not operate without a subsidy if we wanted to promote our own concerts – the price of independence. However, we could take on engagements and, as remains to be seen, we did.

Having made this decision, against the wishes of the older members of the orchestra, I gave notice to leave but agreed to remain for a further three years, subject to a minimum of thirty concerts in the United Kingdom and all concerts abroad. This probably resembled the contracts that major symphony orchestras draw up with internationally renowned conductors, who are mainly interested in boosting their reputations and happy that there are not more concerts. I believe that even world-renowned conductors can be unpopular with their players, who will sometimes sideline them if the feedback is poor. My terms were agreed and, despite a tumultuous three years with the board continuing to display its total and complete inability to cope, asked me at the beginning of the third year to extend the contract by a further year. Arts Council support continued until my departure and then, as I expected, was finally withdrawn.

Back to concerts

Our traditional start to the year was followed by a concert I conducted in Worksop Priory in Nottinghamshire. I remember conducting many concerts in the priory, so believe that the site had been deconsecrated for some time. This particular concert featured John Lill and, since dressing rooms were in short supply, he and I shared one. It was sparsely furnished and, undaunted, John stretched out on the floor to relax before the concert. I followed suit and we lay side by side chatting comfortably. I cannot remember what led to the subject of life after death, but he surprised me by posing the question in reverse. Did I believe in life before birth? Four or five years later, readers will learn there was to be a sequel to this conversation.

Of the many tours we made to Spain, this visit in February remains in my memory. The programme was a demanding one for which I scheduled a pre-rehearsal in London the day before our departure. This was mainly to cover the Dvořák Serenade and the Shostakovich Piano Concerto, which features a trumpet solo we had not played before. Perhaps, more importantly, my leader was noticeably unavailable for the tour and Raymond Cohen took his place. The pianist, Christina Ortiz, was our soloist for the Shostakovich and, as is customary, was scheduled only to join the orchestra at the afternoon rehearsal immediately before the first concert. My rehearsal with the orchestra went well and we met at Heathrow the following day only to learn that our flight was delayed owing to a baggage strike. We ended up loading our own luggage under airport direction and, after a long delay, eventually took off. Despite our late arrival in Valencia, our coach was patiently waiting for us. This left us with just enough time to get to the concert hall and for the concert manager to set up the music stands and distribute the music. Some members of the orchestra decided to change into evening dress on the coach. I spoke to Christina, who had joined us at the airport, and explained we would not be sight-reading her concerto as I had included it in our prerehearsal. She was completely relaxed and said she would at least have plenty of time to change. Such situations inevitably occur from time to time with all musicians, but such is the standard of professionalism that they go completely unnoticed by the listeners.

There were two programmes for this tour, which started in Valencia in the south of Spain, finished in Oviedo in the north, with the final concert in Bilbao in time for our return flight. In the second programme, Christina played the Mozart's Piano Concerto K 449. I recall some towns had a second concert, which necessitated the two different programmes. With regard to my contract there were only two events which, although not entirely the fault of the concert society, I will mention. The first (also a loss for the players) was a week's tour in Sweden. Having just returned from a tour in Spain mentioned above I received a telephone call from Jasper Parrot, a partner in the agents 'Harrison and Parrot'. They were due to manage a week's tour by the London Mozart Players in Sweden, who for some reason were not able to go. The agency also managed Christina Ortiz and knowing of the success of our tour in Spain, asked if we could go in their place and play the same programme. I spoke to Trevor, our concert manager who informed me most of our players could be available, including Ray Cohen, as Jack had again declined. However, there was, a stumbling block which I believe could have been circumnavigated. The Spanish tour arrived back in England just in time for one of our monthly concerts in Nottingham. For this there was a guest conductor, and a problem over his pre rehearsal. I offered to talk to the guest conductor to see if there was any room for manoeuvre only to be reminded of the terms of my contract!

Christina was to play with us again in Nottingham in December. The second event in terms of my contract was when I subsequently received an offer for a second American tour which, although by the time it would take place I would no longer be with the English Sinfonia, was, nevertheless still on offer for the English Sinfonietta. I was given to understand this was vetoed by my leader Jack Glickman for reasons best known to Jack. It is also a sad reflection on his loyalty that he was not present to lead the orchestra for a BBC Radio 3 broadcast scheduled from De Montfort Hall, Leicester the following year. Finally I was sadly left wondering about a conversation between a member of the orchestra and the newly self-appointed chairman, subsequently manager of the orchestra, that was overheard and was not complimentary about me.

In May I should mention standing in for Richard Hickox to conduct his orchestra in Ely Cathedral. The programme included Arthur Wills's organ concerto. I was given to understand that Richard took ill after his pre-rehearsal and, knowing I had given the first performance of the concerto, his manager rang to ask if I could step in at only 24 hours' notice. Arthur Wills, organist and master of the choristers at the cathedral, had written this organ concerto, which had been featured as a first performance at the Nottingham Festival concert in Southwell Minster on 22 July 1970, in a formidable programme for any conductor. See 1970.

Concerts continued regularly until the summer break. Our second visit to the Montreux Festival took place in September and our soloist on this occasion was the oboist Heinz Holliger. The conductor Ephram Kurtz, who I mentioned previously, was in the audience for this concert. He had a residence in Gesdatsch and came to the green room at the end of the concert to congratulate me on the programme. He also had high praise for the quality of the orchestra, and still wondered why I was not better known.

There were three concerts this year as opposed to two on the previous visit. I conducted two of them, the second in Saint-Maurice featuring the organist Georges Athanasiadès who played the Haydn organ concerto in C major. But I must mention how the orchestra had assembled on the platform exactly on time and tuned ready for my appearance to conduct the first item, Symphony No. 46, Haydn. I remember waiting in the wings ready to walk on and start the programme, but the seconds ticked by and then turned into minutes. No panic as it could be just a slight problem, but on this occasion went on long enough to make the musicians just a little fidgety. The problem was eventually explained to me. Although the Swiss Broadcasting Corporation was ready, it was linking up with several other countries in Europe and waiting for their confirmation. I did not know a broadcast was involved in this engagement and I think I prudently forgot to tell the musicians afterwards that this had been the reason for the delay. The third concert in Montreux was conducted by Heinz Finger.

Another highlight of the year was a booking we gave to the violinist Kyung-Wha Chung who was very popular at the time. She wanted to play the Elgar violin concerto and I will confess to being worried by the thought of her playing a work so 'English'. So much so I made certain she came to the prerehearsal. This is not a routine thing for any concerto other than a first performance or a very challenging work. My worries were of course unfounded. We gave two concerts, the first in Nottingham and the second in Hull. The programme also included the Sibelius Seventh Symphony.

1977

Despite the unrest, there were quite a few highlights, though none attributable to the new board of directors. The year began with a QEH concert featuring the American violinist Howard Gottlieb who also came on tour with the orchestra in the Midlands.

With the award of a life peerage to Benjamin Britten in the Queen's birthday honours last summer I had thought it appropriate to give a performance of his *Les Illuminations* with Heather Harper to mark the occasion. Now, with the composer's untimely death occurring a few weeks before, the English Sinfonia decided to give another performance on 21 January in his memory.

In February I conducted a concert in St John's Smith Square with John Lill playing Mozart's Piano concerto No. 20 in D minor and Walter Boeykens playing the Finzi clarinet concerto. Not surprisingly, in view of events taking place with the board of the Concert Society there was a departure from recording with the Sinfonia. On 8 August I recorded four works by Malcolm Arnold, the two flute concertos with John Solum and the two Malcolm Arnold Sinfoniettas. (The third was still to be composed.) These were successful recordings, but unfortunately when released, the flute concertos engaged the wrath of Malcolm Arnold, who had dedicated the flute concertos to Richard Adney and I believe had also promised him the first recording. Sparks flew! But the Sinfoniettas survived, later to be available on CD. I should emphasize the orchestra for these recording was the Philharmonia.

Regretfully, the new purpose built concert hall in Derby had serious acoustic problems and we were now back to giving our Derby concerts in the cathedral. For a concert on 2 October, we had Clifford Curzon to play the Beethoven 'Emperor' Piano Concerto, which followed the 'Corilanus' overture, the concert ending with the Fifth Symphony in an all Beethoven programme. On 7 October, the BBC recorded a concert in the de Montfort Hall, Leicester in which the soloist was John Lill who played Mozart's Piano Concerto No. 21 in C major (K.467.) The programme having started with Haydn's 'Clock Symphony', was followed after the interval with the Fantasia on a Theme of Thomas Tallis by Vaughan Williams and it concluded with 'El amor Brujo' (Love, the Magician) by Manuel de Falla.

Family and boats

Last year, having taken a trip in *Maestro* to France and then a cruise to Plymouth and back, we covered the whole of the south coast of England. In the spring I did the usual courses for New Parks and we took a permanent berth in Lymington Yacht Haven. From there we cruised the Solent, the south coast along with trips to France, the Channel Islands and Brittany. While based in Lymington I completed my shore based theory course for yacht master.

My eldest daughter Clare left school in the summer of 1976. Rather to my disappointment, as opportunities to do so were so much easier than they had been in my day, she was not interested in continuing her studies at a university. She was also reluctant to decide on any sort of career, despite our ample encouragement. Her mother and I eventually laid down the law and, to our disappointment, and near to Christmas, she decided to go into waitressing. The only consolation this gave us was that it was at the George Hotel in Stamford. I despaired at her lack of direction, but after Christmas 1977, Pamela and I discussed her dilemma and reached the conclusion based on two facts (i) Clare's interest in horses and (ii) my experience of being away from the comforts of home due to National Service. This followed a discussion with my friend John Solum who was friendly with an American woman who had married a Frenchman and moved to France. At this point I will introduce readers to Miranda (now) Toulouse Lautrec. She lived with her husband Charles Constantin Toulouse Lautrec in the old apothecary's house adjacent to the Palace of Versailles, but also had a small château with a stud farm near Limoges. CC (as we called him) was a successful businessman and, need I say it, descended from the well-known artist. Miranda managed the farming business in Limoges and, according to John, welcomed students to work with her on the stud farm. John kindly gave me her telephone number, after having warned her that I would be contacting her. When I did, she said that if Clare were willing, she would give her a chance. This satisfied my two aims of letting her work with horses and giving her a break from the comforts of home. It now remained for Pam and me to convince Clare, which we did, and by spring, she was ready to leave. Clare, who was now 18 years of age, 19 in April, was ready to break her home ties, just as I had been at her age. On 5 April, she duly travelled overland to Limoges where she was met at the station and taken to Roussac. I must admit to a slight panic on my part as I could not obtain a connection with the farm and had to ring CC in Paris, who immediately put my mind at ease, as only the French can do, and then all went to plan.

Shortly after Clare's departure I took the practical examination for the yachtmaster certificate with an examiner who spent two nights on board

Maestro over the weekend of 22 April. I was told that we could be friendly before and after the practical test, which lasted all Saturday, but that the examination period had to be formal. We left Lymington with a very strong breeze and I was given the task of navigating the boat across the Solent to Newtown Creek on the Isle of Wight, but wait – I was shut in below deck with curtains drawn and had to direct my examiner with only the chart as my reference. I was ordered to give him instructions on what course to sail. This meant calculating both the direction and speed of the tide, which of course depended on the time of day. Another factor was 'leeway', as the wind was strong. It was also my responsibility to tell him of any buoys that should be visible and for him to report to me the speed of the vessel and what he could see. He promised he would go aground if I was wrong, or at the very worst fail me! That task was completed to his satisfaction and we moored on a buoy in Newtown Creek for a few questions before continuing up the Solent to Cowes. Throughout the voyage there were searching questions and when we passed a naval frigate at anchor dressed overall, he asked me to identify the flags one by one. After a full day of this concentrated examining he finally said I could now be 'normal', and had I got any drinks on board? We then motored back to Lymington fairly late in the evening, cooked a meal, carried on drinking and had a thoroughly pleasant evening. He would not divulge my results, but said that I would be informed in due course. To my relief, several days after returning home I learnt that I had passed.

We decided on a family cruise to France in the summer with Rachel, boyfriend Dick, Gré and Rebecca. The voyage was to meet Clare in Paris. Or, to be more precise, Versailles where the Lautrecs had their family home. We berthed in Cherbourg and I hired a car to drive us to Versailles. Miranda kindly drove Clare up to meet us and we spent several days there together. On our arrival, CC gave each of us a Kir Royale, and, if my memory serves me correctly, he said it had to be champagne and *framboise*. (Some French people I have met dispute this, claiming that it can be any sparkling wine and with any flavour, in other words only the fizz makes it Royale.) I disagree! We visited Paris as a family, saw many sights and ascended the Eiffel Tower. Needless to say, we were wined and dined in several restaurants before we parted company and Clare returned to Roussac.

We, of course, wanted to return their hospitality, so what better than to invite CC and Miranda to Tixover to coincide with the Burghley Horse Trials, which were well known to horse lovers. This is an annual three-day event held at Burghley House near Stamford and classified as one of the six leading three-day events in the world. In previous years, Clare had taken part in some of the junior events. They accepted our invitation and arrived in time for the trials, bringing Clare with them. Miranda had purchased a return ticket for her because she was impressed with the way she handled horses and was more than prepared for her to continue. On their arrival, I met them at the airport and drove them home in time for drinks with our friends Mike and Georgina Saunders Watson. By this time I think that Mike had forgotten that he was a naval commander, at least since his claim that he was a 'farmer!' The party was a great success and Miranda insisted on taking us all for dinner the following evening. Where else could we go but to the George Hotel in Stamford? CC and Miranda had received an invitation to visit Rockingham Castle, which they did before returning to France. Clare opted not to return to France but agreed instead to go to university. However, it was already September and the question was, would we find her a place? Pamela saw Margaret Medcalf, the headmistress at Stamford High School, who thankfully succeeded in finding her a place at Leicester University to read English and biology, which seemed ideal because Clare was good in both subjects. The faculty department at that time was in Northampton and they had a hall of residence on the north side of the town. This was convenient for ferrying her back and forth if she chose to spend weekends at home, which then became her normal routine.

This was subsequently followed by a cruise to the Channel Islands and Brittany with Rex and Elizabeth, who were introduced earlier. It was a longer cruise than expected as, after a fortnight cruising in perfect weather, we departed from Cherbourg in time to make our scheduled return at the end of our two weeks. We left on a night crossing to Lymington but it soon became evident that we were in for a rough ride. With a headwind nearing gale force we were forced to reef and bear away broad reaching up the English Channel – a very uncomfortable night and my first experience of a gale. I was anxious to stay well offshore and know our position, which I could do with my radio direction finder, it was a long night, the wind did not drop and next morning we witnessed just how high the sea was. A decision had to be made as the forecast was still not in our favour. By this time we were off Le Havre, I decided to change course and shelter for the duration of the blow. We arrived safely in the outer harbour and I was able to pick up a buoy and tie up. I knew that the Thompsons had to be back in England, for Rex was on a fortnight's leave and Elizabeth had family commitments. However, Rex told me that he always allowed for this sort of emergency and did not have to be back for another week. He suggested we put Elizabeth and Pamela on the ferry and we sit it out until the wind moderated. This solved the problem and there was a car waiting for them when they docked in England, courtesy of one of Rex's sons. Pam drove to Lymington to rescue Rex and me when we eventually made it back.

Relocation

Following the unrest in Nottingham and my decision to leave the Sinfonia, we decided to relocate near the sea. We looked at property on both the east coast – Suffolk – and the south coast near Lymington. We first experienced difficulty finding a buyer for Tixover, so decided that such a fine property called for an equally fine agent. Knight Frank & Rutley's reputation was second to none, so I arranged an interview with them and took photographs for them to see. I was told that, until recently, they would not have considered a property like Tixover anywhere north of the Home Counties, but were changing their policy and had had recent successes in Oxfordshire and even South Northamptonshire, so would visit the hall to see if it interested them. They sent their representative Richard Gaynor, with whom I found myself on friendly terms. He had a positive approach, which, in short, quickly produced a buyer. Josephine Bourne-May, who viewed the hall on her own, said that her husband would only buy a house through Knight Frank & Rutley.

They eventually bought the property, but gave us little or no time to find another, for an agreement was drawn up scheduling completion within three months. However, while shopping in Stamford on the morning of Christmas Eve, we purchased a *Stamford Mercury*, which Pam immediately opened at the property page and saw that Easton Hall was for sale. We did not know the property, but as it was on the books of a local agent we immediately went to its office and arranged an appointment for that afternoon. We looked over the hall after lunch and loved what we saw at first sight. There was already a flat in the house, which was suitable for my parents and with one or two minor improvements in mind we agreed to buy. I was about to buy another hall! There were mixed feelings from our four daughters – two for and two against, but being a village house the property stood well, was completely walled in, and had about three-quarters of an acre of ground. This was another country house, bought through a local agent, and later to be sold again through Knight Frank & Rutley. Although unknown to me at the time, it was to be soon.

1978

There was a very busy start to the year – a family concert with Johnny Morris, an English Sinfonia Music Night featuring Steve Race and Semprini playing 'Rhapsody in Blue', and a concert in Northampton with Fou Ts'ong playing the Grieg piano concerto. These were followed by a QEH concert, this time featuring Moura Lympany who played Piano Concerto Op. 21 in D by Haydn in the first half of the programme and the Malcolm Williamson second piano concert after the interval. The final item was Mozart Symphony No. 29 in A.

The orchestra had a surprising invitation from the Nottingham Palais to play for an evening of Viennese dancing. Yes – really for people to dance to. I had heard that Sir John Barbirolli had done something similar with the Hallé as a New Year 'thank you' to the city council for its ongoing support of the orchestra. In that case, I believe the orchestra gave its services freely. In our case it would be an engagement. I first discussed this with my leader and several players and the measure of their enthusiasm decided me to accept what I have to say I thought would be a challenge. After many years of playing Viennese concerts, our music library was not short of waltzes, polkas and gallops, but keeping the rhythms in time with the dancing was a slightly different matter. Our dress for concerts at that time was always 'tails and white bow ties' but on this occasion I remember making it rather more relaxed – I wore a green velvet jacket (probably 'Sherwood' green being Robin Hood country) and have to say the evening was a great success and I rather think we repeated it the following year.

Following this, we were again at EMI in Abbey Road recording a Percy Grainger album titled 'Grainger on the Shore'. This had come about through an earlier meeting I had with EMI following the unexpected discovery of an arrangement of the 'Londonderry Air' by Percy Grainger. The discovery was immediately after the first concert of a tour I had been on with the Ulster orchestra. I had not rehearsed anything special (a mistake) in the event of an encore, so when it became clear from the tumultuous applause that the audience wanted one, I turned to the leader and said 'last movement of the symphony'. He whispered, 'no problem, we have one – the Derry Air, three times and it starts with the cellos, follow them, three verses!' I smiled and, taking his advice, started the cellos and cautiously followed them and then the main body of players when they came in. For the third verse, the horns suddenly seemed to take over, which brought the piece to an end with a fantastic climax. At an earlier programme meeting, I had mentioned to EMI that I would like to include this arrangement in a future recording of English music. A short while later, EMI asked me to record an all Grainger album, which I agreed to do. To complete the recording, I researched several pieces that Grainger had intended to make into a 'suite' but never completed.

In July, and now settled at Easton Hall, Pamela and I decided to open the garden and have a concert on the terrace. The programme comprised eighteenth-century concertos, which the Sinfonia principals played in costume with guest soloist Hugo D'Alton on the mandolin. (I should add at this point that Hugo was frequently in demand by the Royal Opera and others whenever a 'serenading' mandolin was required.)

BACH	Violin concerto in A minor
HUMMEL	Mandolin concerto
TELEMANN	Flute suite in A minor
BACH	Brandenburg Concerto No. 5

Towards the end of the year, in November, I again conducted the Philharmonia in a recording of 'A Bouquet of Romantic Flute Music' with soloist John Solum. I have a particular memory of finishing the morning session a little early and not wishing to waste any of my valuable time, decided to take the opportunity of rehearsing a short flute work 'L'Oiseau des Bois' (Bird in the Wood, Idyll) by Doppler, which only required an accompaniment of four French horns. The rest of the orchestra quietly left and I simply conducted a run through without any stops. On my return to the studio after lunch, the sound engineers invited me to listen to a take they had made of the run through, and I had agreed with their judgement, there was absolutely no need to do it again. I listen to it now and my admiration never falters. I question why this recording never seemed to be generally available in the UK as it sold well elsewhere in the world, in America alone, more than 18,500 copies. (It appears from time to time on eBay and Amazon.) See copy of email from John about the recording in the Appendix.

It was a sad moment for me when John eventually decided to return to America, particularly as it coincided with the last stages of my stay with the Sinfonia. As already mentioned, there should have been another extensive tour of America with the English Sinfonietta but sadly this never took place.

Apart from concerts and our move to Easton Hall, the early part of the year had been hectic. I did a New Parks sailing course in Majorca and *Maestro* unexpectedly sold, but too late to be replaced by the Westerly 33 I had ordered but had to cancel while waiting for the Nantucket Clipper to sell. Fortunately, we did not lose our deposit, but Westerlys told us that its order book for 33s was now full. As a stopgap we bought *Vitalba*, which stayed with us for only four months, but during that time we sailed to Holland and visited our usual haunts on the east coast of England. *Vitalba* sold very quickly, in fact to a couple who would have bought her before had we not arrived there first. She was replaced by *Killicrankie*, a 35-foot masthead sloop and among the last built in wood by Moody's. A 35-foot yacht in those days was really something. Our short experience of *Vitalba*, an early East Coast Buchanan designed wooden yacht convinced me there was still a place for wooden built vessels, a sentiment I confess did not last long. However, *Killicrankie* was a superb example, wheel steering, long keel, teak decks and Moody's pride and joy. We were to be well looked after by the company, but events took on a cruel change.

Chapter 9

Wilderness Years
1979–1981
Loss of Pamela, chaos, Philomusica

1979

At the start of this year all seemed normal, if anything bordering on the busy side and starting with an emphasis on animals. Johnny Morris, the well-known broadcaster about the animal kingdom, who had already appeared with the orchestra on numerous occasions, particularly when we gave school concerts, was the speaker at one of our families concerts in Derby narrating *Juanita: The Spanish Lobster*. A later concert featured the well-known ITV newscaster Anna Ford in a controlled performance of Prokofiev's Peter and the Wolf. The 'controlled' moment was when, in a very quiet voice, she warned Peter to 'look out'. I mention this as our other readers usually shouted out this warning causing great surprise in the auditorium.

Loss of Pamela (20 November 1930–19 April 1979)

Sadly, Pam never really sailed in *Killikrankie*. The last time I saw her alive was after a week of fitting out, just Pam and me together, before Easter 1979. She drove home to Easton leaving me to skipper a week's cruising instruction with a trainee crew from New Parks College, Leicester. On my return to the Hamble the following Friday, I rang home to be told that Pamela had been found asleep on the bed during the afternoon by Gré and Rebecca and, on being unable to wake her, called the doctor, George Hattersley, who came at once and ordered an ambulance to take her to Kettering General Hospital. I immediately rang George and shortly afterwards was on my way to Kettering Hospital. When I arrived at about 11 p.m. Pam was still unconscious and I was told that if she regained consciousness she would be taken to London. After an agonizing Saturday and Sunday for my four daughters and myself, without regaining consciousness she died of a meningioma (intrecerebral haemorrhage) around midnight on the Sunday. My daughters had heard the telephone call and I gathered them together in Clare's bedroom to tell them the sad news. The hospital rang me again the following day to say that, for the sake of my four daughters, the cause of her death was not hereditary.

Later, I heard that our doctor had alerted the coastguard who had radioed all the ships in the Solent area.

Only a few days later, from 22–28 April, I was scheduled to make a return visit to conduct the Göttingen Symphony Orchestra. My agent would normally have found my replacement, but it was very short notice and I chose to call my first horn in the Sinfonia, Tony Randall, to see if he would take my place. The previous year he had approached me about his plan to form a Welsh Sinfonia – needless to say he was Welsh – and would I mind him using the term Sinfonia? I was moved by his thoughtfulness. I knew that Tony had been doing some conducting and had heard from several colleagues that he knew his job. I thought I would give him one of those rare opportunities we all dream of, so I called him, told him the programme, and he immediately said he would, without changing the programme, which included Elgar's Enigma Variations. I received a deeply moving letter from the management of the orchestra telling me that Tony had commemorated the Nimrod Variation to the memory of Pamela, which had occasioned my absence.

Words would have escaped me to describe my sad loss and still do but somehow life had to go on and at this time I had a formidable diary of concerts still to conduct in this 'added year' to my initial contract.

There were three interesting concerts during the summer – two with the soloist Fou Ts'ong in Nottingham and Chesterfield respectively and an international pops concert that included Liszt's First Piano Concerto and Britten's Young Persons Guide to the Orchestra. Then, in Bakewell and Melton Mowbray, there were two evenings of eighteenth-century concerti, which I directed from the harpsichord, one including Hummel's Mandolin concerto played by Hugo D'Alton. In Kettering parish church, I featured Anna Shuttleworth playing Haydn's Cello Concerto in C, Lynda Coffin playing the Quantz Flute Concerto, and two Brandenburg concerti, No. 3 and No. 5, which I directed from the harpsichord. The summer season ended with a concert set in the forecourt of the seventeenth-century Holland House at the Court Theatre in Holland Park, London.

At this time, both Clare and Rachel were at university, Gré would take her 'A' levels at the end of the summer term, which was about to start, and

Rebecca still had two years of schooling. When the summer term started, there were only three of us at home, for by this time Clare had moved out of the college residence and was living with other students in a rented Northamptonshire cottage, and Rachel was still in a hall of residence in London. Nonetheless, they all came home every weekend. By this time, Gré had learnt that she had a place at Goldsmiths College, London, and when the time came for her to leave I drove her to her hall of residence.

By September, only Rebecca was left at home to share my life during the week, and she completely took over where Pam had left off and was cooking all my meals. However, realizing that this was no life for her, I arranged an interview with her headmistress Margaret Medcalf, who had always been friendly with Pam, to see if I could (weekly) board Rebecca for the rest of her time at the High School. This was duly arranged, and now there was only one! Nonetheless, there is no doubt in my mind that it was the best thing I could do for her future.

In mid-September, Michael Saunders Watson invited me to spend a week with him on his boat, a Westerly Berwick he kept moored on a buoy on Loch Craignish close to their cottage at Ardfern, which was visible from the loch. He also invited Rachel and Gré to crew for us. We spent a memorable week exploring the islands and, on one, we met a woman I suspect was the sole inhabitant, but nevertheless known to Mike. We remember passing between two islands where there was a notoriously strong tidal current, though thoughtfully in a favourable direction, and later we entered the Crinan Canal for a night. The weather was kind, and we saw much of the coastline and enjoyed observing many species of seabirds.

John Kempe, who I still met from time to time and who had come to Pamela's funeral, lent me a book by Arthur Koestler called *The Ghost in the Machine*. I was already deeply concerned about what life meant (still am) and started to read several books in succession on philosophy. In fact, on 19 September, while driving to London for a prerehearsal with the Sinfonia, I decided to try to enrol as a mature student to read philosophy (having missed out in my early life it would have to be Cambridge) and that it would have to be now! Fate, however, determined that I would follow an entirely different path.

With time to spare on my arrival, I popped into a coffee bar near the rehearsal venue in Conway Hall and joined Anna Shuttleworth who was already there. Shortly thereafter, a violinist I had never seen before walked in and, spotting Anna's cello, asked if she was with the English Sinfonia.

Introductions followed. I was rehearsing for a concert in Nottingham the following evening with a repeat performance in Northampton the next day.

Elgar	Introduction and Allegro
Schumann	Piano Concerto in A minor
Beethoven	Symphony No. 5 in C minor
	Soloist Anthony Goldstone

At the end of the Northampton concert I strolled into the band room to thank the musicians and stopped to talk to our new violinist. I learnt she had been with the Ulster orchestra but was now working in an administrative capacity for the BBC in Belfast, but was keen to return to England and take up freelance work. She was at the moment staying with her parents in Sheffield for a few days before returning to Belfast. Decide in haste, repent at leisure, as alas, against all my principals (fraternising with the female members of the orchestra), I suggested perhaps we could meet in Sheffield and take a walk in the Peak District. It was agreed, and I drove to Sheffield on 27 September, met her and then dove to the village of Thorpe to walk through Dove Dale. It was a lengthy walk and we arrived back at my car to enjoy a picnic that Janet had thoughtfully prepared before leaving her home. This was in a field close to the Peveril of the Peak Hotel near the foot of Thorpe Cloud and we decided we would stay the night there. Janet called her parents and we drove back to Sheffield the following afternoon – actually, Janet drove back as she was fond of cars but had never driven an Audi before. I met her parents and her father rather dryly remarked that it must have amounted to more than a 'friendly' meeting if she drove my car. Her interest in cars was evident when we arrived in Sheffield to recover hers, it was a Healey Sprite, which of course was very familiar to me. (But I was never allowed to drive it!)

My interest in and fascination with philosophy continued and, in October, I attended a Hull University course on 'Mind and Body' held in Horncastle. The course gave me food for thought and I remember the lecturer saying that most of us had experienced things we could not explain and invited a show of hands from those who had. Very few raised their hands, but we listened to each who did. The lecturer went on to say that he was certain that at least half of us would have had such experiences, but were too embarrassed to admit to them, which was correct in my case. Several years earlier, while at Tixover, I awoke one morning to see my grandfather Dilks gazing down at me in our bedroom. He spent three months with each of his sons, but at that moment was in fact in hospital in Derby. My first thought was that he had wandered into the hall from my parent's cottage, my second that it was a dream. I therefore turned over and thought no more of it until later that morning when my father received a telephone call from his younger brother saying that their father had died.

I will add at this point that John Lill, following a piano concerto I conducted with him, described clearly seeing Pamela lovingly standing at my side while I was conducting and describing in perfect detail the pale blue dress she was wearing, which he would not have seen but which was a particular favourite of mine during her life.

Concerts followed in Leicester, Keyworth, Grimsby, Derby, Wellingborough and Newark. Janet was able to fly over from Belfast to play with the orchestra in several of them, thus affording us more time together and resulting in my proposal of marriage. We were married in Sheffield on 1 December and went to Majorca for our honeymoon. It could have been a memorable time, but despite having a friend's sailing yacht at our disposal and a hotel overlooking the harbour, it was a complete and unbelievable disaster! What had I done?

Returning by air to England we had just enough time to prepare to travel to Ireland for Janet to complete her contract, which still had a week to run. I had booked the Sunday night ferry crossing so that we had the use of my car for the week we were to be there and Janet could return to work on the Monday. She had arranged for us to use a friend's flat and I patiently occupied myself catching up on scores and telephone calls. Our return crossing was scheduled for the following Saturday, but was informed at the very last moment that our stay had to be extended because of a farewell party. Since our relationship was already at breaking point, I suggested I return as planned and she make her own way back, which she did, but to her parents' house in Sheffield. The following weekend I drove there with my four daughters knowing they were impressed by Janet and would join me in persuading her to return, but if my memory serves me right, I do not think we were invited into the house, though Janet did eventually appear at the front door to join her parents. I was shocked by her appearance – she looked as it she had just emerged from bed. There was a Sinfonia concert sponsored by the Trustee Savings Bank for New Year's Eve in Nottingham on 31 December and Janet was playing in the orchestra. We agreed that she would return with me to Easton Hall after the concert.

PROGRAMME

Strauss	Overture 'Die Fledermaus
	Perpetuum Mobile
	Thunder and Lightening Polka
	Emperor Waltz
Saint-Saëns	Carnival of Animals

INTERVAL

Tchaikowsky	Nutcracker Suite
Henry Wood	Fantasy on British Sea Songs
	Patricia Taylor Mezzo Soprano
	Marlene Fleet Piano
	Neville Dilkes Conductor and Piano

1980 Chaotic year

Following my rebound marriage, Janet, now Dilkes, was very unhappy at Easton Hall and never once set foot in the very beautiful walled garden. She clearly disliked the house and probably also the furniture in it, so suggested we move. In the hope that this might solve the problem, I put the house on the market with my friend Richard Gaynor of Knight Frank & Rutley. At the outset of my relationship with Janet, my parents who were living in the flat, said that they were uncomfortable with the dramatic change to all our lives and had decided to return to Derby. I reasoned that having four daughters, Easton Hall and a hungry husband was not the best environment for an inexperienced partner 12 years my junior. Nonetheless, things should not have been that difficult for her as my three eldest daughters were at university and Rebecca was now boarding during the week at Stamford High School. Sadly, finding life difficult, Janet spent most of her mornings in bed. She finally left without a word on the evening of 21 February and, shortly there-after, in an effort to save the marriage, I invited her father to have lunch with me in Sheffield. He warned me that it would just be the two of us and we met in a Sheffield hotel. I explained that Janet was frigid and that I could no longer even hold her hand. In short, he told me that he was not surprised because her mother was too, as was his sister-in-law. To my astonishment, his only advice was to live as happily as I could and make my own arrangements, just as he had always done. He was a pharmacist with his own business and, I should add, was also a church warden.

Enter Rupert Bear – a Nottingham solicitor and friend of Philip Vine, whom I have already mentioned, but to recall was a solicitor by training but now town clerk to the City of Nottingham. There was no talk of divorce proceedings at this point, but I thought it prudent to prepare myself before things got out of hand. Rupert Bear was a specialist in divorce and I will be eternally grateful to him for how he handled my case with only his fee.

Life without Pam had changed things for us all. My parents had sunk some of their capital from the sale of their Derby house in 1968 into the cottage conversion at Tixover, so it was my responsibility to rehouse them. They spent some time in Derby and found a property a stone's throw from where they were living before retirement. I bought the house on 16 June, but they insisted I put it in my name as it would ultimately come to me. I took on a small flat in St John's Wood in London and resolved to spend more time in the capital. But it was a lonely life and, I confess, I spent more time at Easton than in London.

The sale of Easton went through remarkably quickly, which rather wrong-footed me, but fortunately my buyer had requested a delay to completion until July. Interestingly, at this point I decided to see a marriage counsellor, but after several sessions found it a complete and utter waste of time. July came and I put all the furniture into store, leaving just enough to furnish two bedrooms, a sitting room and kitchen in a cottage in Collyweston, which James Thompson, son of Rex and a merchant seaman who was away most of the time, had converted. I subsequently moved to a rented bungalow back in Easton on the Hill.

Concerts with the Sinfonia continued, including those at Queen Elizabeth Hall. Then, on 8 May, I flew to Naples to conduct the chamber orchestra of the 'Domenico Cimarosa' Conservatory in concerts featuring Patricia Chitti, an English soprano married to the controller of music for the Italian Broadcasting Company in Rome. The invitation followed an opera night in which she had sung with the Sinfonia at an earlier Nottingham Festival. She had been booked to sing the first performance of a hitherto neglected song cycle by Respighi and was to ask, with my agreement, for me to be the conductor. Following two repeat concerts, I travelled to Rome with Patricia and subsequently had the pleasure of meeting Respighi's widow in her apartment and playing her late husband's piano. While in Rome, I visited several tourist spots, including the Vatican, and returned to England on 21 May.

In the August I crewed for Tony Simmonds when he was taking his boat from the south coast to Holland, where we spent an enjoyable bachelor fortnight. It was a remarkable friendship, particularly after we discovered that his wife Audrey had died from exactly the same affliction as Pamela. They were having a drinks party and she collapsed while carrying a tray of drinks into the drawing room. That was exactly seven years before I met him, and he was exactly seven years older than me.

Filling in time, I suppose, in the September I drove some of my family to London to see *Riddle of the Sands* sailing again, but I have to add that I did miss the carefree days I had spent with Pamela. I continued to take *Yachting Monthly* and in the past had frequently been amused by the advertisements in the magazine's personal column for crew members, usually a male skipper requesting a female crew. I read one that was different. It was from a woman living on a 40-foot Ketch in Malta and, still short of female company, I answered it. It goes without saying that this was standard practice in those days, although nowadays many couples seek prospective partners via the media and internet. I sent her my details, including a photograph and my age, for which she particularly asked, also my sailing CV – she wanted someone who knew how to sail. I booked a cheap return flight to Malta, which allowed me two weeks on the boat.

Before flying to Malta I had arranged to spend a short spell on Tony Simmonds's yacht, which he berthed in Moody's marina on the Hamble River, and from where we could visit the Southampton boat show. We spent an interesting day there and I met Des Sleightholme, the editor of *Yachting Monthly* who had known Tony for a long time because, apart from their mutual interest in boats, Tony had purchased Des's house in Southend. Returning from the south coast I had a few days to sort out my life and prepare for Malta. I arrived there in the early evening and was surprised to be met by a taxi. The driver told me he knew my host to be and delivered me safely to her boat. When I met her I realized that I had sent her my photograph, but that she had not sent me hers. I know my readers will understand my mistake, but how I was to escape was another matter. We dined on board, it was a good meal without any shortage of wine, and she made it clear that I was more than welcome. I ran over my problem before eventually getting to sleep and after breakfast the following morning made an excuse to go into town for the bank. My first call was to a travel agent to see if I could get a return flight to the UK with a refund from my present one. This was not possible and the cost of a single flight back to the UK was considerably more expensive than the return flight I already had. It was time to pause for thought. How much would a hotel cost me? The net result was that I booked into a hotel for the rest of the fortnight and hired a car. In other words, to turn an error of judgement into a holiday was exactly what I did. Returning to the boat I apologized, but said that I did not think that the situation in which we found ourselves was quite what I had expected. She was sitting in the cockpit with a friend when I returned to the boat, and our conversation was in the privacy of the saloon. I packed my luggage and left. The weather in Malta was, predictably, very hot, and the lack of green fields depressed me enough not to choose the island as a place to which to retire!

Returning to England, in the autumn I started looking at properties for conversion in the Stamford area and, with the help of Michael Williams, a cousin of Pam's who was a successful architect, I purchased Adam and Eve Barn in South Luffenham on 3 November. Michael drew up plans following my brief, which had been to include a music room and he astounded me with his creation. I should say at this point that plans for an up-market four-bedroom house, which I seem to remember would have meant lowering the Collyweston roof, were given to me as part of the sale. Michael's ideas were very different. I employed Curtis, a Stamford builder, to do the conversion under Michael's direction and was able to move in in 1982.

I am informed that nothing should be left out of a biography! So this short period of my life will be dealt with swiftly as it involves a relationship I had with Sue who worked as a reporter, or perhaps sub-editor at the *Stamford Mercury* – interestingly the oldest newspaper in Great Britain. She had come to live with me in the bungalow at Easton on the Hill and subsequently at South Luffenham when the conversion of Adam and Eve Barn was complete. As it was now a house, I decided to give it a name based on a stone carving of Adam and Eve set in the wall above what was now the front door, with an oriel window above. There is a story behind this because, although the property was not listed, it was subject to some protection order. Since I did not want to lose the planned oriel window, the question arose over the need to keep the stone carving in place. Michael had designed a brick built extension to the kitchen to accommodate the central heating boiler, and was able to satisfy the county surveyor that, by having a wooden enclosure built with a latch gate to a tiny courtyard, which also conveniently hid the oil tank, that the stone carving could be removed without any damage, and this was carefully and satisfactorily accomplished. The only other stipulation was that it was to remain in the house for all time. I made this clear to my purchaser when I sold the house and I sincerely hope it is still there today. I think I always made it clear to Sue that our relationship would never be permanent, and inevitably there came a point when I needed to make that clearer.

Philomusica

Keith Diggle, who would have been well informed I was shortly to leave the English Sinfonia, rang me to say the that David Littaur, the conductor of the Philomusica of London, was having a bad time in both obtaining concerts and finding players and could Keith help or give him some advice. Keith rang me to ask if I would be interested in talking with David, to which I agreed.

Philomusica was formed out of the Boyd Neel Orchestra, which disbanded when Boyd Neel left the country in 1954 to work in Canada. He would not allow this very successful chamber orchestra to continue under his name, but so successful had the orchestra been that the players were determined to keep it going. The leader and a few members approached Thurston Dart to see if he would be interested in taking charge of them. I gather this was over a pint or two in a London hostelry, together with a representative from the Arts Council. They chose the name Philomusica, so the now renamed Boyd Neel, like other London chamber orchestras, could offer its services to music societies, provincial authorities, and city and county councils. It should be remembered there were only five or so professional orchestras in the British Isles outside London, hence instrumentalists wishing to make a career out of playing in an orchestra found it preferable if not necessary to live in London. With the exception of the BBC orchestras and the Royal Opera House, all the remaining symphony and chamber orchestras worked on a freelance basis. The London Concert Board had funds from the city to give grant aid to orchestras playing at the Royal Festival Hall, Queen Elizabeth Hall and other venues on the South Bank. They are of course faced with the challenge of maintaining a high standard of playing and management. To this day London orchestras tour the regions and tour abroad giving concerts where provincial councils and concert societies can afford to engage them.

From 1955, Philomusica was a great success under Dart, specializing in baroque music which, at the time, was being played on modern instruments. His scholarship, however was to result in a new awareness of the value of baroque music, but there was a considerable gap before the emergence of performances using ancient instruments, or more often copies of them. When Dart left in 1959, Granville Jones, violinist and former leader of the Boyd Neel, took over the orchestra. He filled the gap until George Malcolm took over in 1962. Like Thurston Dart, George was also a very fine harpsichordist. I had attended several of his concerts in London and saw, in my early days with the Sinfonia, an opportunity to give orchestral concerts using a very small number of players. I had taken on directing performances from the harpsichord, which was the fashion in the times of Bach, Handel, Haydn and Mozart, to name the best-known composers. However, it was never my policy to delve back even earlier as I knew there would be considerably less audience appeal. George, however, had personal ambitions to conduct from a rostrum and increased the size of the orchestra to facilitate playing later classical and romantic symphonies. Following an invitation to become associate conductor of the BBC Scottish Symphony Orchestra, George left in 1966. Niels Gron then took over the Philomusica, but some time later, following the advice of the Arts Council in 1969, the London Orchestral Concert Board withdrew its subsidy for Philomusica concerts in the QEH and this finally led to his departure. David Littaur then took over the orchestra.

Keith kindly arranged for me to meet David in London and the three of us met at the Saville Club on 15 November. I understood the problem, not to mention the challenge, and said I would help. David offered me a 50/50 share of all the concerts and joint administrative direction. Later, under the new regime, Keith very kindly found us our first engagement in Lewisham Town Hall.

1981

However, first and foremost was the need to gather together an orchestra. Thanks to the loyalty of my old friends in the Sinfonia this was happily not a problem, and it was made even easier for us with the help of Trevor Ford who had both played in the Sinfonia and for many years 'fixed' the players. David and I met Trevor for lunch at the Saville Club, and finalized arrangements for him to manage and engage the players we would need for each concert we were to undertake. He also expertly managed our finances and took on the role of concert manager and librarian. This was all agreed and it simply remained for the orchestra to find work.

Having invited Trevor Ford to 'fix' the players for Philomusica, I suppose it was inevitable there would be a substantial number of musicians from the Sinfonia who would be happy to continue playing for me and I was confident they would be equally happy with David. Adrian Levine, who was everything David and I could have wished for, was appointed as our leader and he continued to lead until the last concert. These were happy, interference free years. Being based in London, the orchestra could not receive direct support from the Arts Council, so, apart from sponsored concerts, we were reliant on bookings. The promoters of these, in many cases, did in return receive public support, as for example, the Eastern Authorities Orchestral Association.

David and his wife Joyce lived in a beautiful house in Stormont Road, Highgate and I drove to London, usually once a week for meetings with them; Joyce was our secretary. They thought it would be good for us to have an occasional dinner party at their house to entertain some of our patrons. I knew the value of such occasions from my frequent experiences with sponsors of the Sinfonia and from our privately entertaining members of the Artistic Council. I further arranged to meet an old friend, Tony Burley, manager of the Eastern Authorities Orchestral Association, to enlighten him on the background to my association with Philomusica.

David had an impressive array of patrons who were pleased to be associated with the orchestra. I was quick to notice Clive Thornton, chief general manager then chief executive of Abbey National and a frequent broadcaster on money matters, who even capitalized on the company's address at 221 Baker Street, by marketing Sherlock Holmes souvenirs. I suggested we approach him, which David did by inviting Clive and his wife Maureen to dinner at their house. He lived just north of Peterborough, where I believe he also owned a very successful pig farm. He expressed an interest in sponsoring the orchestra and the company generously did so, promoting six provincial concerts with the help of Bill Kallaway, mentioned earlier. Unfortunately, all took place in cathedrals as we could not find enough abbeys. (Westminster Abbey was totally uninterested!) The series was brought about following my experience with the English Sinfonia and the sponsorship we had received, principally from John Player of Nottingham, but also many others for individual concerts. On learning that Abbey National would sponsor us, David and I took Bill Kallaway to lunch, and I refrained from commenting on the Bournemouth conductor's competition! Bill now ran a successful enterprise and was not, as he had been before, connected with any specific company. He simply devoted his company to all the aspects of the event in the interests of both the sponsor and the performers and, having introduced Bill to Abbey National, everything now lay in his hands. To his credit, he did a wonderful job for us, including publicity and programmes, which resulted in full houses at very location.

It was soon apparent to all and sundry in the profession that the orchestra, with the exception of its leader, was in fact largely composed of my old colleagues from the ESO. These were happy years, with no board of dictators, (sorry directors). We were now in competition with all the other freelance orchestras and could not expect to be spoon fed by direct grant aid. Our future now depended on our playing and management. David and I drew up a brochure of programmes with costings for performances in the provinces and we quickly succeeded in obtaining bookings. These concerts took place throughout the Midlands and north of England and the region covered by the Eastern Authorities Orchestral Association, and we did not neglect London. There was also a tour of Northern Ireland. Referred to later, as it coincided with a memorable event there in November 1987.

Also known to me was the well-known broadcaster Richard Baker, who in addition to reading the TV news was known and liked for his interest in music. Indeed, I had wanted a well-known personality to participate in Walton's Façade Suite and had invited Richard to read the text with the Sinfonia. He was at first hesitant so I suggested we met and I would give him some piano rehearsals. The result was very successful and was followed by many repeat performances. I introduced Richard to Philomusica in order to 'chair concerts', which became known as 'Programme Master Concerts', which proved to be extremely popular with our audiences. Richard would talk about the music, rather like the Proms concerts, but sitting through the concert at the side of the orchestra. If there was a concerto he would have a short chat with the soloist, the conductor or sometimes a member of the orchestra if there was something of interest he could highlight. At the end of the concert, the audience were invited to meet Richard, David or me, and the musicians afterwards.

* * *

Back to family matters. Rachel, daughter number two, had graduated in July and stayed in London to work for the travel company, Gulliver's Travels. Her boyfriend, with whom she was now living, had left college the year before and was now well established as a photographer in London. He shared a studio with an already successful photographer and rapidly got to follow in his footsteps.

Being without a boat, I had chartered a Moody 36 centre cockpit sailing boat and sailed to the Channel Islands and the north coast of France, thus keeping my connections with the ocean 'blue'. This was a part family holiday for my, as yet unmarried daughters, Rachel and Rebecca, along with Rachel's boyfriend Dick and an old schoolfriend of his.

Earlier in the year Corby Choral Society had approached me to take over the choir in September from its retiring conductor, Sam Muir, whom I had known in my grammar school days. I agreed, but stipulated that I would only conduct concerts requiring an orchestra if the players were professional. I was confident this would be possible and it indeed proved to be. However, it turned out that they were committed to an annual carol concert in the Corby Festival Hall, which the Beanfield School band traditionally accompanied. I was hesitant, but was assured I would not be disappointed by the standard of their playing and that they would be happy to arrange for me to hear them. I did and was reassured. The band accompanied all the carols sung by the choir and audience, and really did excel themselves. The choir also sang the Malcolm Sargent four part settings of traditional carols (unaccompanied) from many countries, thus reflecting Sargent's great love for the choral tradition.

Now, having time on my hands, so to speak, I learnt that Stamford High School needed a piano teacher for a small number of weekly lessons. I no longer had any daughters there, but the headmistress remembered me, as did the then director of music who had taught three of my daughters. Christine Allen was a member of the music staff and, in addition, taught the flute. We soon became friendly; she sort of looked after me and we talked regularly over morning coffee. The talk became increasingly friendly, so much so she is here with me today as my wife. My proposal to her will be dealt with in due course.

Chapter 10

Brighter Future

1982–1984

Moving on, family and leisure, decisions

1982 Moving on

David and I continued to follow our policy of connecting with our patrons. On the social side, Joyce would arrange an occasional dinner party and I recall meeting Lady Bliss for the first time. I also met Lady Boult, whom I already knew from several encounters after concerts, at the Royal Garden Party and also quite by chance at the Manor Hotel, Blakeney during a summer holiday when our caravan was parked a short hill walk away from the hotel. The last time we met, she spoke sadly of her husband's last few years sitting in an armchair listening to his many recordings. (Now 90 myself, I fully understand this pleasure.)

David had conducted the first concert of the new partnership in Peterborough (home ground for me) in December last year with the following programme:

ELGAR	Introduction and Allegro
CORELLI	Christmas Concerto
HANDEL	Water Music
VAUGHAN WILLIAMS	Fantasia on a theme of Thomas Tallis
MOZART	Symphony No. 40

For my first concert with Philomusica, which Keith Diggle in fact organized, we were booked to play in Lewisham's 'subscription' series of concerts (seven concerts for the ticket price of five) in the Town Hall as part of the Lewisham Celebrity season. It was in fact their inaugural subscription series of concerts.

In July 1982 I had to face my first real challenge with Corby Choral Society. As it was 250 years since Haydn's birth in 1732, I decided to celebrate the occasion with a Haydn anniversary concert, which we were to give in the Festival Hall Corby. The concert would mean a departure from its normal routine as I was determined to use professional soloists and a professional orchestra. All credit to the committee for the concert, which went ahead with the help of the Corby District Council and New Towns Commission. Philomusica was engaged and the programme commenced with the Surprise Symphony, followed by the Piano Concerto in D Op. 21 with soloist Allan Schiller. Part 2 was devoted to the Mass in G major 'in temporee belli' with Elizabeth Lane, soprano, Maty King, mezzo, Mark Curtis, tenor and Mark Rowlinson, baritone.

This was later followed with my next concert with Philomusica in 'The Orchard' concert hall in Dartford conducting:

MENDELSSOHN	Nocturne and Scherzo, Midsummer Night's Dream
PROKOFIEV	Peter and the Wolf (Johnny Morris)
BARTOK	Adagio for Strings
BEETHOVEN	Symphony No. 1 in C minor

Four days later I was invited to conduct the Derby Radio Orchestra in a broadcast concert from Repton School in its concert series featuring two 'Young Musicians of the Year', Karen Jones (flute) and Jean Owen (bassoon).

Family and leisure

In April I undertook a New Parks cruise skippering a Moody 36 that belonged to one of the college instructors. We sailed over to the Channel Islands and, on our return from Jersey, berthed for a night in Alderney. Going ashore for a drink, in the bar I met Bryans and Anna Rendall. Bryans was a sea pilot at the Port of Harwich and Anna a music teacher in Clacton. She also ran the county music school and asked if I would be interested in conducting the Clacton Schools Orchestra. This was a successful enterprise and extremely well supported by both the education committee and local sponsorship. I agreed I would rehearse and conduct a public concert over a three-day period and found myself in demand annually for several years thereafter. The first concert was at the end of June and a great success.

In May I gave notice of my intended departure from the bungalow I was renting in Easton on the Hill and moved with the small amount of furniture I had into Adam and Eve House. My Bechstein grand piano had gone to Nottingham after the sale of Easton Hall and the rest of the furniture into store, apart from what I required for my immediate needs. The piano was completely overhauled, including the casework with a new music desk, square legs and, most importantly, a modern black polished lacquer finish. When the work on the piano was completed, being reluctant for it to go into store I arranged with friends, the Lanes to give it space at Tickencote Hall. Their second daughter, Charlotte was a friend of Gré's and as they both had piano lessons I encouraged them to make use of it. Stamford Decorators undertook the decorating of the music room, as it was complicated due to the high ceiling and gallery, so there was a delay before the furniture could be delivered and I arranged for the piano to be picked up en route.

I spent part of that summer on the west coast of Scotland having been invited to join Rex and Elizabeth on their boat in Plocton. I arrived on a very hot weekend and, within minutes, went over the side for a swim. Not usual for me! To my surprise, there were three already on board, me making four of us in total. I was introduced to Barbara Markham with whom I remained on Christian name terms even when I found her to be Lady Barbara. She lived at East Colne in Essex and at the end of my holiday, as Rex and Elizabeth were staying on board *Seacure*, Barbara took the opportunity to return to Essex with me via the Thompsons' house where she had left her car, having travelled to Scotland with them. So it was simply a case of driving her back to my home ground, so to speak. During the drive I learnt that she and her husband had separated, so suggested we might meet again. I had an invitation from a company sponsoring a concert in the Barbican and was able to take her to that and to the reception afterwards. We saw each other several times, including me visiting her in Essex where, to my surprise, she lived in a house that Pamela and I had looked at back in 1977 when first trying to sell Tixover. I remarked on this and she confirmed that they had bought the house at that time. Barbara subsequently came to a concert I was conducting in Southwell Minster and we entertained the Gurlings afterwards in the hotel where we were staying. Ken and Monica both approved of my new partner!

This concert was memorable from a musical point of view, as, despite an impeccable performance by John Ogden in Mozart's Piano Concerto No. 9 (K271) he had a memory slip in the first movement when he left out exactly four bars. I always conducted the concerto from the score – and displayed four fingers of my left hand and gave the orchestra four rapid 'down beats' and hoped for the best. It worked! Apart from the orchestra, no one mentioned it to me, and I believe the incident went completely unnoticed by everybody, including the most knowledgeable ones I knew to be in in the audience. (I should add, I believe even John was unaware, as there was no mention of the incident.)

This reminds me of a situation earlier in my career in 1971, when the pianist Clive Lythgoe had a memory lapse at a concert in the Corby Festival Hall playing the Grieg Piano Concerto. First, however, my readers must understand the circumstances surrounding this particular incident. Classical symphonies, concertos, sonatas and so forth are composed according to a well-established formula known as 'ternary' form, three parts as opposed to 'binary' two parts. The three parts are known as (i) the exposition, say (a) eight bars in the tonic key and (b) eight bars in the dominant (nearest related key); (ii) development of the ideas just heard, and (iii) the recapitulation which is a repeat of (i) but with BOTH parts in the tonic key. Sometimes an introduction is added at the beginning and a coda at the end of the recapitulation.

Going back to the soloist with the memory problem – note perfect until the recapitulation. Subject 1 tonic, OK subject 2 memory lapse, should have been tonic but was dominant. Soloist realizes the mistakes and stops playing. I carry on. Quick thinking, we are nearer the end of the movement than the beginning, to stop would mean either going on to the second movement or starting all over again; better to continue. Orchestra short 'tutti' just coming up so worth going on to see if the soloist has sorted out his problem. He had and simply came in at the right moment in the correct key.

Going back to Barbara, I was subsequently invited to dinner in Essex and had the pleasure of meeting her four daughters! I pondered over a future with eight daughters between us and sadly my interest waned.

This was the year I took on my first son-in-law, when Clare married Neil Rickett in York. He was a former Stamford Boys' School pupil, who had gone on to York University for his degree. They had gone to live in Tadcaster, which was convenient for York where Neil was working. Thomas, my first grandchild, was born at the end of October, the first of my seven in total.

My youngest daughter, Rebecca had by now left the High School and immediately started work with Peterborough Building Society. All my daughters had learnt to drive, but Rebecca had a slight advantage as she was now living with me and had the use of her grandfather's car, which he gave me when he considered his driving days to be over. The car was affectionately called Arthur.

Early in December I conducted Philomusica in Harlow and finished the year with a Corby Choral Society Concert featuring Britten's 'Ceremony of Carols'.

1983

An interesting start to the concert year – I conducted a concert in Stevenage in February that ITV was going to broadcast. Joyce rang me to say that ITV wanted to know what my broadcast fee would be? I replied that it was usually half my concert fee, which was my arrangement with the BBC. As far as I am aware, they never replied, but it was to my utter, but pleasant surprise, considerably more than I expected. The soloist was John Lill.

Noteworthy, this year marked the Silver Jubilee of Philomusica and also 150 years since the birth of Brahms. We celebrated both with two concerts at the Queen Elizabeth Hall, one in February and one in April conveniently filling a gap in the South Bank's celebration of Brahms with his two Serenades, as I believe these were the only two orchestral works by Brahms that had not yet been included.

The BBC wanted to interview David and me about our contribution to the orchestra's 'Jubilee' and the 150th anniversary of Brahms's birth. John Humphrys, at that time the main presenter of the BBC 9 o'clock news interviewed us. Judging from the interview, his interest was mostly in our relationship as 'joint associate conductors'. We assured him we had never fallen out, but I jokingly said we could help each other over 'difficult starts'. Not of course true! There was a brief mention of the Brahms Serenades.

I returned by train to Peterborough and while completing my journey home by car decided to stop in a lay-by to listen to the broadcast in comfort. Almost immediately a police car drew up behind me and an officer came to the window and asked if I needed help. I explained I had stopped to listen to a broadcast in which I had taken part that same evening. Perhaps just interested, or suspicious, I do not know, but another fellow officer joined him and they remained to hear the broadcast. I think their final comment was 'well done, sir!'

David conducted the first of the two and included in his programme the Strauss Oboe Concerto with soloist Malcolm Messiter. For my part I conducted the second of the two Serenades and included in my programme the Strauss Second Horn Concerto with soloist Ifor James. In May there was a concert with Corby Choral Society and the Academy of English Music. The programme included Purcell's trumpet overture from *The Indian Queen* and 'Come ye sons of art' and Vivaldi's Concerto Grosso No. 3 and 'Gloria'.

Not wishing the choir to engage a 'named' orchestra involving management fees, I chose a programme that I could direct from the harpsichord and restrict to a small group of players. These were naturally Philomusica musicians, but I fixed the players myself. I had agreed with David at the outset of our relationship that I would not undertake concerts directing from the harpsichord with Philomusica, particularly as we wanted the image of the orchestra to be 'symphonic'.

* * *

At the end of May my second daughter Rachel got married in Tixover church, familiar territory after spending her teenage years in the village. The church is isolated in the middle of a field so we had decided to have a decorated tractor and trailer to carry the married couple from the village road. This was followed by a more conventional journey to South Luffenham where the reception was held in our large galleried music room.

* * *

Later in the year saw the first of the Abbey National series of concerts, which David conducted in Canterbury Cathedral.

MOZART	Overture Don Giovanni
MENDELSSOHN	Violin concerto (soloist Leland Chen)
ELGAR	Serenade for Strings
BEETHOVEN	Symphony No. 7

I was able to attend this concert, which I enjoyed immensely, and it left me in no doubt about the quality of our orchestra and, judging from its size, the very large audience agreed with me. I was further impressed with the overall presentation, programmes, sellers and ushers, all thanks to Bill Kallaway. His attention to detail became evident at every concert in the series.

The orchestra's next concert was in Swindon where I conducted the Beethoven Second Piano Concerto with John Lill as our soloist. I will just say a few words about the piano cadenza in this concerto as it ends without the usual preparatory trill. Listeners will be familiar with the trill signifying the end of the cadenza and it is customary for the conductor to give the soloist a bit of time trilling before bringing the orchestra in for the final bars. Beethoven does not afford us this luxury with the cadenza in his Second Piano Concerto as the orchestra has to be brought in at the end of a very rapidly ascending scale at precisely the moment of arrival. This is not a 'treatise' on conducting technique, so I will spare readers that, but it would be one of the tests to which I would subject a conducting student, the other two being the last movement of the Schumann Piano Concerto, and the last movement of the Dvořák Serenade for strings, both involving down beats. In one case, the soloist is playing continually in 'triplets' with the orchestra coming in on the second of the group and in the Dvořák where there is no soloist but there is a 'tied note' over the bar and it is necessary to place the down beat, incredibly difficult. The orchestra can really take the conductor for a ride at this moment by over accentuating the note following the 'tie'. Waving vaguely and letting the orchestra do it will certainly work as the players can be relied on to keep together but this means being ready to re-engage when the bars return to normal.

Meanwhile, the board of the Sinfonia was giving James Allaway a tough time, probably because his time as manager was limited. He rang me to ask if I would be interested in undertaking a tour of six concerts with Moira Anderson, a well-known light music soprano with whom I had worked in my Sinfonia days. Remembering advice given early in my career never to turn down work, and having got to grips with exactly what was required, I agreed. His budget was limited, hardly surprising considering Moira's fee, but she was necessary if he were to fill seats. His idea was for me to form an ensemble and lead from the piano. Looking back at the programme, I note that he referred to himself as 'London Virtuosi Productions (Director James Allaway)', but I have to say the tour was very successful. The ensemble – a total of six including a percussion player – was led by Adrian Levine. We would have a prerehearsal in London and just one full rehearsal for the first venue. We played in Sheffield, Derby, Mansfield, Northampton, Eastbourne and Leicester.

My concert year finished with Christmas carols with Corby Choral Society in which I included Vaughan Williams's 'Fantasia on Christmas Carols' with my friend Michael Rayner as soloist. I also confess to including a few more of Sargent's settings of carols from four countries.

Other events included giving a talk to the Kettering Gramophone Society, of which I had been a member since the formation of the Kettering Symphony Orchestra – both groups were formed on the same day. I have to say that the members were always more interested in hearing about a conductor's life than in what the music was all about.

From time to time, the Kettering Symphony Orchestra held social gatherings at Islip Mill, the location of the sailing club of which Pamela and I had previously been members. When free to do so, Christine and I would attend these events, which usually included the odd solo item from one or two of the players. I mention this as it was sometime during this period that I was able to introduce Christine to my old friends.

In the summer of this year, my dear friend Rex took *Seacure* from its mooring in Plocton, Scotland to sail to Gibraltar. I knew he was planning this but did not know he had actually started out. He radioed me from the Irish Sea to say he was on his way to Gibraltar – and was there any possibility of joining him if he stopped off in Cornwall? I could not oblige, but he later asked me to assist him with 'fitting out' the following year in Gibraltar. When the boat was eventually launched we were due to sail to the Balearic Islands, where I would leave and he would await Elizabeth's arrival to complete the voyage to Malta.

1984

It was four, if not five, years since I had started the new year with a Viennese concert in January. This was mainly due to Philomusica not being linked with a specific town or city. However, my old orchestra, English Sinfonia, asked me to conduct one in Corby Festival Hall and, wishing to include a chunk of Strauss's *Die Fledermaus* in the programme, needed a choral backing. So, I was with my old orchestra again. I should say at this point that there had been several other such occasions since the troubled times of my departure, and it was to be by no means my last.

My close friend Michael Rayner, the head chorister at St Werburg's Church in Derby when I was assistant organist, subsequently principal baritone in Opera da Camera, and later a focal point (star if you like) of the D'Oyly Carte Opera company, married Joy following his divorce from his first wife Sylvia. He had met Joy while producing a G&S opera for the local Gilbert and Sullivan theatre group in Ilkeston.

Following a concert by Philomusica in Aylesbury with Ralph Holmes playing the Mendelssohn violin concerto, I was invited to conduct the English Sinfonietta in Amersham. The orchestra was led on this occasion by Raymond Cohen, who I knew well (sadly he died in 2011) and featured Howard Shelley playing Mozart's Piano Concerto No. 21 in C (K.467).

Corby Choral Society liked to be kept busy and we gave a 1 May concert in St Andrew's Church of Scotland in Corby. The programme was divided equally between unaccompanied singing and organ solos. It commenced with early organ music and madrigals and concluded with organ music by Pietro Yon and modern part songs by Thiman, Quilter and Vaughan Williams.

I cannot ignore a concert in Wolverhampton on 9 May that James Allaway concert promotions organised with the London Virtuosi Orchestra. I think that, notwithstanding a very reasonable audience, he had to face a sizeable loss. I conducted without a fee, but my soloist, Peter Donohoe, who played Mozart Piano Concerto in D (K.537), was rapidly gaining a name for himself in the music world. Peter may also have helped as, while a student in Manchester, he had played the celeste in a performance of Bartok's Music for Strings, Percussion and Celesta at one of our Nottingham concerts. He had spoken to James on that occasion about his ambition to be a concert pianist and, as a result, I gave him an engagement to play the Grieg Piano Concerto at a subsequent schools' concert. Later, after leaving the Sinfonia, James promoted a series of concerts, 'music in quiet places' in the Midlands. In spite of several invitations to participate, I declined.

Having kept my ties with the Stamford area, I continued to meet friends and came to know Albert and Susan Wheway. Albert was chairman of the travel company, Hogg Robinson and had purchased Beaumont, Michael Jackson's old house in Duddington after selling me Tixover Hall. (Michael had taken my advice to sell through Knight Frank & Rutley.) Albert was interested in sponsoring Philomusica, but sadly it never got past two concert performances in the Duddington church with principals from Leicester opera. This year, 1984, there was a concert performance of Mozart's *Marriage of Figaro* and later, in 1986, Mozart's *Magic Flute*, both of which I directed from the harpsichord in company with a string quartet. We became close friends and remained so. They finally retired to Italy, thus limiting our friendship to Christmas cards and telephone calls. Both have now sadly died.

During spring, Rex and I flew to Gibraltar and, because of thick fog, were diverted to Tangier. While killing time in the airport lounge, we met Kenneth Lewis and his wife, friends of Rex and Elizabeth who lived in Preston in Rutland, just outside Uppingham. They were staying at the Rock Hotel in Gibraltar and kindly invited us to dinner the evening after our arrival. Ken Lewis was Conservative MP for Rutland and should, we thought, have been in 'the House' at the time (no further comment!). Rex and I worked on the boat and completed everything down to the antifouling. We were surprised when a port official came to the boat after receiving a telephone call from Derby in England saying that my mother was very ill and I was needed. Rex warned me to expect the worst. I flew back home and immediately drove to Derby to find, as expected, that she had sadly died. My father, a devout Christian, was very calm, something I had not failed to notice when Pamela died.

Decisions

In May, I agreed to skipper a New Parks instruction cruise on the Solent in a steel boat – very uncomfortable so not an enjoyable cruise from that point of view. I had then arranged for a crew member to take me to the Solent because I had invited Christine to meet me on the Hamble for a weekend together. Our talks at the High School had become increasingly friendly and I had taken her to dinner at a restaurant in Stamford renowned for its duck. Christine is an expert cook and I wanted to impress her, but alas the meal was poor. The owner of the restaurant, who knew me, apologised profusely, but he would have done better to have given us a bottle of wine! However, to return to the cruise, we were sailing back to base at the end of the week and, standing alone on the foredeck having just taught the crew how to fly a spinnaker and, realizing how much I was looking forward to the weekend, I decided to ask Chris for her hand in marriage. I knew that she had planned to book a hotel conveniently near the Solent that a couple she knew managed in Fittleworth in Sussex. She was waiting for me when I berthed the boat, but on arriving I noticed that she was not in her own car. As she drove to the hotel, she related the saga of how, the previous night on her way to Fittleworth, she had reached Brackley in Northampton-shire when the car developed a wheel problem. She limped on at a slow speed as far as Basingstoke from where she rang her friend Carlos at the hotel for advice. He was reassuring and the next thing she knew was that a police car arrived in the lay-by where she was parked, quickly grasped her problem, and convoyed her to a hotel with accompanying siren. The next morning she found a Renault garage that could both undertake the repairs within a week and rent her a car to meet me as arranged near Poole. That evening at dinner, I asked her to marry me. I must say that it was the best dinner ever because she accepted. She wryly remarks in retrospect that it was subject to asking Sue to leave Adam and Eve House and, of course, divorcing Janet!

Early in July I went to Clacton for my annual visit to the Schools Orchestra and this time of course, took Chris. She did a bit of coaching for the woodwind and played in a performance of Haydn's 'Toy Symphony'.

By this time, Rex had taken on another friend as crew and sailed *Seacure* to Corsica. However, there was an emergency and he had to return to Peterborough General Hospital. He rang and asked me, if I had the time, would I continue his cruise on to Malta. He suggested I took friends or family to help. I had the time and I thought that the very least I could do for Sue was take her for a holiday, explain the situation and hope she would understand. She was able to take a fortnight's leave and, since our relation-ship had by this time become totally platonic, I asked her if she would kindly leave Adam and Eve House when she returned. We flew to Corsica on 14 July. There were no flights to the north coast of the island so we had to fly to Ajaccio. From there we caught a train and travelled to Calvi on the north coast. The train stopped at the harbour where there was also a seaside resort and we witnessed holidaymakers crossing the line after an afternoon on the beach dressed very scantily, and I mean 'scantily'. It is a worthwhile journey by train, half ascending, and half descending with wonderful views. Next morning, we took a taxi into Calvi to visit the bank and provision the boat in preparation for our departure. Looking over the harbour wall the next day, the beach was crowded with nude sun and sea bathers. I was going to enjoy the Med! Our departure was delayed for a day or so by high winds, but we eventually set sail, making one stop down the eastern side of Corsica to Port Macinaggio and mooring alongside a yacht on which a nude female was showering on the foredeck.

For the next fortnight we sailed, visiting many ports, including the island of Elba, from where we sailed to the Italian mainland and then south to Coppola Pinetamare, just north of Naples. I paused at this point, as I had to arrange Sue's return to England and Naples was perfect for flights. We had a few days in the harbour and during this time I received a visit from a young Italian who greatly admired the boat. I invited him to come aboard and showed him round. He said, in passing, he was the son of the owner of the large hotel in the port and could I possibly take him for a sail. There was not much to do as the marina was rather isolated so I agreed. We had a good breeze and I was able to put the yacht through its paces. We met him for a drink in the hotel and I asked for his advice on getting to Naples airport as Sue had to return to England. He immediately said 'I will take you'. Interestingly, this was my first experience of being driven in a diesel powered car. I mentioned to him that I had another crew member flying in the next day and, without hesitation, he offered to take me to the airport for a second time to meet my new replacement crew, of course Christine. If he was surprised that I lost one female crew member only to be replaced by another he did not show it!

This was Chris's first experience of sailing out to sea in a small boat, in this case to Ischia. We saw a great deal of the island, including William Walton's former residence, and several days later we returned to Naples to await the arrival of two of my daughters – Rachel, now with her husband Dick, and Rebecca with her boyfriend Guy Longbone. On the way to meeting them at Naples airport, I was robbed in the main street of the city of my passport, credit cards and other important documents, not least the boat keys. On returning to the boat, Rachel was fortunately able to get access through the partially opened fore hatch, and I was able to open the main hatch when she located the spare key inside. This did not solve starting the engine, however, as the one key for this had also been in my stolen handbag. A marina engineer managed to solve the problem, but it caused a short delay. Meanwhile, I had met the British consulate who gave me a transit document allowing me to leave Italy, but only to travel to the UK. Interestingly, the receptionist to whom I had spoken, took my details to an inner office and returned with a man, who was presumably in charge, who asked me if I was *the* Neville Dilkes who conducted the English Sinfonia. He loved English music and had several of my recordings. He, however, said we could remain in Italy with his authority and return to

England, but could not in the meantime visit another country. We parted good friends.

The family stayed on the boat and we sailed to Ischia, the Isle of Capri made famous by Gracie Fields (loved by my mother), and several other ports down the coast. We had been having trouble with Rex's paraffin cooker, which we finally had to abandon, which left Christine to cope with the single portable gas burner that we were able to purchase. We all agreed that it took a genius to manage such a feat! We finally dropped our crew off at Sapri so that they could travel by train back to Naples for their return flight home. We pressed on down the coast to anchor in the bay at Tropea, thus giving us an opportunity to clean the hull and generally get the boat ready to hand back to Rex a few days later.

We then got underway to sail to our final destination in Italy, Scilla, but this was much trickier than expected. On sailing through the rough and choppy waters of the legendary Scilla and Caraddi (the sea monsters that created the whirlpools and whirlwinds around the Straits of Messina), the wind started to strengthen and one minute we were surrounded by rough and the next minute oily, sea. I had to go on the foredeck to change the sail to a storm jib and reef the main, leaving Chris on the helm shouting to her to keep the boat heading into the wind. Eventually, I started the engine, lowered both sails with great difficulty and motored into Scilla. To moor stern to, it is first necessary to drop the anchor with at least three boat lengths of chain on the bottom. This requires judgement, which is not easy in high winds. Having dropped the 'hook' I put the boat astern and we would normally reverse in, but due to the strength of the wind it was necessary to keep the engine in forward gear, steer and keep the boat from moving backwards too fast. I had found a convenient slot between two fishing boats to which we were eventually tied. Owing to a high harbour wall our only way of getting ashore was to cross the deck of one of these adjacent boats. This I did to tie the shore lines. Breathing a sigh of relief we went below for a 'cuppa' and listened to the wind getting even stronger. Going on deck and looking around the harbour there was not a soul in sight. The wind by this time was, at a guess, probably force 10 if not more. Furthermore, everything had turned red, so I shouted down to Chris that I thought it was the end of the world! Afterwards, we learnt that we had experienced a sandstorm, which happens from time to time in those parts; it had travelled all the way from the Sahara Desert. Worst of all, the boat was continually rocking from side to side at an alarming angle, which we had to suffer for the next 24 hours. Even when the storm subsided the rocking continued, but we eventually managed to scramble ashore for provisions. On stepping from the fishing boat onto *Seacure* on our return, the handle of one shopping bag broke and the contents dropped to the bottom. The water there is clear and a bottle of Gordon's Gin I had purchased for Rex could be seen lying on the sand.

We then awaited the arrival of Rex and Elizabeth to complete the voyage to Malta. Elizabeth was horrified when she saw the boat still rocking from side to side. Rex and his family had flown to Palermo in Sicily, the nearest airport, and hired a car to cross to Italy. We took over the car and returned it to the island. Anticipating being questioned over the change of driver, I asked Christine to hand the car back to the hire company on my behalf. I kept out of sight, knowing if I had to show my passport all would be revealed. The car was checked and as there were no problems with it we went on to face the next problem of getting a flight back to the UK. This meant flying to Rome and then booking a flight to London, which was easier said than done. Eventually, however, after having been taken into the back rooms of the airport, we were booked onto a flight with a South African airline. This was to leave before daylight, which prompted us to stay in the airport. We were not alone sleeping on the airport floor, which for us continued to rock like the boat we had left. On my return to the Adam and Eve House at the end of August, Sue was still there and so that evening I kindly left her my car 'to keep as a gift' and started walking to Stamford, having phoned to ask Christine to meet and rescue me en route.

We took Rex and Elizabeth out for dinner when they returned to England. Rex told me that the first thing that his son James did after we left was to dive to the bottom of the harbour to recover the gin. Second, when Rex 'weighed' the anchor, it had gone! Fortunately, he had a spare one.

Before our return, we had both decided to purchase new cars – a new Renault for Chris and a replacement Audi for me. Chris had kindly looked after the registrations for both vehicles during my absence and had managed to register them with consecutive number plates.

On 13 October, I conducted Philomusica in Wells Cathedral, part of the Abbey National series. We had agreed with the BBC to give a concert to the winner of the Young Musician of the Year contest. The programme in Wells was to feature Britten's Serenade for tenor horn and strings with Robert Tear as soloist. The winner of the brass section this year was Naomi Atherton, a student at the Royal Northern College of Music, so we gave her the engagement. Otherwise, this was a strings only programme featuring Elgar's Introduction and Allegro, the Britten Serenade for tenor horn and strings, Vaughan Williams Fantasia on a theme by Thomas Tallis, ending with the Tchaikovsky Serenade for Strings. My next Philomusica concert was in Swindon and the season ended with the usual Christmas festivities.

Chapter 11

New Lease of Life

1985–1989

Spring Song, wedding bells, a new venture

1985 *Spring Song*

Sue had still not left Adam and Eve House so I was now living permanently and happily with Chris in Stamford. Her house was close to the centre within a short walk of the town and High School. Our Italian voyage had certainly left an impression on Chris and our conversations inevitably got round to the possibility of having our own boat. I now knew if we did I would have a good and competent crew. Westerly boats had a good reputation and were sound and practical, they were also excellent value for money. The range was extensive and indeed, as previously mentioned, Pamela and I had tried to buy their newly launched centre cockpit 33-foot ketch when we put *Maestro* on the market. It will be remembered that *Maestro* took longer than expected to sell, so I had had to withdraw from the purchase.

I needed little encouraging to revive my desire to own a boat again and started looking at advertisements. I saw a 1979 Westerly longbow ketch for sale in South Ferriby on the River Humber, so we drove there to see her. She was out of the water, which meant having to climb a ladder to look inside. Opening the hatch I was overjoyed to see a wooden interior as opposed to the usual fibre glass, and she also had wheel steering. *Roewerwater Silver* was one of the last of this build at the time and Westerly was improving its interior finishes. The decision was made quickly and we purchased the boat on 1 April from a couple we unfortunately never met because theirs was a rather sad story. They had sailed up to Holy Island just off the Northumberland coast in the North Sea and were at anchor for the night. Next morning, while weighing the anchor, the skipper, whom we only knew as Norman, had a heart attack and had to be taken off by helicopter, but unfortunately died. We gathered that he had been a director of education and, though we never met him, we grew fond of him because he left behind so many useful tools and belongings, which we came to think of as Norman's this and that. We changed the name of the boat, not because of the event leading to its sale but because we purchased it at the beginning of spring.

We made several visits to South Ferriby to antifoul and get her ready to be launched and, after launching, berthed further along the river bank. This meant a longer walk to the Hope and Anchor, a pub by the lock where we spent many happy evenings, but at least we were no longer subject to the cement factory on the bank opposite the marina that had been responsible for depositing cement dust on our decks and rigging. This could only be removed when it got bad by a mild solution of sulphuric acid, which we could obtain from the marina, which had a special licence. We brought the interior of the boat up to our liking and made our first trip upriver to Brigg. We made a final trip to the yard to have the masts stepped and then we were ready to leave for the voyage to Woolverstone, my old stamping ground and home of the Royal Harwich Yacht Club of which I had been a member for many years. The trip was memorable as the forecast was not brilliant. We locked out very early into the River Humber, which is a very sickly brown due to all the mud, and motored down to the mouth of the estuary. There was an almighty storm – not wind, but vicious thunder and lightning. However, it soon passed and we sailed on. I had, for the first time, self-steering and was anxious to get it working, so carefully set the course I wanted. The boat dutifully altered course but strangely by 180 degrees, which meant we were sailing exactly on a reciprocal course. After several attempts I solved the problem and was able to rely on it from then on. These early self-steering units were belt driven from a motor programmed to activate a belt attached to a drive on the wheel and would operate to keep to a correct course according to a pre-set compass heading. Present-day ones are less evident as they work directly on the rudder. The voyage was slow, and the wind, having dropped, required us to motor. The result of this meant reaching Lowestoft shortly before midnight. I decided to opt for a night's sleep in harbour as we were by now tired and cold, huddled in the cockpit under the spray hood with a blanket around our knees, so we motored in and moored alongside an unoccupied yacht tied to the harbour wall. Chris hesitated to clamber aboard and remembers me shouting 'do it'. We did not go ashore the next day but made an early departure and suffered a rough but invigorating day's sail; in other words, we had a 'real dusting' all the way to Woolverstone.

We had a ship to shore radio on the boat for which we needed a licence, so we both decided to take a correspondence course, which we listened to on our tape recorder and in the car, later travelling to Grimsby on 2 July to take the test, practical and written, which we both successfully passed. Concerts had been ongoing but finished for the season in Clacton with the schools' orchestra on 11 July.

Following our voyage from Ferriby, I was happy with the boat and decided in August we would sail to Holland. We invited Tony and Pat Simmonds to have a holiday with us and agreed to meet them in Veere. We made an early start and, reaching the end of the estuary, tried to put up the mizzen sail. I had not used this sail coming down from Ferriby and had a problem with the rigging supporting the mizzen mast. On closer examination, I realized the riggers had mixed up the stays, which meant finding a buoy or anchoring. This was going to cause a delay so I thought it prudent to call Tony before they left to warn them we would be late. So, for the first time I tried my hand at making a ship to shore call requesting a line to a private telephone – no problem, the learning curve continued to grow. I eventually changed the position of the stays and we moved off with the sail setting perfectly. Tony and Pat joined us and we were able to explore some of my favourite haunts from the past. I had promised Chris perfect summer weather, which I had always had in the past in Holland, but not this year.

After Tony and Pat Simmonds left, we sailed to Bruinisse and took a stern to mooring to explore the town, climbing the tower that overlooks the harbour and then shopping in a chandlery store where we bought a clock and barometer. Returning to the boat, I fitted them on an inside bulkhead and during lunch checked the pressure, which had suddenly dropped dramatically. I remarked to Christine that since there was no change in the weather it clearly was not working and would have to go back. Barely had I spoken, when suddenly a huge gust of wind heeled us over, causing complete chaos all around us and in the port. We were glad to be in harbour but some boats were not so lucky. We read later that boats on anchor were uprooted and swept ashore and some lives were lost. My faith in our barometer was restored and we enjoyed the rest of the cruise, which was uneventful. We decided on our return passage to stop off at Ostende before crossing the North Sea. While comfortably moored up in the outer harbour, to my surprise a Westerly 33 bridge deck sloop motored in, the skipper of which was Peter Wakefield. There were no moorings left in the outer harbour so he had to lock into the inner one. However, before he did, we arranged to meet before sailing back to Woolverstone in company. In the event, we were held up for several days by very high winds, but eventually got out. I say we sailed in company, but his was the faster boat and so he gradually vanished over the horizon. We had decided to return to Woolverstone rather than Woodbridge where we had taken a permanent berth, as I was not happy with either the state of the tide or the entrance to the River Deben, which has a notorious bar. When we finally docked in Woolverstone, we discovered that Peter had also taken a berth there, so we met again. He had always berthed in Brightlingsea, and in fact still did. Peter was a doctor and we first met when having a trial sail in a Halcyon 23. Much to our surprise, we met again in Veere when, as explained in Chapter 7, I took my entire family to Holland for a month. As I mentioned, when buying *Maestro* there were three Nantucket clippers 'in build' and it transpired that Peter had bought the other one of the three. Also having bought the original Halcyon 23 he had joined the Offshore Yacht Owners Club and eventually reached the dizzying height of becoming its chairman, so our paths were frequently criss-crossing. We stayed one night in Woolverstone before leaving the following morning for a short sail to the Deben River and entering at exactly the right time in terms of sandbanks to go to a new berth in the marina at Woodbridge, a decision we had made some time before.

The new concert season started on 7 September in St Albans Cathedral. Abbey National was the sponsor, David Littaur the conductor, and Heather Harper the soloist. It concluded with Beethoven's 'Eroica' Symphony.

In October I conducted two more Abbey National concerts, the first in Ripon Cathedral and the second in Durham Cathedral, both featuring young award winning soloists in the programme. The first half was devoted to the eighteenth century with Abigail Young playing Bach's A major Violin Concerto and the second half to twentieth-century music with Jack Brymer playing the Finzi Clarinet Concerto. I concluded the concert with Tippet's Concerto for double string orchestra. Chris came with me on this short tour and I must say it was a joy to have her company, which continued for many concerts. She quickly became friendly with the players, soloists, promoters, sponsors and audiences, thus reminding me of Pam's contribution in my early days. They say that 'behind every great man is a woman', but I think 'in front' would be more apt!

On 11 November I went to the National Sailing School at Cowes for an instructor's course. Passing this qualified me to certify successful candidates after my instruction. Later, following a weekend in Woodbridge, we returned home to find that Sue had finally left Adam and Eve House, so I was able to return there with Christine. Work could now commence, as I had planned to have a tiled floor in the entrance hall, foyer and passage to the ground-floor bedrooms and bathroom. I should have mentioned before that Adam and Eve was an 'upside-down' house, apart from the principal en-suite bedroom, which was on the second floor off the galleried music room and over the drawing room.

There was a large open front barn with parking for several vehicles, so both cars were now garaged with a large expanse of gravel for turning. The garden was on two levels and I eventually built five steps in a pyramid semi-circle arriving at the point of entry with two urns eventually planted by Christine who loves gardening, leaving me to cope with anything power driven!

1986 Wedding bells

I had been too occupied to think of my personal responsibilities and indeed my promise to marry Christine, but they were to be solved when, on 23 January, a letter arrived from Janet's solicitor requesting a divorce. I had no doubt that my musical colleagues would have kept her abreast of developments in my personal life, as she was of course still a member of the Sinfonia, which, as mentioned before, now formed the basis of Philomusica. My former players, including principals, were all with hardly an exception outstandingly loyal to me, but as they say 'there's always one!' Equally, we also know that no one is irreplaceable.

Following Janet's letter, I rang my old friend Rupert Bear for his advice, reading out the documents from her solicitor. I followed his brief to take the papers to my local registry office and simply agree. Apart from putting my signature on some document this completed the break and shortly after, on 14 February, I found myself a free man, but not for long as wedding plans were on the horizon.

The next day, after conducting in Southwell Minster, Christine and I met the Gurlings, who had remained dear friends of mine since I first met Ken, a consultant at the Derbyshire Royal Infirmary and dean of Medical Studies at Nottingham University, after a concert in Ilkeston Town Hall many years earlier. Given that he lived in Derby it was inevitable that I would see him again because we frequently played in the city, although then it was only a town. Ken's wife had died a few years earlier and he was now married to Monica. A new friendship with Christine now started and we were to spend many happy summer holidays sailing with them in the Channel Islands and France.

In March I met, at his request, a former Corby Grammar School music pupil of mine, Brian Snary. He was now music adviser for schools in an area of South Wales, and ran an annual summer school in Exeter. He wanted me to take charge of the orchestra, which we discussed in the comfort of the Saville Club. I undertook to do the course that summer and took Christine with me. It was a splendid week and I was impressed with the work he was doing, particularly with the enthusiasm of his pupils and staff for singing and playing.

On Saturday 12 April I married Christine at Surfleet Church (near Spalding), where for more than seven years she had been the organist, and was still driving from Stamford every Sunday to play for the morning service. It had happy memories for us, as it had been our first excuse to meet socially. The organ had just been renovated and I was to have the pleasure of doing an extemporization on it. Good move Christine! My colleague David Littaur was our best man, and there was a reception at the Toft House Hotel situated between Bourne and Stamford. We left in the late afternoon to spend two memorable nights in the Inn at Fittleworth before flying to Nice for our honeymoon on the Monday.

On our return, Chris went back to teaching. I did the usual New Parks course and, in June, we attended a Kettering Symphony Orchestra concert, perhaps the first since I had become its president some time before. In fact, I am still its president and Christine and I attend its concerts whenever we can. In July, in lieu of a wedding present, Albert and Susan Wheway took us to dinner at Hambleton Hall Hotel near Rutland Water. This was what Albert would call the 'We Way' of doing things. If readers care to look at the menu, they will understand why it has become a lasting memory. Guest menus did not reveal the prices, but I already knew them. We were curious to know how the four waiters who served each of our courses individually, each plate covered with a silver salver, miraculously always gave them to the right person. Albert had to know how they did it, and probably as a result of a handsome tip was told – by the colours of the men's ties and ladies' dresses. I seem to remember having a touch of indigestion during the night, but this was probably due to me helping Susan out with her magnificent dessert! These were real works of art.

The summer saw the first of many cruises in company with the Gurlings aboard *Spring Song* from Woodbridge. Later, we sailed to the Walton Backwaters in the company of Tony and Pat Simmonds.

At Woodbridge in September we visited the Maltings at Snape, home of Benjamin Britten and his well-known festival, and noticed that a two manual harpsichord by William De Blaise was for sale. EMI had provided me with a De Blaise harpsichord for my recording of the Walter Leigh Harpsichord Concertino and, though admittedly bigger, the instrument particularly impressed me because the recording had the benefit of a 16-foot stop as well as the usual 8-foot and 4-foot ones. We bought the instrument, which has certainly earned its keep over the years, and it is still with us.

Autumn saw some more concerts, including one in St Albans with Marisa Robles the harpist and one in Luton with Susan Milan who played the Mozart flute Concerto in G major. Peter Wakefield, previously mentioned in connection with sailing together from Ostende, came to the concert at our invitation and kindly offered us a bed for the night afterwards so that we could talk 'boats'.

In December, thankfully, new carpets were finally laid at Adam and Eve and the hall area tiled with a choice of white tiles with black diamond inserts at each corner. I would love to have the same here in France.

1987 A new venture

In January I learnt that Oakham parish church needed an organist and, knowing it was a fashionable church with a good choir and organ, offered to fill the vacancy. Christine had by now given up Surfleet as it was too far to travel for the early services. I enjoyed getting back my old skills, but hasten to add that this was not because of the time lapse since I had last played an organ, but because the console in Oakham Church is separated from the pipes by the length of the nave, with the console in the choir and the pipes on the tribune at the opposite end. This means that the distance causes a delay in the organist hearing what he is playing, so needs to be allowed for. It was of course not a new experience for me and I knew that for a short time at least I had to discount the delay, and simply not listen to what I was playing, not easy. I had an assistant to help with the choir, Margaret Bennett, who I probably overworked; she taught singing at Stamford High School and is a close friend of Christine's. This was convenient for Margaret as she also taught singing at Oakham School. She rehearsed the trebles during the week leaving me just the Friday night practice, which seems to be the tradition of every church I ever knew. We tackled a cathedral like repertoire and I included in the short time I was there Stainer's 'Crucifixion', but confess to adding a bit of professional 'stiffening' with a tenor and bass choristers from Peterborough Cathedral. My soloists for this were two of my old friends from Opera da Camera days, David Cound, tenor, and Michael Rayner, bass baritone.

I should mention that at the end of last year's sailing season we put *Spring Song* up for sale. On a very cold January morning in Woodbridge, we were surprised to have a couple to see the boat, but what was more surprising she sold immediately, so we were once again boat searching, something that was to become rather a habit. It was not long before we purchased a centre cockpit Westerly 33 ketch, *Rosetta of Wyckham*, the class of boat with which Pamela and I had so much wanted to replace *Maestro*. At this, point we said goodbye to the east coast and took a berth at Hamble Point Marina. We loved both the marina and the location and Chris was glad to escape the east coast mud.

The concert year had started early for me on 9 January in Bradford. The programme included Mozart 'Don Giovanni Overture', Berkeley Serenade for strings and the Rodrigo Concerto 'de Aranjuez' with soloist Carlos Bonell, guitar. After the interval the Respighi Airs and Dances and to finish the programme Mozart's Symphony No. 40 in G minor.

July was a sad moment for Chris when Robert Gilman, then head of music at Stamford High School, left after several years at the end of the summer term and was replaced by John Worthington. In 1982 a lot of changes had taken place at the schools. Graham Johnston, the director of music at the Stamford School for boys, had retired and it was decided to bring the two schools' music departments and sixth forms closer together, so an overall director of music was appointed. This was Paul White and both schools now became known as the Stamford Endowed Schools. Each would now have a head of music under the direction of the overall director Paul. Robert Gilman, who had previously been organist at Newark parish church, challenged me to listen to a recording of Carlo Curley playing the Reubke 93rd psalm, a work I mentioned in connection with the opening organ recital at the Royal Festival Hall. He wanted my opinion but was not specific, so I listened for wrong notes, choice of stops and was curious to know what I was missing. He revealed it was an electronic organ, which took the wind out of my sails. I must take my hat off to progress! I envy the present generation of organists who can have an electronic organ in their home with the full RCO pedal board (radiating and concave pedal board of precise measurements, Royal College of Organists standard), a large variety of stops and programming for stop combinations, plus a discreet volume control or headphones for the sake of the neighbours.

During the summer holidays this year we drove Christine's mother and my father to Hamble Point and took them on a weekend cruise to the Isle of Wight and Beaulieu, which they both loved. We spent our main holiday cruising across to Cherbourg then the Channel Islands. Ken and Monica Gurling joined us for two weeks – the first cross channel trip for them and Chris's first of many to the Channel Isles. Guernsey is a wonderful island with a breathtaking southern coastline and lovely bays. On this occasion, we took a boat trip to Herm, which was also idyllic and, like Sark, has no cars. What bliss to take life at such a leisurely pace! After Ken and Monica left, we went on to explore Jersey before returning to Guernsey, then sailed back to Hamble Point. On our return to the marina, we had the boat lifted for the winter and were horrified to discover she had osmosis, which, although seemingly the fashion at the time, was nevertheless an expensive and depressing blow.

We sought legal advice as the boat had been sold to us with a Westerly's survey giving it a clear bill of health. Our solicitor based in Portsmouth, a yachtsman and commander of the Royal Southern Yacht Club, was confident we would win our case and on his advice hired an attorney, only to be beaten at the winning post by Westerly's going into bankruptcy. Nigel Lightfoot was most apologetic when he sent his account and, although no fault of his, split the bill 'fifty-fifty'. We read later in the national press that he had been murdered in the presence of his wife at the front door of his home late at night when answering the doorbell to a former employee.

Towards the end of the year Rebecca's boyfriend Guy, who had sailed in Italy with us, approached me at a party to say that he had proposed to Rebecca and that they were now engaged and would like to get married the following September. I was pleased to be well prepared, but it left me wondering about my third daughter, who was now in Australia after having left her job with Gold Greenlees Trott, an advertising company working with ITV. She had a successful career with the company producing a popular TV advert for Toshiba – readers may remember 'Hey Tosh got a Toshiba'. I believe that her decision to go to Australia arose from the frustration of her on–off romance with her boyfriend Nicholas Duthie not going to plan. More about that later. Her idea was to work for six months in Australia and then spend another six months touring the country. She could not get a job doing that, so she reversed the order by touring first and then successfully finding work in Sydney that was similar to what she had been doing in London. The sequel to this will come next year.

A memorable occasion took place in October when Chris and I had dinner at the Saville Club with Joyce and David Littaur. From time to time, the club relaxed its rules to have a 'ladies night', along with 'candlelight supper', and we enjoyed an extremely pleasant evening. David's wife Joyce was a brilliant secretary and it would be impossible to meet a nicer man than David. Joyce sadly died (in 2018) shortly after having received a card from the Queen congratulating them on their seventieth wedding anniversary. We are still in touch and call on him whenever we travel to our present boat on the Norfolk Broads.

Moving back to concerts, in November we put on another Programme Master concert, this time at the Corn Exchange in Ipswich, which conveniently provided the opportunity to meet up with old sailing friends Don and Kay George, with whom we stayed for the weekend. Being a Programme Master concert, there was a reception afterwards at which, out of the blue I met Graham Bell, a former Corby Grammar School music pupil of mine who, from time to time accompanied for me, usually for the annual Nine Lessons and Carols in the parish church in Corby. I recalled meeting him on a staircase in the grammar school one lunchtime when he was in the sixth form and him asking for my advice on whether he should apply to university to read music or physics. I think I may have said that such a decision really rested with him, but added that maths and physics were my best subjects at school (music was not even a subject in my schooldays). In recent years, I have renewed my interest in physics, but there was never any doubt at his age that my choice would have been music. To my surprise, he chose neither and became a vicar at Wickham Market near Woodbridge in Suffolk. I thought his choice excellent, and felt certain he would have opted for a parish with a good church organ. Now, having decided to return to his roots, he has retired to Northamptonshire and, having obtained my address from my friend John Peck through the Kettering Symphony Orchestra, recently contacted me by email. I later received a copy of a book he had written, along with several CDs of recordings of organ music he had made in Kettering. His love of music has clearly not waned.

In November I was due to make a short tour with Philomusica to Northern Ireland. We were scheduled to fly from Heathrow on Monday 9 November for the first concert that night, but the day before we heard on the news that a bomb had exploded at the war memorial in Enniskillen, County Fermanagh, our first venue for a Programme Master concert. I received several phone calls from musicians to ask if I would still go and my reply was 'yes', as there were still other concerts booked. By Sunday evening, our management had established that, despite the incident, the Irish wanted the concert in Enniskillen to go ahead. I rang Richard Baker who immediately said he would go. By midnight on the Sunday, one or two of the musicians had lost their nerve, but Trevor, our concert manager, managed to replace them in time to be at Heathrow for our departure with all the players we needed for the tour. The concert was much appreciated by the people of Enniskillen, who said that it brought their community together.

The Philomusica, originally the Boyd Neel Orchestra, had over the years accumulated a large music library with orchestral parts and full scores dating back to its inception. We were using the library and it was particularly interesting to read notes on interpretation, bowings and dynamics. It had started life as a chamber orchestra with probably between 25 to 35 players depending on repertoire and venue. It travelled extensively in the provinces and clearly filled a gap in the country not shared by our European partners where most large towns and cities had an opera house with orchestra in addition to a resident symphony orchestra. The orchestra's repertoire was baroque to modern, Bach and his contemporaries taking in Haydn, Mozart and Beethoven and a broad repertoire through to the twentieth century. There was a healthy repertoire of English music, which probably reflected Boyd Neel's interest. However, the change that took place when Philomusica emerged from the ashes, so to speak, was dramatic to say the least. Thurston Dart was an academic at Cambridge and a brilliant harpsichordist. He was an authority on baroque music and Philomusica rapidly became known as a baroque orchestra specializing in the seventeenth and eighteenth centuries. I remember a television broadcast he made talking about Bach's Brandenburg Concertos, and in particular No. 3, which is for strings and continuo only. In one, if not my first concert with the Kettering

Symphony Orchestra, being a Bach fan, I conducted a performance of this particular work. We hired the parts, which I noted Sir Henry Wood had edited and presumably performed at a promenade concert. His arrangement divides each of the string sections, with the exception of the double bass, into three. Imagine this being played by a full string section of a symphony orchestra with 30 violins, 12 violas, 9 cellos and 6 basses. I recall my performance was more modest, if my memory serves me correctly it was probably nearer to 9, 6, 3, and 1 bass.

Dart insisted that in Bach's time it was played with single instruments and harpsichord continuo, and this he demonstrated. He succeeded in catching the public's interest in baroque music, but failed to go further into using only old instruments, so the pitch was still A440. For some time after this a wave of new interest in baroque music emerged. I followed his thinking with the Midland Sinfonia, for there was a wealth of instrumental music that could be performed with just 11 strings and harpsichord. As mentioned, we purchased a harpsichord and took on many engagements in the Sinfonia's County Plan concerts, as well as in other parts of the country. This surge of interest in baroque music, however, later began to demand that it should be played on original instruments, or perhaps I should point out, mainly copies, which were tuned approximately a semitone lower, A 417 instead of the now universal A 440. I have never quite seen the point of going this far and certainly question the inclusion of Beethoven's 'Emperor' Piano Concerto played on a straight strung piano that may have been 'square' as well!

1988

This was a hectic year. Starting with boating, Hamble Point Marina, owned by a Dutchman, was to be sold to a company by now well known in the boating world as MDL – Marina Developments Ltd. It was well known because berth holders had to meet the cost of its developments, so we correctly foresaw a significant rise in the cost of our berthing. Since we seemed to spend every summer sailing to the Channel Islands and France, it seemed logical to save ourselves the channel crossing there and back, sometimes more than once a year, so we decided to go to Guernsey where berthing costs were considerably lower than the south coast of England. Furthermore, we could fly from Southampton to Guernsey for £17 return (sometimes less if the flight was underbooked) and car hire was just £5 for the weekend. The seeds were beginning to be sown for leaving England, but it was to be another seven years before they were planted.

Family developments. My second grandchild Sophie, was born on 17 September. Rachel and Dick were now living in Kingston upon Thames. Dick had decided to have a change of career so he went back to university and took a B.Sc. in computer studies.

April finally saw *Rosetta* launched, having had the hull completely dried out and treated by Don Smy in the marina, a specialist in the treatment of osmosis. Life was certainly busy. Concerts were still taking place in, for example, Leicester, Norwich, Bradford, Leeds and St Albans, but they were fewer in number. Also, finding sponsorship was difficult and local authorities seemed to have smaller budgets.

At this time we saw quite a lot of Rebecca and Guy as they were living in Stamford. I remember an upsetting evening when Guy came for supper, as Rebecca had been working away but was due back later that evening. I received a phone call from the police in Spalding to say that she was in hospital after her car had crashed into a lorry that had apparently reversed out onto the road in front of her without lights. We immediately drove to the hospital, saw that she was comfortable though clearly shocked, but to our relief knew that she would make a full recovery. They were still planning to marry in September.

Early in the summer, we heard that Gré was to make a flying visit to London from Sydney. This was to make a TV advertising clip with Felicity Kendal, who had been scheduled to go to Sydney, but being pregnant had refused to fly, so the Australians decided to fly their team, including Gré, to Britain to film in London. Apparently, when Gré arrived at her hotel, her room was filled with flowers and a note from Nick saying could they meet? Shortly after hearing this, Chris answered a phone call from Nick saying that he would like to come and see me. Chris was certain that he wanted to marry Gré, but I said 'nonsense, he more likely wants advice on buying a boat!' Chris, of course, was correct as indeed it was to ask for Gré's hand in marriage. Nick followed this by saying that he was shortly going to work in America and then apologized for taking her away again, as Gré had agreed to join him there. I was delighted but warned him that they would have to take their turn as we were already committed, with Rebecca having already reserved a date in September for her marriage to Guy. It should be noted that Gré returned to Sydney determined to finish her contract but later followed Nick to New York.

On 26 July, we left the Hamble for Cherbourg, then to Guernsey where Ken and Monica later flew to join us. This time we ventured down to Saint-Malo and the North coast of Brittany, well known to me but new to Chris, Ken and Monica, who had never visited these harbours by boat. You get a completely different aspect when approaching somewhere by sea. After their departure, we continued to enjoy Guernsey and settled into our new berth in Beaucette in the north of the island. While on Guernsey, we walked along the well-known coastal path and pretty well covered the whole south coast. A road runs parallel with the coast, and a regular bus service made it possible to catch a bus at our starting point and then subsequently pick up another one after a very strenuous cliff walk, gradually over several days we covered the entire length. The views from the cliff path were stunning. In August, Rachel and Dick joined us with their au pair and baby Sophie.

Property prices in the Channel Islands are normally considerably higher than those in the UK, particularly as in Guernsey there is a two-tier system where only a limited number of houses are available to non-residents of the island, and we noticed at this time that the prices of these properties had fallen behind those in England. On our return home, the sailing season finished, we had Adam and Eve House valued and, on the basis of the staggering increase, the house immediately went on the market, as did our Westerly 33. We just did not feel the same about the boat, the osmosis had left a nasty taste in our mouths. We earmarked a Seafin 41 to replace it but this proved the start of the most frustrating period of my life. Christine applied for a music appointment in Guernsey and was told a job would be possible if we moved there. We knew a property we would have liked, and I looked forward to reducing my work load. Sadly, the price of houses in England started to fall and despite some interest we could not sell, in other words we had 'missed the boat'.

We did, however, have plenty to keep us busy, including two weddings. On 7 September, Rebecca and Guy were, like Rachel, married in Tixover Church and we had a marquee on the lawn at Adam and Eve House. The organist for this occasion was Paul White, director of music at the Stamford Endowed Schools. With no electricity in the church, he struggled to pedal the bellows to provide wind to play the old harmonium organ, which I gather was also missing some notes, one being top C, which was vital in the wedding march. He will never forget that moment!

My routine continued with Philomusica concerts, Oakham church, and a modest list of piano pupils at Stamford High School, plus another wedding to be organized for Gré and Nick, which was to be in London and needed a large church and facilities for a very large gathering for the reception. Gré and Nick wanted all their old friends there as they would see so little of them in the future. They were to live in America and in fact remained there for more than 13 years. I was able to arrange for the marriage to be in the fashionable St George's Church, Hanover Square. This was made possible by Ken Gurling whose brother lived in London and was a friend of the rector, the Revd Bill Atkins. I seem to remember he was also an honorary member of the Saville Club, though I was unaware of that at the time. I was careful to warn Gré that I had already paid for three daughters to marry and that it would be unfair to treat her and Nick disproportionately. Being the gentleman he is, Nick agreed.

While Gré was in London I took her to the Saville Club to see the facilities and to choose the menu and drinks. I agreed with the club's secretary that its champagne would be ideal for the reception, but as Nick was an 'authority' on the subject, Gré was dubious. The secretary gave Gré a bottle for Nick to try, but despite careful refrigeration and serving it was, I am told dismissed out of hand. However, I took the precaution, as a father should do, of asking the head waiter to keep me informed on the levels of champagne consumption, which I knew was expensive, requesting if it was Buck's Fizz to make sure they used something cheaper, and to keep me posted on the number of bottles in circulation. The wedding took place on 10 December and was a memorable occasion, especially since many of my old friends and colleagues from my Corby days were there. Gré and Nick left for their honeymoon in Kenya testing my overdraft, but at the airport kindly posted me a cheque to cover the excess cost of their wedding before their departure to the States.

Chapter 12

Good Times

1989–1995

Changes, Holy Trinity, more decisions

1989 Changes

Changes were on the way. We were now once again boatless and so in January snatched a short holiday to Marbella for a winter break and search for another boat. We saw a superb Formosa 41 in Estepona and a lovely bridge deck Moody 42, but this had had osmosis, so was a definite no. The Formosa was built in Taiwan, which seemed too much of a risk.

In April we had finally decided on our replacement for *Rosetta*, a new centre cockpit Moody 346, but changed our minds after seeing the Moody 376. We were still to sell Adam and Eve House, so all thoughts of a Seafin had to be shelved. While visiting Moody's boatyard, we negotiated to get a favourable deal and ordered the new boat on 2 May. We visited the Marine Projects factory in Plymouth to see her in build, but were disappointed when we saw only the keel. However, we were shown round the factory and saw the impressive build sequence, so it was quite a memorable day. The boat was finished on time to be launched and ready for handover on 11 July. I had opted to buy the boat without paying VAT so we had only seven days to prepare the boat and leave England for our berth in Guernsey. This was a valuable week as we were berthed in Moody's marina on the Hamble and had its workers on call if anything was wrong, or needed. We left on time, with Ken and Monica having joined us the day before our departure, for our maiden voyage to the Channel Islands followed by the north coast of Brittany.

Just a brief catch up on family as a new member arrived on 19 November. A second daughter for Rachel and Dick – Lara, my third grandchild.

Concerts this year had certainly diminished, partly due to talk of the forthcoming poll tax. Local authorities and councils were reining in their expenditures, and being cautious over their commitments concerning grant aids and subsidies. Consequently, they were either not booking concerts, putting them on hold, or, in the worst cases, cancelling them.

1990

I felt there was a cloud over the country, which I attributed to the leadership of the prime minister, Margaret Thatcher. Politics had never really interested me as I calculated one vote in a million, not to mention the total number of voters in an election, could make no difference to the outcome. If the word democracy has any meaning, common sense dictates that there is a limit to the number of people who can benefit from it. Though probably a socialist at heart, I did, however, vote for Margaret Thatcher in 1979 shortly after my bereavement. It will be remembered that I had a crew for sailing tuition on the Solent the week before Pamela died. There was one member who was very 'left wing' and made life for me and the rest of my crew unbearable, especially in the confined space of a yacht. He focused for me what I then realized was a prevalent mood in the country at the time, and I came to the conclusion that the Callaghan government was partly responsible.

The introduction of the poll tax triggered large-scale protests in London with 250,000 people marching into Downing Street in March of this year, followed by riots just before the tax was due to come into force. The threat of the tax had already in many ways had a devastating effect on local authorities, but not least in their distribution of subsidies to the arts. They were, of course, Philomusica's main source of finance for concerts everywhere in the UK. We struggled on for a while, but finally agreed it was time to look at retirement pastures.

I am pleased to write that the cloud over the country lifted in November when John Major replaced Margaret Thatcher, but the harm had been done. I believe that Margaret Thatcher took a perverse pleasure in destroying the miners and their communities and to do so turned the police into an army of the state. Arthur Scargill was perhaps a poor leader, but when he said there was a 'hit list' of pits destined for closure, which Margaret Thatcher denied, we discovered which one of them was a liar! In 1986 Thatcher, along with Ronald Reagan, freed the banks to play irresponsibly with our money, which we still feel today. Thanks to North Sea gas, I do not think that any prime minister had more revenue than she did at her disposal, which was wasted because she had to win the Falklands War because it was her incompetence that encouraged it in the first place, and did so by selling off all our energy assets to foreigners who are now screwing us!

It was frustrating not being able to sell Adam and Eve House, but nevertheless, after my gratifying experience of directing the music at Oakham parish church, decided to explore the possibility of finding another parish church with a good choir and potential for combing music with my impending retirement.

I found that the parish church in Colyton, East Devon, had a vacancy. I was invited to audition and was given a surprisingly ambitious schedule and repertoire to rehearse. I was to play at both the morning and evening services. We were invited to stay with one of the church wardens, so arrived in time to settle in before driving to the church for a rehearsal with the choir on the Friday evening. I was prepared to rehearse the setting for the Eucharist and evensong plus an anthem. It was, however, the anthem that had surprised me as it was to be Parry's 'Blest pair of sirens', which involves an eight-part choir. Arriving at the church I was even more surprised to see so many people in the building and wondered if I would have an audience. It was in fact the choir, or should I say choral society? The organ console was on the screen with good vision down to the choir stalls and I enjoyed playing for both services. I later learnt that the organist before the present one, who had been asked to stand down, was none other than Arthur Hutchings, mentioned earlier, who took on the job when he retired as the professor of music at Durham University. His appointment probably explained the 'choral society'! I was informed I would have their decision in about a week's time.

Holy Trinity

The following weekend I had an audition at Holy Trinity Church in Folkestone. This time I had a conventional choir of boys and men, together with an assistant organist who would be leaving shortly to go to music college. Again, choral Eucharist and choral evensong were to be rehearsed on the Friday evening followed by a pleasant session on the very fine three-manual Walker organ during the Saturday. We were invited to spend the weekend with the Revd Robert Stroud and his wife Dawn with whom we immediately became friendly and on Christian name terms. I played for the services, and conducted the settings and anthem at evensong. Holy Trinity was not the parish church of Folkestone and not in the centre of the town. In fact, we had mistakenly gone to the centre of Folkestone where the parish church is situated and, while impressed with the church were disappointed with the organ. Holy Trinity, however, which was Victorian and a short drive from the town centre, was at first disappointing to me until we went inside. It was undoubtedly the focal point of the town in that it had very large congregations, an accomplished choir and was extremely popular for marriages. I was offered the appointment before lunch on the Sunday, but since our house in Rutland was still on the market, thus entailing a weekly commute until we could complete our sale, I was given a little more time to reach a decision. Chris, of course, had a full-time job at the High School and I some commitments with Philomusica, but retirement was certainly in the air, at least for me, so we soon opted in favour of Folkestone. I accordingly wrote to Colyton, which had by then offered me the appointment, to explain my decision to go to Folkestone. Another consideration in favour of Folkestone was that it had a Friends of Music association in the church that extended to choral concerts, recitals and each year a summer series of organ recitals, which I would be expected to organize.

I took up the appointment in September and Chris was able to arrange her timetable so that we could travel down on Friday afternoons and arrive in time for choir practice at 19.00, often sharing a pint with several of the men afterwards. Meanwhile, Chris would be socializing with Bob and Dawn Stroud, our hosts at the vicarage, with whom we stayed as guests until other arrangements could be, and were, made. Once it was discovered that Christine was a music teacher, she was offered work teaching recorder at Dover College Preparatory School. This was perfect as she could fill her Saturday mornings while I was occupied at the church. Later, had we been able to move there permanently, it was likely that she could have filled the post of deputy after the present one's forthcoming retirement.

I do not think Chris could avoid the temptation of taking on pupils; she loved teaching. She was incredibly popular and despite her full timetable at the High School had private pupils at home. We set up a teaching room for her on the ground floor in the largest of the bedrooms, which, having French windows, was designed to be a sitting room if required.

To mark my appointment at Folkestone I gave the last in the series of organ recitals already arranged for 1990 on Wednesday 26 September. My programme included:

BACH	'Great' prelude and fugue in G major
BALBASTRE	Noel with variation
MENDELSSOHN	Sonata No. 2
RHEINBERGER	Sonata No. 4
MUSHEL	Toccata

My work and our weekly visits to Folkestone were soon to be a punishing schedule, but trusting that our house would soon sell were spurred on, spending our spare moments looking at property in the area. I travelled at my own expense but the stipend was very generous, which, with weddings, if nothing else, kept me in the VAT category with regard to my total income.

The summer holiday was spent cruising in northern Brittany, this time round the corner and south to Brest and Concarneau. We had decided to bid farewell to Guernsey and find a berth in Brittany. Port-la-Forêt, a large marina with first-rate facilities, fitted the bill perfectly and we were given a berth there. We had flown to Guernsey to collect the boat so all that remained was to fly back to England. From Folkestone at this time we found we were able to cross by ferry to Bologne and drive to the south of Brittany. It was a long drive but since the ferry left very early, time was on our side. This early boat usually carried very few passengers, so few in fact that the crew frequently gave us waiter service in the self service. However, despite our early start, we did not arrive at the marina until long after sundown, but we thought that *Mattinata* made it all worthwhile.

1991

The Stamford–Folkestone routine continued, but it was not all work. Chris enjoyed shopping and we found an excellent curry house, which we now remember as probably the best we have ever known. We were made very welcome everywhere, but alas had still not sold our house, which would have lifted the burden from Bob and Dawn, plus other members of the congregation who had come to our rescue. We still communicate with several of these people, but must mention Betty Heppenstall, a widow with a large house who served us excellent sherry and cooked wonderful meals. There was also Rupert and Sarah Bristow, whose two sons sang in the church choir. Sarah made the best breakfast muesli I have ever known, delicious. Margaret Williams, a colleague of Dawn Stroud's at Folkestone High School, and her husband Rob, offered us the luxury of their house for several months while they were on a long cruise. Rob was quite an eccentric person and when visiting them to pick up the keys, we recall that they kept the bath filled with hot water. On asking why, he said 'to heat the bathroom.' It seemed that they had other eccentricities as well. For a start, we found money all over the house, sometimes under cushions, but often on an armchair or settee. We had been warned that there was only one saucepan in which to boil eggs, which should not be washed out after use because it was full of calcium – there was barely room for the eggs. We also found a brick on the dressing table for use in case of burglars! They were a kind couple, but alas our stay there was curtailed after a short while by a telephone call from Folkestone saying that we could not stay there again because, following a spell of intensely cold weather, the header tank in the roof had burst, causing the ceiling to collapse and the house to flood. It was made clear to us that the events were in no way due to our tenancy, and that their son would see to the repairs without telling his parents because he did not want to spoil their holiday. Thanks to a generous insurance claim, they arrived home to a newly decorated, carpeted and curtained home.

We were really enjoying *Mattinata* and sought to make full use of her at every opportunity. Christine was of course limited to school holidays, but as we all know public schools enjoy longer breaks than state schools. We were able to make use of short breaks by leaving Folkestone on Monday morning and arriving back in time for choir rehearsal the following Friday. Although I did not have my original sixth form assistant, there was an organist, John Hurd, who lived in Hythe who would be available to play if needed, as he had done before my time. He enjoyed the opportunity to be let loose on the Walker organ!

My first series of concerts at Holy Trinity included three concerts. The first featured Christopher Hyde-Smith accompanied by Jane Dodd on the piano in a 'Summer Serenade' for Flute and Piano, the second 'An English Song for a Summer Evening' with Lyn McLeod soprano with lute and guitar, and Philomusica, which unfortunately never materialized.

My contract with Holy Trinity allowed me four consecutive Sundays away in the summer, during which John Hurd would take over. This year we were joined, I think I can say 'as usual', for our summer cruise with Ken and

Monica. They were great company on the boat and the girls shared the cooking on a one day on, one day off basis, with Ken and me helping out from time to time, but usually going to a restaurant. This year we explored the beautiful Morbihan, after having battled with the notoriously strong tide at its entrance, so strong in fact that as we sailed in we witnessed a boat trying to leave but in spite of motoring forwards was in fact going backwards! This was with Rebecca and her new partner Glenn McMillan (sadly her marriage to Guy was over). This introduction to sailing, to which Glenn took like a duck to water, changed his life from then on and, as we shall see later, sowed the seed for their future together.

In March, I agreed to give a concert in our music room at Adam and Eve House. It was a large room, the full width of the barn and almost its full length apart from the drawing room at one end. Over the drawing room a minstrel gallery formed a large landing for the staircase to the second floor. We had come to know Isla and Errol Matthews who lived in the village. Isla had flute lessons with Chris, and Errol was a violinist who, while at school, had played with the Welsh National Youth Orchestra. I had on several occasions accompanied Errol, which reminded me of similar such sessions with my father as a boy. He suggested a concert for the benefit of the village. We added a very good local cellist and played as a piano trio, other pieces being devoted to solo items. It was a joy to use the music room for the purpose for which it was built and to entertain a large gathering of village neighbours.

As part of the annual Oakham Festival, I conducted Philomusica on 25 June in an all string programme, which included Mozart's Eine Kleine Nachtmusic, Britten's Simple Symphony, Finzi's Clarinet Concerto played by Emma Johnson and the Tchaikovsky Serenade.

On the family front, Gré and Nick came over from the States with their baby daughter, Georgina Gré who was born on 7 September (the same day as my second daughter Rachel). My daughters are certainly sticking to the tradition of having girls. Georgina was christened in Rhyall Church near Stamford on 22 December – a good day for a family reunion.

1992 More decisions

Our routine continued but we were frustrated by still being unable to sell the house. Thanks to long school holidays, we were at least able to enjoy our boat, which included one cruise to Bénodet and the Glénan Islands with our friends Tony and Pat Simmonds, another with our usual sailing friends Ken and Monica Gurling, and finally a third with Rebecca and Glenn.

Decisions had to be made and, sadly, after three years of commuting to Folkestone, we realised that we needed to look closely at our lives. As a result, we very reluctantly decided (i) to give up going to Folkestone, and (ii) to sell our 37-foot Moody, *Mattinata*.

There were good reasons for both decisions. We had spent three happy years driving up and down to Folkestone and Chris loved it there. We even saw the construction of the Dartford Bridge and suffered the endless traffic jams. Bob Stroud was due to retire and did so shortly after I left, retiring to live in Canterbury where in the cathedral he was made a canon. We felt it unfair to have to rely indefinitely on the amazing hospitality we had received from these wonderful people. We had made many friends, the surviving ones of which we are still in touch. With regard to this decision, Christine had to forego taking the position of assistant director of music at Dover College, which had been offered to her. The concerts this year included Holy Trinity Choir and the Academy of English Music, a programme by South East Arts Young Musicians, and the band of the Royal Scots Regiment. I gave my last organ recital before leaving in September.

GUILMANT	Grand Choeur
SAMUEL WESLEY	Allegretto in F major
BACH	Prelude and Fugue in A minor
REGER	Ave Maria
RHEINGERBER	Sonata No. 7 in F minor

In January the following year, Britain was finally to become a member of the European Union, which meant that from 1 January we were liable for the VAT we had avoided paying when purchasing the new boat. Christine was very disappointed with this decision, but I was a little more realistic, for I had always regretted having insufficient funds when we bought *Mattinata* to pay for extras such as a furling foresail, central heating, auto helm and sophisticated navigation equipment, never mind the VAT. She was duly advertised and we decided to spend Christmas on board. We were fortunate to find a buyer who came over from Sweden to view the boat and decided there and then to purchase her while we were on board. We arranged for the boat to be skippered to Guernsey for him in case there was a possibility of paying the tax.

1993

On 8 January we made a quick dash over to Guernsey, where our crew had safely delivered the boat, though they told us it was the coldest sea passage they had ever made. Our agent, Peter Pearson, whose bureau was in St Peter's Port, had all the papers and cheque to complete the sale and, after clearing the boat, we made a swift return home. Not wasting any time, we met Ian McIntosh on Cobb's Quay, Poole to view his Moody 422. She was a recent build, fully equipped with all Navionics and the layout we wanted plus, for the first time, full central heating. However, no decision was made as there was a Moody 425 for sale in Majorca with a slightly different layout, namely two ways into the aft cabin, one on the port and the other on the starboard sides of the cockpit. Moody's had made this change as the 422 starboard approach passage had two bunk beds, which, if occupied had to be passed from the aft cabin to go to the galley and saloon.

We decided in February to fly over to view her. The visit was arranged by the broker, Alan Wilkinson, in Essex. (Chris had hoped for a quiet half term at home.) The boat was lying in Puerto Pollensa, a very attractive marina and there we met the owners who left us on board to look around. The boat was exactly what we were looking for except for a broken vertical wall mirror in the aft cabin. I queried this and was told it was the result of rough weather on the last voyage they made back from the Canaries to Majorca. We subsequently discovered that there were divorce proceedings taking place and wondered if there might have been another explanation. The other consideration for us was whether the boat was configured with a fin or scheel keel. The owners did not know the answer. You can sail closer to the wind and have a little more stability with a fin keel, but the disadvantage is the deeper draft. We would have sailed back to France across Biscay, but with less draft could have taken the short cut through the Canal du Midi, though at that time there were notable shallow sections. The wife pressed us very hard to sail off to an island with them and have sardines for lunch, which seemed more important to her than selling the boat, but we declined before moving on to enjoy the rest of our holiday.

We spoke to Alan Wilkinson on our return home and he, having a photograph of the boat out of the water, confirmed it was a scheel keel, so we made an offer. The vendors did not seem keen to sell, or at least from what we were given to understand, the wife was not as she was spending quite a lot of time on the boat alone. Alan Wilkinson was frustrated at having a buyer wanting to buy and a vendor unwilling to sell, but the problem was later reversed when the sellers wanted to sell and we no longer wanted to buy.

We decided to contact Ian McIntosh again about the 422, his boat was still for sale so we would go ahead. She was surveyed on 24 April and, as expected, the survey was brilliant. *Moody Minx* – 'pert young girl' – was purchased on 15 May followed by four fitting out days. Chris thought this particular boat was the most boring we had ever bought but only because it was so immaculate. There was absolutely nothing to do to bring her up to her exacting standard, or to mine, as the bilges were spotlessly clean and dry and the same with the engine room.

She was launched on 25 June and set sail on 5 July, eventually reaching Port-la-Forêt, berth C51. After our long summer cruise, we were finally joined by Ken and Monica who drove to France and were able to take us home at the end of August.

When I left Folkestone, I decided to take my private pension early and, in March, much against the advice of my accountant, started the process, but I was glad I did as the following year there was a sharp decrease in interest rates. (The 'lump' sum from my pension fund had enabled us to invest in the ocean going Moody 422.) This, to some extent an involuntary decision, left me to fill my time at home while Christine battled on teaching at the Stamford High School. 'Battled' is the wrong word for her as there was never a moment she did not enjoy her work. However, there were things to do and the dream of France was never far away, so it may prove surprising to readers that we decided to take Adam and Eve House *off the market*. I had made provision for an Aga when the plans were drawn up for the conversion and in the outside barn there was a second-hand one I had purchased that was never fitted. I resolved to have it fitted, together with a new kitchen and tiled floor. As then, now, and forever more, I left the choice of everything to Christine and, since I have never been able to convince her about an Aga this was not to be included, so I sold the one in store. My expert chose the new kitchen and together we selected the tiling for the

Adam and Eve House (above).

New cars with consecutive registrations (left).

Wedding day with best man David.

Our wedding at Surfleet.

Me with Mike Rayner and David Cound.

Enjoying our sailing days.

Philomusica at Enniskillen.

Nicholas and Gré's wedding (facing page).

Holy Trinity, Folkestone (below).

Mattinata.

On holiday with Ken and Monica Gurling.

Sailing with Glenn and Rebecca.

Relaxing on *Moody Minx* with Tony Simmonds.

Arthur, Georgina and Camilla (in christening gown) (above).

Sophie and Laral (below).

La Graineterie (above and below).

Glenn and Rebecca's wedding.

Cru Classe (below).

New Canaan
(left and below).

Annabel, Georgina
and Camilla.

My 70th birthday.
(Left to right) Rebecca,
Gré, Rachel and Clare.

Enjoying the
Bechstein at La
Graineterie.

La Noue.

Lions Club Concert and programme (below).

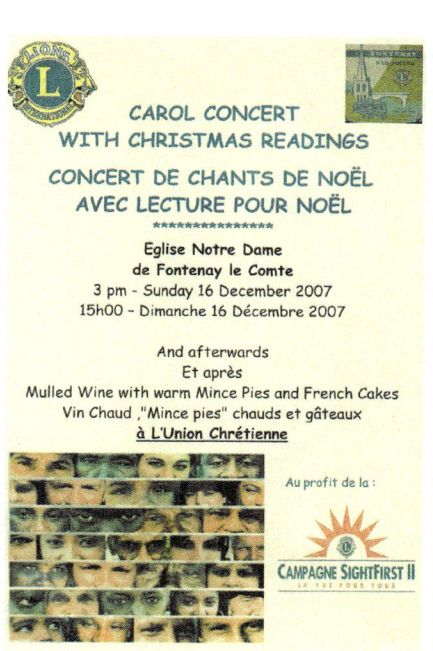

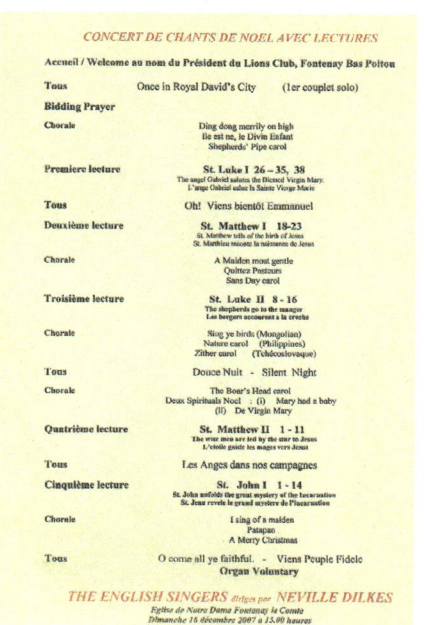

CAROL CONCERT
WITH CHRISTMAS READINGS

CONCERT DE CHANTS DE NOËL
AVEC LECTURE POUR NOËL
****

Eglise Notre Dame
de Fontenay le Comte
3 pm - Sunday 16 December 2007
15h00 - Dimanche 16 Décembre 2007

And afterwards
Et après
Mulled Wine with warm Mince Pies and French Cakes
Vin Chaud ,"Mince pies" chauds et gâteaux
à L'Union Chrétienne

Au profit de la :

CAMPAGNE SIGHTFIRST II
LA VUE POUR TOUS

CONCERT DE CHANTS DE NOEL AVEC LECTURES

Accueil / Welcome au nom du Président du Lions Club, Fontenay Bas Poitou

Tous	Once in Royal David's City	(1er couplet solo)
Bidding Prayer		
Chorale	Ding dong merrily on high	
	Ile est ne, le Divin Enfant	
	Shepherds' Pipe carol	
Premiere lecture	St. Luke I 26 – 35, 38	
	The angel Gabriel salutes the Blessed Virgin Mary.	
	L'ange Gabriel salue la Sainte Vierge Marie	
Tous	Oh! Viens bientôt Emmanuel	
Deuxième lecture	St. Matthew I 18-23	
	St. Matthew tells of the birth of Jesus	
	St. Matthieu raconte la naissance de Jesus	
Chorale	A Maiden most gentle	
	Quittez Pasteurs	
	Sans Day carol	
Troisième lecture	St. Luke II 8 - 16	
	The shepherds go to the manger	
	Les bergers accourent a la creche	
Chorale	Sing ye birds (Mongolian)	
	Nature carol (Philippines)	
	Zither carol (Tchécoslovaque)	
Tous	Douce Nuit - Silent Night	
Chorale	The Boar's Head carol	
	Deux Spirituals Noel : (i) Mary had a baby	
	(ii) De Virgin Mary	
Quatrième lecture	St. Matthew II 1 - 11	
	The wise men are led by the star to Jesus	
	L'étoile guide les mages vers Jesus	
Tous	Les Anges dans nos campagnes	
Cinquième lecture	St. John I 1 - 14	
	St. John unfolds the great mystery of the Incarnation	
	St. Jean revele le grand mystere de l'Incarnation	
Chorale	I sing of a maiden	
	Patapan	
	A Merry Christmas	
Tous	O come all ye faithful. - Viens Peuple Fidele	
	Organ Voluntary	

THE ENGLISH SINGERS dirigés par NEVILLE DILKES
Eglise de Notre Dame Fontenay le Comte
Dimanche 16 décembre 2007 a 15.00 heures

Ste Hermine Festival in costume (above and below).

Music Box at Chateau de Ste Hermine.

Concert at Le Pigeonniere.

At the organ in La Caillère.

Azimut in Holland (left).

Map of the route through the Netherlands (below).

Summer Concert at la Caillère (below).

Stamford Singers
at La Caillère
2012.

Thomas and Darren with my grandchildren, (left to right) Annabel,
Georgina, Sophie, Darren, Thomas, Lara, Ben and Camilla (above).

Nautie Buoy
on Norfolk
Broads.

Christmas concert 2019 at la Caillère, (Toy Symphony).

La Noue 2020.

floor. This was to be a major job (one I have experienced twice since) and the necessary contractors were engaged. Meanwhile, to accommodate our large dining table under the gallery, we changed the layout of the music room. It was a little inconvenient, but I had thought of installing a food lift down to the kitchen, although it did not materialize. The smaller round table was moved to the entrance hall.

Notwithstanding this decision, the dream of moving to France one day continued and in the September I decided to attend evening classes in French. This had not been not my best subject and readers may remember Polly Wood from my school days. Chris spoke no French, so it would be up to me when we finally arrived there.

On 19 December there was another family reunion as Gré and Nick's second daughter Camilla Clare, born on 6 June, was christened in our church in South Luffenham. Rachel and Dick's two daughters, Sophie and Lara, had not been christened, so it was decided to have them christened at the same time. I now had four granddaughters as well as four daughters plus one grandson. With Christmas over, on 28 December it was back to the boat before the new term, never a dull moment.

1994

This year followed the normal routine. Chris continued teaching, with her long holidays allowing us time to take extended trips to France. *Moody Minx* was really a second home for us, albeit a floating one, and I suppose we spent some four months a year on her. I cannot say that Chris was lazy in France, as she seemed to find schoolwork while we were there. She was responsible for organising a rota system for the many visiting instrumental teachers who gave lessons in the music school. It entailed a huge number of pupils being timetabled for lessons, so to say the least it was a complicated job. Imagine juggling 40-minute lessons around so that pupils do not miss the same academic lesson each week, she loved it.

At the start of our summer holiday on the boat, in my role as an instructor I was able to qualify Glenn for his coastal skipper certificate with the RYA. Rebecca and Glenn skippered the boat from the marina at Port-la-Forêt on a night passage without a stop to La Rochelle. There were no problems in spite of a bit of a blow off the Quiberon peninsula, which woke me up. Well done, Son! Following their return to England we were joined by Clare, husband Neil and Thomas who drove down to La Trinité-sur-Mer, where we had sailed to meet them. They loved the boat, despite being awakened when we had to re-anchor in another bay off the island of Hoedic. It turned out to be a holiday with strong winds, even on our return trip to Port-la-Forêt.

On our return home to Adam and Eve House, the new kitchen was fitted in time for Christmas but not the tiling of the walls behind the work surfaces and the floor. To our good fortune. Read on.

Chapter 13

Retirement

1995–1997

A momentous year, Nalliers, *Cru Classe*

1995 A momentous year

We were in France for New Year, which we spent with David and Jennifer Saxton, sailing friends I had known through Tony Simmonds in the days he kept his boat in Moody's marina. They had sailed to France and bought a house just outside Bressuire in Deux-Sèvres, the next department to the Vendée. On New Year's Eve, we were all invited to a French *reveillon* meal at 9 p.m., with intermittent dancing throughout the night. This proved quite a marathon as we were put through six courses and the dancing; we also suffered midnight twice, as at 1 a.m. I was overheard saying, 'It is only just midnight in England.' This was an excuse for the French to leap onto the tables once again with even more champagne to drink to *les Anglais*. We learnt at breakfast that onion soup was the recipe for sobering everyone up. The French, as we have now learnt, really do know how to party, and can add that our experience of French weddings confirms this as they are even more of a marathon.

Back home in the UK and on my own at Adam and Eve House on Thursday 19 January, a very wet Thursday, I unexpectedly received a telephone call from an estate agent in Peterborough asking if I could show a Mr and Mrs Whittle around the property. (I believe he was in some way related to the Whittle associated with the development of the Rolls Royce jet engine.) Curiously, I was to learn that they knew the Kempes as John later told me they subsequently had dinner with the Whittles at Adam and Eve House after we had moved to France – small world! The Peterborough estate agent who called had not been our main agent and I had assumed had not been told of our decision to leave the market. As you have read, the kitchen had been completely refitted in accordance with our decision to stay, except for the tiling and a new floor. Other rooms in the house had been rearranged so the pictures in the sale brochure were different from how it was now. The interested party duly arrived and within 20 minutes they had gone. She was, I understand, a very keen gardener, but so far as I was aware barely looked at the garden or barns. About 45 minutes after they left I received another telephone call from the agent saying the Whittles liked the house and would like to buy, subject to us not going ahead with the tiling for the kitchen as it was their intention to replace the entire NEW kitchen for one of their own choosing. Their offer was £500 less than the advertised price, which, for the life of me at that moment I could not remember. He advised me to accept and I replied that my wife was out at that moment, but I would discuss it with her and ring with our reply. Chris returned from the High School at about 6 p.m. I took her to the drawing room where, to her surprise, there was a large log fire and bottle of champagne ready for drinking. On hearing the news, this time to my surprise, she burst into tears. We now had serious decisions to make.

After getting over our shock we decided to accept the offer and further pursue our interest in buying a property in France. For my part I felt, now approaching 65 years, it was time to seriously consider retirement. They say 'musicians never retire' and the following chapters will to some extent, bear that out, but life was to prove very different.

Moody Minx was berthed at Port-la-Forêt in Brittany, so we decided to look seriously in that area. Meanwhile, we would need somewhere in England as Christine wanted to continue teaching. David Wilson Homes had a small new build project in North Luffenham on a tiny estate off the main lane round the village. Its show house was in fact for sale and that is what we bought with all the fixtures and fittings, the perfect pad.

Britannia Pink & Jones packers arrived on 18 April, and worked quickly, especially the women, who specialized in the smaller objects such as glassware and kitchen utensils. The men constantly bombarded me with questions about what was going into store to go to France eventually and what was going to North Luffenham immediately. It was difficult to keep up with them. Christine was at school, but when she returned, several things had gone, and some that should not have gone had. We relocated to our new home on 26 April.

Travelling to France during the Easter break, we came to terms with how French *immobiliers* (estate agents) sold their houses. It is difficult to persuade them to give you an address so that you can view a property from the road, and if, on arrival for a viewing, you say you are not interested, it is difficult to escape without spending some time in the house pretending to *be* interested. We viewed several properties in Brittany but could not find anything we liked and returned home a little disappointed.

On our return to England we commenced looking at the market and, reflecting on our sailing experience, decided to head further south, 'South of the Loire'. We were familiar with the coastline and harbours all the way down to La Rochelle, so it made sense to look at the Vendée. I knew from my research that it could be very flat – I was not a lover of South Lincolnshire for that reason – but I came to learn that the department had a varied landscape and that the 'Bocage', being hilly and wooded, had considerable beauty. I had to be convinced and eventually was, but having been born in Derby and familiar with the Peak District it would have meant pushing down and inland to the Dordogne to achieve anything similar, so we had to look. Deux-Sèvres lies to the east of the Vendée and our friends the Saxtons were already living there, so we resolved to look in their vicinity on our next visit to France. During the half-term break the French search continued and, on 2 June via an *immobilier* in Luçon, we found La Graineterie, a *maison bourgeoise* in Nalliers in the Vendée. With the right sized walled garden and magnificent cast-iron *verrière* (conservatory), it was love at first sight. At right angles to the house and forming a large courtyard was a coach house with a garden wall to the main boundary. Behind this wall a gated access led to the main garden. The garden in front of the house was also walled with a wrought-iron pedestrian latch gate to the road. There was a railway line on the opposite side of the road, which should have stopped me from purchasing the house, but being head over heels in love with it and on being told that it was a local line and trains were infrequent, we decided to go ahead with the purchase. Following this decision we decided to take *Moody Minx* down to the La Rochelle area during the summer vacation, particularly as we knew from experience that, with 2,500 hours of sunshine per year, the climate south of the Loire and of the city of Nantes is considered second to the Mediterranean. In pondering on this statistic it is as well to remember that the sky has to be virtually cloudless to qualify. However, before accomplishing this we had to return to England for Christine to finish the summer term.

An interesting development had taken place in our absence as Rebecca and Glenn had been searching the market to buy a boat and, on 14 June, had bought a Moody 33, *Foxy Lady*. The boat was lying in Moody's marina and we were invited down to it on Saturday 17 June, which coincided with Moody's annual 'meet'. Like us, they were now members of the Moody Owners' Association. After an evening meal, Moody's boat designer Bill Dixon gave a talk and that night we slept on *Foxy Lady*. We left early the next morning to return to Rutland and I recall advising Glenn to make a shake-down sail to Poole and perhaps circumnavigating the Isle of Wight the following week. We returned home to North Luffenham and quite late received a telephone call from Rebecca that took the wind out of my sails; they had just arrived in Cherbourg!

At the start of the summer break we drove to France and immediately sailed down from Port-la-Forêt (boat owners should note that our annual mooring fee for the time we were forfeiting was repaid to us). We knew that there was a marina at Bourgenay, so broke our journey to see if we could have an annual berth in the port. We could, but not until the end of August, so we pushed on to Rochefort, having already decided to avoid the vast marina at La Rochelle. Rochefort is a lovely town, but a long approach up the Charente river before locking into the port, which we knew from the chart to be limited to about an hour before and after high water.

Nalliers

We were due to complete the purchase of La Graineterie on my 65th birthday, 28 August, at that time the day of my official retirement. We arrived earlier in the month and lived on the boat, but had found the present owners of the house very friendly. We had explained, with difficulty owing to the language, that we planned to make the coach house habitable not least because we had a concert grand piano to accommodate and could an English builder we knew through our English friends in Deux-Sèvres do a little preparatory work for us? They agreed, we duly introduced him to them, and were given keys to the double doors into the courtyard. I should mention at this point that, although originally a coach house, it had a hayloft with a bedroom off it, below which was a room with a corner stone fire-place, which had served as the surgery for the original owner who had been a doctor. The centre of the coach house had double doors to accommodate the coach and there was a passage at the side for access to the fireplace room and upstairs bedroom. John Pate, our builder, set to work, and the next time we visited the house he was already on the roof replacing tiles.

Little did he know it at the time, but this was the start of a major project. Perhaps I should say at this point what while we describe it as a coach house, which is exactly what it is in English terms, the French call it a *grande dépendance*.

On 28 August, my 65th birthday, vendor and purchaser met at the *notaire*'s office in Luçon and I completed the purchase simply by signing the various documents and handing over a cheque – how wonderfully simple! We now owned an empty house and had prepared for it by bringing a blow-up mattress and two plastic chairs. We had arranged for Pink & Jones, our removal and storage company in Northampton, to deliver the rest of our belongings on the 31st and they duly arrived on time. After a hectic five days, we returned to Rutland and Christine afterwards resumed work at the High School. From this moment I resolved to retire from music and enjoy a completely new way of life. We shall see.

In November Clare, my eldest daughter and I flew to New York to see Gré, Nick and their now three daughters; Annabel Alice had been born on 21 August 1994. They had a flat in New York where we spent the first night, and the following day took a coach to Long Island where they had purchased a bolthole. This was a typical American build for that area constructed in wood. There was a swimming pool and pool house with full overflow accommodation. This was entirely for me! We spent a real family week there. I managed to take two bottles of Château Desmirail, a troisième cru, with me hoping to impress my son-in-law, but he put me in my place by later serving a deuxième cru! You cannot win, though at that time I think I was probably the only one of us ever to have tasted a Château Margaux premier cru. Just before we departed to return to England, Nick treated the four of us to dinner at the American Hotel on Sag Harbour, which boasted one of the best wine cellars in the New York area. I was honoured by being given the choice and asked to choose with my head not my heart. Page one of the wine menu was devoted to cru wines only and to my utmost surprise they had all five premier crus for drinking. My first reaction was that they were all too young. I debated putting Nick to the test but resisted the temptation and turned the pages to see if Château Margaux's second wine was on the list. It was, and Nick was certainly correct about the wine cellar at this hotel. I chose a Pavillon Rouge and it came to the table with the cork removed. To my surprise, Nick did not query this and when questioned just brushed it off as being usual in the States. I was reminded of an incident following a Nottingham Festival concert when being dined by our sponsor. On the next table a party was entertaining another celebrity from the festival, Clement Freud, who refused to accept a bottle of wine that was not corked at the table. I do not know if he was the guest or host, but the waiter broke down in tears, I suppose in the knowledge that he would be responsible for the cost of the wine.

At the end of the school term, we excitedly looked forward to spending our first Christmas at our house in France and departed on 14 December via Plymouth to Roscoff. We had been friendly for some time with Robert and Sue Evans, boat owners we had met in France who lived in Leicester. This was one of those occasions when you meet people who are friends of friends. They had relocated to Plymouth, although Robert still had business connections with Leicester and had joined us from time to time at our house. They now lived in an apartment overlooking the marina and could enjoy seeing their boat, a Moody 47, lying peacefully there. We sometimes stayed overnight and caught the day ferry as was the case on this occasion. We drove from Roscoff and, approaching midnight a few kilometres short of Nalliers, could not believe our eyes when it started to snow. Had we got things wrong? Suffice to say, there was little sign of snow the following day and in all our time in France, touch wood, '*touche le bois*' we have seldom been troubled by this element.

1996

In retrospect, our new build in North Luffenham was perfect for our needs and prompts me, as I write this diary, to ask why I was not content to settle for that and enjoy a *secondaire* in France. One cannot go back and judge whether one or other decision was the right or wrong one for the simple reason that any decision necessarily affects all future decisions. This reflects on my interest in science, mentioned in the Foreword, as it prompts the question of parallel universes, quantum physics and string theory.

For my part, I continued with my French classes and with coming to terms with my new toy in the form of a computer. Christine had her teaching, in my view more than a full-time occupation, although I was in no way ignored. We both enjoyed the house and were able to continue to enjoy the company of our friends. Rebecca and Glenn had bought a cottage in Wansford. This was the same village in which John and Barbie Kempe lived, as did Stanley Vann, former organist and master of the choristers at Peterborough Cathedral, but now retired and content to play the organ in the village church. We were able to renew our friendship with all these people.

It was a difficult time for my eldest daughter Clare, whose marriage to Neil had ended and who was finding the separation traumatic.

On returning to France for the summer half term, an old school friend of mine (my namesake Neville) Johnson came to stay with us with his wife Olive. I had rather lost touch with him over the years, but he never failed to remind me whenever we met that it was he, over a pint at the Friary Hotel in Derby, who had given me a cutting of Watney's announcement that they were going to finance a conductor's award. He had worked in catering and read the article in a magazine. We had learnt that they too had left England and retired to the Dordogne, which was why I had contacted them and invited them to pay us a visit.

There was of course plenty of work to do at La Graineterie, for we chose to modify the principal bedroom to include an en-suite shower room and walk-in wardrobe. The double entrance gates to the courtyard needed renewing and we replaced the 500-litre oil tank in the wine cellar with a 2,000-litre one, which necessitated laying a pipe across to the garage on the opposite side of the courtyard.

As we still had plenty of exploring to do, we set July aside for our main sailing holiday. There are two islands off La Rochelle, Île d'Oléron and Île de Ré, but harbours are few and tidal – that is they can only be entered or left for a short period before and after high water. We found the alternative to anchoring in this area less appealing than in Brittany, and what at first seemed a very attractive sailing area and likely to be every bit as popular as the Solent in England, is often in fact virtually deserted.

We were of course back in England for the start of the school term but we made one more visit to France before Christmas during half term and managed to get up to date with hedge clipping plus seeding the newly prepared garden area to take a lawn.

In November, I played for Nick's youngest sister's wedding in Rhyall, a village just outside Stamford, which meant being able to catch up with Nick, Gré and the girls who were over from the States. At the start of the Christmas holiday it was back to France again, but a shorter stay as we felt some obligation towards my father in Derby.

1997

We had my father stay with us for the New Year and, after he left, went to a sherry party hosted by John and Janet Peck in Burton Latimer. John was chairman of the Kettering Symphony Orchestra and was still playing the horn in the orchestra, which he had been doing since joining when I was its conductor. I met a young German girl at the party who spoke perfect English, thus prompting me to tell her that we had a house in France and I wished I could speak French as fluently as she spoke English. She replied by saying that her school allowed pupils a choice between English and French and without hesitation she chose English because it was so much easier. I think this was the first time I came to realise that French is really the most difficult of all Western languages. I would add I can always detect a French person speaking English but this is by no means 'always' so with the Germans, Dutch and Scandinavians – I rest my case.

Still on the subject of language, I continued my French classes, but now had Rebecca with me. From the moment they joined us to sail in France, it became evident that Glenn had some command of French because I once heard him chatting over the pushpit (stern handrail) to the owner of a French boat. Since Glenn's company worked with a French publishing company, he frequently went to Paris, and had done a business course at INSEAD in 1996. I suspect at that time that the idea of living in France had already crossed his mind, perhaps even been discussed, but knowing that I took French classes, Rebecca asked if she could join me when I went to Peterborough. I could pick her up in Wansford and drop her off afterwards, usually after a pint. Glenn, who had previously worked in Peterborough, had been promoted to a subsidiary company, Seymour International, which was based in London.

An old friend from my school days, Denis Evans and his wife Joan invited us to their ruby wedding anniversary in February. It was a memorable evening because I met so many of my old friends, most of whom Chris was to meet for the first time.

Life suddenly started to get busy again. After our last sail in *Moody Minx*, we realised we were unlikely to sail any more long sea passages and had exhausted our knowledge of our immediate sea area. As they say, when the stress outweighs the pleasure, it is time to change. Change is the right word here, for it was not our intention to give up boating altogether, but we had decided to switch to a motorboat. *Moody Minx* duly went on the market and early in May we made a quick visit to France to meet a potential buyer arriving by private plane. Peter Pearson, a yacht broker in Guernsey, had alerted me to a potential client flying in from England, and asked me to let him know of an airfield close to Port Bourgenay and the length of its runway. I did my research, rang him back and agreed to pick his client up at the airfield I had located. We agreed a date and arrived there at the appointed time to find the airfield deserted of any human presence. We parked outside the gates and waited. About twenty minutes later we heard the sound of a light aircraft approaching. It duly appeared and, after circling the runway, came down to land. The pilot and a passenger (male) stepped out, closed the door of the plane and walked over to the gate where we stood. I was astounded it could all be so simple. The pilot had apparently tried to call the airfield in Nantes to log his journey, but on receiving no call back, just pushed on. He was completely relaxed about it. The boat had been lifted for the winter and was not due to go back into the water until everything was settled. This was to the benefit of any buyer who might want a survey, or wished to access the hull. The two men were matter of fact, took a quick look round, liked the boat and said 'where can we take you for lunch?' We said we were pushed for time but would have a quick drink with them in case they wanted to discuss the boat. His only remark from what I recall was how nice it was to sit in the cockpit with a gin and tonic! As we expected, there was no sale and we courteously returned him to his aeroplane. We decided the whole thing was just an expensive reason for a day out!

Believe it or not, it was not long before we had a second enquiry that involved another trip to the same airfield. This time our potential purchaser lived in London and wanted to fly a surveyor over from Guernsey to look at the boat on his behalf. This certainly sounded more promising. I felt superior when the pilot of the plane being chartered rang to ask if I knew of an airfield near Port Bourgenay and was able to impress him with the exact GPS location, plus the length of the runway. He flew down in a much more organized way; the airfield was prepared for his arrival, and we drove the pilot and surveyor to the boat. The surveyor did a thorough inspection and told us he had no hesitation saying the boat was in first-class condition and he would be recommending our buyer to go ahead. The matter was now in the hands of our broker, from whom we expected to hear after we returned to England. When we returned home, Peter Pearson eventually rang to say that the buyer had confirmed his intention to go ahead, but along with his wife would like to see the boat for himself. There was a problem because we had the only hatch key and they wanted to see inside, so given that he was travelling close to where we lived in Rutland, he suggested calling on us to collect it. We expected him in the late afternoon, but at about 11 p.m. Peter

Pearson called to say that our buyer had been taken ill and was in hospital – we later learnt with a brain tumour. The sale inevitably fell through and rather than continue in this vein we decided that it would simplify things to have the boat sailed to Guernsey, where Peter would have it on his doorstep. This was arranged and the boat was safely delivered there, where she was eventually sold, though subject to being returned to England.

We arrived at Nalliers for the Easter break and were slightly put out to see one of the main stone gate posts on the point of giving way and the gates at a strange angle. This was John's first job when he arrived a few days later to work on the coach house.

* * *

Back in England in mid-June, the 17th to be exact, Rebecca and I had gone to Peterborough for our weekly French lesson and customary pint, and were sitting enjoying our drink when the landlord came over and asked if I was Mr Dilkes. There was a telephone call for me. How could this be possible? I asked myself. It was from Chris who, aware of our routine, was urgently trying to contact me to say that our house in Nalliers had been burgled. I immediately returned home to hear the full story. Our key holder had gone to the house very early (5 am) on his way to work that morning and dis-covered the shutter to the kitchen door had been wrenched off the wall and the glass panel smashed to gain entry. The gendarmes were immediately alerted and we later learnt that there had been considerable activity around the property for most of the day. Neither of us had been at home during the day, so it was not possible to contact us until the evening. We made an instant decision at midnight to take the early morning Brittany Ferries crossing to France and arrived at the house in the late afternoon. We had visions of a *cambriolage* (with pretty well everything taken), but things looked fairly normal at first sight. The new wooden gates had not yet been fitted, so the present ones were still temporary, but untouched, which ruled out any form of transport being used. A six-foot wall completely surrounded the property, so logically there would be a limit to what had been taken. On closer inspection, the intruders had concentrated on smaller valuables and, to my horror, these included the clock movements of two longcase clocks, a crystal chandelier, a pair of antique pistols, and of course the television. On reflection, we conclu-ded it was very much an amateur job, but I have to say a costly one. Our house insurance was with our French bank and we can have nothing but praise for their help and generosity in events that were to follow. We had to report to the gendarmes in L'Hermenault and were introduced to an Englishman, André Slatter, who was there to translate for us. Afterwards, we took him for a coffee at the local bar tabac. He had been in catering and his last job before coming to live on the continent – first in Andorra and now in the Vendée – was head of catering at the Royal Festival Hall. In fact, he had been there when I played at the QEH.

Having left in haste on the Wednesday, Christine rang the High School to explain that she would not be returning until the following Monday. She in fact returned to England at the weekend to finish the term and I remained in France. I was to be carless for the period. While in England, Christine kindly drove to Derby to collect my father and take him to Bourne to stay with her mum Evelyn where, following previous visits, he was made very much at home and enjoyed meeting her chatty friends. Just before returning to France she drove him back to Derby and unfortunately had an accident on the way home running into the back of a jeep as a result of brake failure.

I knew nothing of this until she arrived back in France on the Saturday, sooner than I had expected as the ferry had docked early. When she saw me she burst into tears, worried about telling that me she had written off her car. I was just pleased to have her back safe and sound even if rather bruised.

About a week later, we received a call from the gendarmes to say that a farmer had found all our belongings at the bottom of a hedge in one of his fields close by. We were asked to go over and identify the stolen property, but it was several days before they returned everything to us. The clock movements had been adversely affected by dew and damp, the wooden pendulum on the Whitehurst clock was broken and the silvered dial considerably 'worse for wear'. We duly reported this to our bank, which authorized us to have the work carried out following our estimate of the cost. Taking into account the re-silvering and stripping down all the clock works and the cost of a new wooden pendulum, this added a substantial amount to the cost of the repairs to the kitchen door and shutter. The crystal chandelier miraculously survived undamaged but the antique pistols, now probably in someone's pocket, were not retrieved. The bank advised us to consider fitting a burglar alarm, which I have to say we did.

* * *

Foxy Lady, Glenn and Rebecca's yacht, was now in the Les Minimes marina in La Rochelle. They had decided to get married in Nalliers in August. The boat had been there for some time and they had come to know this part of France well. Nalliers had been a useful retreat for them when fitting out. They had asked me to suggest a suitable local venue for the reception and we had shortlisted one or two, which we introduced to them when they came over. During their time in La Rochelle, however, they had frequently dined at Bar André and it was clear to us that we could do no better. However, we decided to go there together before making the final decision, which we did. We had a splendid meal and agreed that, despite the distance from Nalliers, they would settle for that. Being well-known diners there, I seem to remember a free bottle of champagne arriving on the table to greet us. They knew all the waiters who in turn knew they were being vetted for a wedding reception menu. Knowing how vigilant the French are, Christine had opted to go easy on the drink in order to drive home. It was a memorable evening and, on leaving, Chris found our car hemmed in by neighbouring cars, so I elected to manoeuvre it out and, feeling competent, continued driving. Chris was furious as she had drunk very little. Within a short distance, we were stopped by the gendarmes who came to Chris's door. She wound the window down and was asked to breathe into a bag, which she did while pointing to the steering wheel in front of me, on the right-hand side of the car. He fortunately had a sense of humour and saw the funny side of it, but nonplussed walked round to my window and gave me a bag to blow into, then walked to the front of the car to read the result in my headlamps. On his return, he asked if I had been drinking, to which I replied, 'Yes, but only with the meal.' He gave me a wry smile and waved me on. Phew! On the return journey, we decided that we could not subject their guests to a similar challenge, so Rebecca asked me to arrange for a coach to transport everyone to La Rochelle and back to Nalliers again after the reception.

The wedding took place on 5 August and, following French tradition, we walked to the *mairie* (town hall) where the ceremony was held. Being a legal institution, marriage is a matter for a registrar and is usually carried out by the local *maire* (mayor). If a religious celebration is needed this takes place afterwards in a church. We assembled at La Graineterie and walked to the *mairie*, where the officiating mayor met us. It was a very hot day and after the ceremony we walked back to the house for champagne and iced cold melon on the front lawn. The coach duly arrived and drove us to La Rochelle for the reception. I should note at this point that all Rebecca and Glenn's friends who arrived from England, whether by rail or car, had sensibly reasoned that it would make sense to stay in La Rochelle, so only my immediate family came back to Nalliers after the reception.

The day before the wedding, Glenn had asked me to move *Foxy Lady* from the marina and to berth her in the Vieux-Port in the heart of La Rochelle, a stone's throw from the restaurant. This I had done by motoring the boat the previous morning. We had also purchased a complete set of signal flags and I had prepared the rigging to display them after the reception. Everything went according to plan. I slipped away unnoticed from the restaurant for a short time and dressed the ship overall. In his speech, Glenn invited everyone to go aboard *Foxy Lady* for a digestif after the reception and, much to the surprise of the married couple, we were greeted with fairy lights and a dressed ship. In spite of the number of people on board the boat stayed afloat!

When the party finally came to an end, just my family of six returned to Nalliers by coach. About a third of the way back, we drove through Marans and I remember the traffic lights just outside the town changing to red when we were alongside them, but thought no more of it until about two kilometres later, the gendarmes stopped us and breathalysed the coach driver. He said that he had only had a beer and sandwich, and seemed to be driving perfectly well, but they nonetheless arrested him. We received the typical French shrug of the shoulders when we asked what would become of us. The keys were temptingly left dangling in the ignition, but we just sat there wondering what was going to happen next. The good news was that it was not that long before a taxi turned up to put an end to our worries. But one small taxi for six people is also against the law!

Following the advice of our bank, before leaving in September we had *télésurveillance* (remote monitoring) fitted to the house. We took the precaution of making sure that our key holder knew how to work it as, in addition to looking after the garden, he routinely checked the interior of the property.

The highlight of the year came for me when on the ferry back to England, Christine told me she would resign from her teaching at Stamford High School and come to France permanently, France had won.

A little forethought at this time would have halted my immediate decision to sell our North Luffenham house, which in retrospect I think we should have kept, if only to rent out. There was clearly no point in regarding it as a *maison secondaire* as we were still interested in spending all our secondary time, so to speak, sailing, now boating, and I had never been convinced about renting. In any case, my decision to move to France was to leave England and, within a short time of arriving here, I did eventually become a taxpayer – you cannot be more resident than that!

Peter Pearson had just sold *Moody Minx* and, being committed to bringing the boat back to England, we had commissioned a crew in Guernsey to sail her back. It could have been a turning point but Christine was, and still is, hooked on enjoying being afloat. PLEASE NOTE – afloat not sailing. For a variety of reasons Chris decided not to leave the High School until the end of the following term, Easter, although our North Luffenham house did go on the market as our previous experience reasoned it would not sell quickly and we would be able to last out for a matter of six or seven months.

Cru Classe

Having decided to abandon sailing and turn to a motor cruiser we commenced viewing the market. We finally settled for a Broom, well known as one of the leading manufacturers in the country. Its 37-foot (10/70) was our first choice and seeing one for sale on the River Thames made arrangements to view. It had all the comforts of our last Moody, centre line berth in the aft cabin with en-suite, spacious saloon down two steps to the galley and forward heads and spacious fore-cabin. Two steering positions, one below, the other on the aft deck with a removable canopy, so a seating area in all weather, or alternatively just a Bimini top if hot. She had two powerful Volvo diesel engines and navigation equipment capable of sensible sea passages. We purchased the boat and, for her survey, had her lifted where she was to remain until we decided how we would take her to France.

Very, very unexpectedly Murrays, our house agents rang us after two viewings to say that they had sold the house and could we complete asap. Quick thinking saved the day. We could live on the new boat, but not on the Thames. Where was the nearest marina to Stamford? Answer Newark. Did they have an available berth, and could we live on her for a short time? The answer in both cases was 'YES'. Arrangements were duly made and the boat was delivered there by road where I met her. She was chocked up, so we planned to antifoul her before launching. We were not going to be homeless.

On 23 October the removers arrived, packed and loaded the last of our furniture to go to France, but to complicate things we had for that evening accepted a fiftieth wedding anniversary invitation from our farmer friend and his wife who lived opposite and made arrangements once again to sleep on our inflatable mattress in an otherwise empty house. Apart from a very late night all went well and we departed the following morning. The one thing we had got right was that the following week was half term for Chris and we would be in Nalliers to receive our belongings.

On 24 October we took the overnight crossing to France and arrived in Nalliers, now our principal residence, at midday. The furniture arrived on schedule a few days later, but before we returned to England on 2 November. We had arranged to stay with Rebecca and Glenn at Downderry House in Wansford, followed by some time in Bourne with Chris's mother. At that time Glenn was in London all week, so Rebecca welcomed our company.

While Chris was teaching, I worked on the boat while out of the water, antifouling and generally making her shipshape for our future occupation. She was duly launched and the yard engineer came with us to our berth. Realizing I had no experience handling a power boat he berthed the boat for us and then suggested I took her out in his company to make sure I knew what I was doing. I now had two very powerful engines to control and was perfectly aware that accelerating the port engine would push the boat, without the help of the rudder, to starboard. What I had not immediately realised until the yard engineer pointed it out to me was that it also increased the boat's speed, which in the confined space between boats, could be disastrous. Reversing the port engine turns the bow to port and has the effect of slowing the boat down. Clever use of the two engines in this way is only necessary where sea room is restricted. Normal steering of a course needs only the helm. Lesson over I had plenty to keep me busy and happy. Our time at Newark was memorable – Chris goes so far as to say that it was fantastic, and would add that she spent nearly six months in heaven. We were handy for the shower block, which was new and warm, and the boat was connected to shore power, which was metered so we had the choice between warm air heating on the boat or electric radiator(s) or both. The boat had a holding tank, but it was not necessary to use our heads (bathroom) unless in an emergency.

We joined the sailing club in the marina and attended its annual dinner on 6 December at a golf club in the country outside Newark. Chris commuted daily to the High School, and aperitifs awaited her every night on her return. We could not resist the temptation from time to time to make the short walk down to the Navigation Inn for the odd pint and, from time to time, supper.

At the end of term we retreated to France and were joined by our sailing friends Colin and Jan Lillywhite on 27 December for a great New Year. We reflected – what a year!

Chapter 14

Transition
1998–2004
Move to France, debut,
never a dull moment

1998

On arriving back in England, we drove to our English *secondaire* — *Cru Classe*, Newark Marina, telephone mobile, no internet. This was a new year and a new beginning. It is not a short walk into Newark from the marina but we never avoided it if we wanted to go, only taking the car for shopping. I knew the parish church, having played the organ there at the invitation of Robert Gilman, who had been its organist and choirmaster before becoming director of music at Stamford High School. I also knew the theatre, where I had conducted the Sinfonia in a concert featuring Leon Goosens, in what I believe was his first public appearance after a serious car accident. The town itself is lovely and features many antique shops, which became a regular haunt for us and the Saturday market was a must.

February saw us in back France for the half-term break. We now had only a few weeks left in Merrie England before catching the ferry to live in France permanently on 18 March. To mark this occasion I had promised Chris a Commodore class cabin for the night crossing. Christine had started teaching at Stamford High School in September 1979, so had completed a total there of 19 years.

On 17 March, Margaret (Maggie) Maclennan (piano teaching colleague) organized a farewell party with other members of the music staff at her home and presented Chris with some Tutbury crystal glasses. The next morning I was with her on the stage for assembly at the High School and recall it was a very emotional moment, particularly as the school presented her with more Tutbury glasses to complete the set. She left on a HIGH.

Move to France

We drove to Portsmouth for the night crossing to Saint-Malo and I will never forgive myself for not keeping my promise to book a Commodore class cabin. I had left it too late, even to book any sort of cabin and could not believe so many people would choose to travel at that time of the year. To make matters worse we could not even find a reclining seat and had to sleep, albeit quite comfortably, on the floor.

On our arrival at Nalliers we set about making our presence there legal. This first involved obtaining a *carte de séjour* and then registering our car in France. This went smoothly and we were soon able to put French number plates on the ZX car and had the necessary changes made to the headlamps as we were now driving permanently on the right. At the same time, I purchased a new Citroen AX to replace the previous one. I had the new car fitted with a tow bar as we had been made aware of the French system of disposing of rubbish, for us the *déchetterie* principally for garden waste, but there were, and still are, bins for pretty well everything else. When the car was delivered one of the first jobs we toiled with was getting rid of empty wine bottles, literally hundreds of which had been left (lazily) for us by, I think, not only the owner before us but also the one before him.

We were aware that we needed to think about speaking French and were not slow to enrol for French classes at AVF (Accueil des villes françaises) in Fontenay-le-Comte. The AVF exists throughout France and offers classes in various things – art, dance, and language to name a few. There we met the first English couple to become our friends, Ken and Eileen Lytton. We have been friends ever since, although they recently returned to live in England for health reasons and to be closer to family support. Since writing, Ken has sadly died.

Readers may recall that moving to France was to seal my retirement. I did not know any musicians there and envisaged a quieter lifestyle for my twilight years. However, not long after arriving there permanently, the doorbell rang and a Frenchman at the gate introduced himself as Gilles Clergeaud. He lived in Nalliers and wanted to introduce himself because he understood I was a musician, conductor and organist. To my surprise, he said there was an organ builder in Nalliers, or perhaps more accurately a restorer with a workshop, who was restoring an organ that he was giving to the church. When he had finished it, would I give the opening recital? Not forgetting my resolution, but curious, I said I would at the very least like to meet him and see his work.

This was arranged and I visited the workshop where I met Monsieur Claude Madigot. He invited me to play a two manual with pedal board pipe organ with some 12 stops including a very fine trumpet. Such was the quality of this instrument and, knowing the rarity of organ recitalists, I agreed. When I knew the date of the recital, I learnt it was to be shared with a Gregorian chant choir. I prepared a programme that definitely had to include a work to feature the trumpet.

Debut

I was once again back in my old routine of preparing a programme. There may have been a grain of relief in my decision, but I was not consciously aware of it. I do, however, confess that the experience was not unpleasant and good for my ego.

The organ was moved into the church a few days before the concert and I wandered down for my first rehearsal. Imagine my surprise when I found, not the organ I had played in the workshop but a chamber organ with one manual and no pedal board. I realized too late that my French had not been up to understanding on the occasion of my visit to the workshop that the organ I played was simply an example of his workmanship. Could I play this instrument? I tried it there and then. It was beautifully voiced and an absolute joy to play, so the concert went ahead on 17 July and was to seal my fate for the next twenty years! A repeat of this concert followed a few weeks later in Sérigné, a small village close to Fontenay-le-Comte. Our organ builder friend had many connections with churches where he had been responsible for rebuilds and this gave me contacts for other recitals further afield.

As a result of these two concerts I met Josef Vité, a priest at Notre Dame in Fontenay-le-Comte. Father Vité was such an organ enthusiast that he put his hands to rebuilding the organ in Saint-Jean Baptiste, the second church in Fontenay-le-Comte, and I believe also had a hand in restoring the organ in the Union crétienne chapel in Fontenay. At this time I had seen, but not played, the organ in Notre Dame, but was now invited to do so in the company of Father Vité. The organ is placed high on the tribune at the west end of the church and looks very impressive from the nave. He told me he had been in charge of the specification when this organ was restored a short time before. We met at the church and I followed my routine of extemporizing and stop changing and, like most organists, could not resist finishing with the full organ, a term used when all the stops are out. Organ lovers will know the sound of the tuba pipes. On the Fontenay organ there are three tuba stops each at a different pitch, a 16-foot which produces a sound an octave lower than concert (normal pitch), an 8-foot at concert pitch and a 4-foot one an octave above concert. I was later invited to give a recital on this organ and permission to practise any time I chose to do so.

In September, we once again travelled to *Cru Classe*, our second home in England, to have a boating holiday, our lives really were now in reverse.

In some respects, our first cruise on the Trent was a shakedown trip to the River Humber to get the feel of the boat. I had recently spoken to my old schoolfriend Denis Evans, whom I knew for several years had chartered canal and river boats for his annual holidays, and I seem to remember that he was rather proud of having covered the bulk, if not all, of the inland water-ways of Britain. I spoke about the possibility of him having experienced the River Trent. He said that he had, but only from where the River Witham which they were cruising on joins the Trent. He advised me he had difficulties there with strong currents, but had not continued further to the Humber. I did a careful check of the River Trent chart and the Tidal atlas and planned the proposed voyage in detail.

We locked out at Newark just before high water and arrived at Cromwell lock. We passed through the lock and continued with the ebb as far as Torksey on the Fossdyke, which eventually joins the River Witham at Lincoln. We turned into that river and moored for the night on a floating pontoon. We reflecting that this was where Denis had walked to the pub and enjoyed a welcome pint! The next morning, we made an early start and continued down to the Humber where there is a huge expanse of water just short of the entrance, which is challenging for navigation, especially if visibility is poor. There was no problem on this occasion, so we eventually reached the upper reaches of the Humber and passed Ferriby where we had bought our first boat, but noted that the water looked just as muddy here as further down; it was that sickly chocolate colour. The final approach was well buoyed and we made Hull marina while keeping to starboard of the river, and enjoying the last of the ebb before being safely berthed. We celebrated in the comfort of a restaurant. I had spoken to several berth holders at Newark, who frequently made this trip before going across to Holland, and, indeed, the marina owner's son had built up quite a business for himself by taking the ferry, buying Dutch second-hand cruisers and motoring them back to Newark to be sold. Being plentiful in Holland, steel cruisers meant that he was able to buy them at a realistic price. It was quite a lucrative business.

Our return was uneventful up to Keadby on the Trent where we locked into a canal for the night. Leaving at low water the plan was to carry the tide as it was essential to arrive at Cromwell lock before the river became too low to navigate. It should have been a straight forward run but at one point we suddenly hit something very, very hard, underneath the boat, almost stopping us in our tracks. We felt very nervous from that point onwards as, along with the collision or whatever it was, from time to time we could hear the props turning in, what sounded like gravel. I was keeping well to the middle of the river and could only conclude there was not as much water as there should be. We, however, finally returned safely to the marina and when I spoke to the engineer about, our experiences he said they had been told there was a sunken car in the river at that point. He was not the slightest bit worried by the props grinding in gravel and said we had probably polished the keel a little! The boat was later due to be lifted for the winter and when it was there was no sign of any damage.

Denis and Joan were keen to learn about our adventure and came over to Newark for a chin wag. It was good to see my old schoolfriend and we managed to persuade them to visit us for a holiday in France, which they eventually did.

Back in France we had a special weekend on 21 October when Rebecca and Glenn invited us to meet them in Paris to see a performance of Strauss's *Der Rosenkavalier* at the Paris Opera. Glenn was working in Paris and Rebecca was flying over to join him. They are both fond of 'grand' opera and they could not have chosen better for me. Glenn booked the hotel for us at business rates and generously paid all our taxi fares for the very wet weekend. We travelled effortlessly to Paris by TGV from Nantes.

On 21 November, Josef Vité phoned to inform me that the Sérigné concert had been recorded and that there would be two separate broadcasts of it on the radio, the first with the Gregorian chant and the second as an organ recital. I was asked to meet Father Josef in La Roche-sur-Yon to record an interview for the broadcast. This worried me as my French was inadequate for those high levels, but nevertheless I obliged and all went well with the help of an interpreter. The interviewer was amused when I said that I had chosen my programme for an organ without pedals, but that the 'Echo and Humoresque' by Pietro Yon did have them, and confessed that my wife, sitting beside me to turn pages, played the pedal notes for me. I should add, I was unaware at the time that the concert was being recorded.

In November we also went to America – Chris's first visit – to see Gré and Nick with their three daughters on home ground. They were now living in a large house with extensive grounds, in a row of other equally large houses, in New Canaan to which we were driven at breakneck speed, including through the toll barriers thanks to an electronic payment system, now of course common, though here in France there is a speed limit of 30 kilometres per hour. The Silvermine Tavern, a local landmark and hostelry, was near their house and, having settled in for our first night, Gré drove us there for an aperitif. Nick, who since arriving in New York had risen to dizzying heights and now needed to travel extensively to both Europe and the Far East was not with us. We unanimously decided on red wine and I chose a Cabinet Sauvignon, the waiter took me to the bar and asked, 'Which one?' They were all Californian so I took his advice with a guarded reply, but was still shocked by the high cost of just three glasses.

Nick was home by the weekend and we all went to the local church for Eucharist. It was a very large Episcopalian church and, having observed the number of cars in the car park, I was not surprised by the size of the congregation. I was surprised, however, once we found seats, by the layout of the church – rather like a cross between a Methodist church in England and a concert hall. A platform led to rising seats crowned with an organ and an impressive array of pipes. It took time for all this to sink in. A full four-part choir sat on the tiered seating behind the orchestra on the platform (at that point busy tuning). Was this to be a concert or a service? The appearance of a priest suggested it really was going to be a service. The surprises were ongoing, as next we were greeted by a woman in a low-cut sequinned dress being applauded by the congregation! We heard a Haydn mass played as part of the service and I was left wondering why so many masses were written for the concert hall, or if performed in a church, why they never included the sacrament. I have concluded that the important element is the 'concept'.

Following an enjoyable week, including a trip to New York, lunch in Bloomingdales, and some sightseeing, we returned to peaceful France after a pretty hectic time 'keeping up'.

* * *

Returning briefly to my Derby days, at the beginning of November the *Derby Evening Telegraph* announced its publication of a new magazine for the Derby Heritage Society, *Bygone Derby* – first edition Wednesday 3 November. I of course knew nothing of this at the time, having lost touch with events of this sort, but suddenly out of the blue, over several days we received nearly a dozen or so press clippings from relatives and friends of an article relating to me. From the text, it was evident who had written the account, which brought back fond memories of my early days at the Central School. I immediately rang my old friend Denis Evans, who would also have known this person, to see if he could find his address so I could write to him. There was nothing in the clipping to suggest that its author was also the editor. Later, when visiting Derby, we had lunch with Denis and Joan at their house in Little Eaton, a village on the east side of Derby. Denis had thoughtfully invited two more guests and, while we were having our aperitifs, who should join us but none other than John Garrett, the author of the article whom I had known from my school days, and his wife. We then discovered that John was also the editor of *Bygone Derby* and he kindly presented me with an 'Old Boys' tie.

John has an enormous sense of humour and we are never without a smile when we hear from him. He has a wonderful 'turn of phrase' and I later tried to interest him in ghost writing this book, or at the very least editing it, but on both counts he judged that in our twilight years it would spoil our friendship as there would inevitably be disagreements. Maybe he was right but it was a disappointment. He told me he gave credit for the headline 'Toast to a Hero' to his chief reporter (see article on page 206).

1999

It was an interesting start to the year when in January we drove to Spain to join Ken and Eileen Lytton who had rented an apartment in El Puerto de la Selva, on the Costa Brava, only just over the French border and not too far from Perpignan. The final part of the journey took us over a mountainous route with magical views. It was quite a tortuous drive and there was only one road down to the port. We always enjoyed their company and had a pleasurable time exploring the region, which they knew quite well.

Toast to a hero

Former Derby Evening Telegraph journalist and Old Centaur John Garratt describes the terror of 'big school' through the eyes of an 11-year-old first former

in 1944 – and half a century on the heroes of that era at Derby Central School pay special tribute to five memorable years at Darley Park.

D-DAY was three months old and the Battle of Arnhem was about to begin. September, 1944, was an epic month in the course of the war and an epic month for an 11-year-old schoolboy – my induction to senior school.

I was selected for Derby Central School – a world away from the back streets of Firs Estate Junior School and the cosy proximity of my mates.

The school was a daunting two bus rides away if you went through town, a 15-minute walk to catch the arterial road bus along Kingsway, Queensway and Broadway.

Luckily I had a mentor, a senior boy who responded to my mother's entreaties to make sure that I actually arrived at the right school at the right time in the right state of dress on that fateful first morning.

My guardian's name was Neville Dilkes. In later life, he became a distinguished musician and conductor of one of England's great symphony orchestras – but, back in 1944, he was one of the great men of Central School.

To me he was the epitome of the heroic English schoolboy – tall and slim with that casual air of confidence and authority of men at the top of the school. Indeed, I was astonished to discover he was not captain of the school.

He was no mere mortal; he was a god, he possessed all the qualities of greatness, save one – he had no idea of time.

When I presented myself promptly on his doorstep on that September morning 54 years ago, trembling with fear at the ordeal ahead, I was horrified to discover that he was not ready. Far from it, he sat there eating toast and marmalade with the air of a man for whom time is of no consequence.

I stood there in a blue funk, shifting from foot to foot, clutching my new satchel and sweating with indecision in my thick new grey shirt as the great man continued to crunch his toast.

Should I go on ahead? Should I run for the bus? But which bus would I be running for? Suppose I was late on my first day? Would I be flogged in front of the whole school?

My protector left the table, presumably to brush his teeth, while I dwelt on the possibility of expulsion before my school career had even begun.

He reappeared suddenly at the door with a grin. "Come on, mustn't keep the school waiting on your first day," and he strode out of the gate and up St Albans Road, leading me to my date with destiny.

Happily we caught the bus – it was the start of a school year in which I watched my mentor eat a mountain of toast, blissfully confident that Derby Corporation buses would be running late.

During this year, André Slatter, the French-speaking Englishman we met following our robbery, and with whom we had become friendly, invited us for drinks at his house in the countryside near Saint-Cyr-des Gâts with a view to introducing us to Adrian and Judith Evett. Adrian had purchased a *maison secondaire* in France some time before, but they were still committed to working with the BBC in London, and spending their free time here when time permitted. Adrian was the manager of the BBC Concert Orchestra and Judith sang with the BBC Singers. We exchanged a few pleasantries and hoped our paths would cross again. Little did we know!

We missed having a boat to escape to, so had *Cru Classe* brought to France and she was now in Rochefort. We enjoyed the town of Rochefort and visited many interesting places in it. These included the residence of the writer Pierre Lotti, who as a naval officer had travelled around the world amassing a rich array of objects, decorations and souvenirs with which to adorn his house – hence the Renaissance hall, Gothic hall, mosque, Turkish lounge, Arabic room, Japanese pagoda and mummy room, all of which transport visitors to the exotic worlds of the Middle Ages and the East. Another attraction that caught our attention was the reconstruction of the *L'Hermione*, the frigate known as 'La Fayette's liberty ship of 1780'. It was built to take La Fayette to America to join Washington and the rebel colonists and was wrecked and lost off the coast of France in 1793. With the help of public bodies, a faithful replica of the original was built in the same dockyard. The construction had begun in 1997 and was completed in 2013. During its construction the boat was open for visitors to go aboard, which we did. Unfortunately, we did not get to Rochefort to see the boat being launched. She has since made the voyage successfully.

We would happily spend any weekend in Rochefort enjoying the Saturday morning market and, by extending our stay, could also attend French classes at a language school conveniently situated on the harbour front. This was a considerably better experience than the AVF in Fontenay, and could be combined with a dictation class, which was very popular and essential in France. In English we can hear the verb endings so have no problem writing them down, but not so in French. I now understood why the French attached so much importance to their grammar. In England, I doubt we would even think of having a dictation competition, at least not at a national level, but the French do and I understand why. It is frankly impossible to spell verbs correctly from dictation without first understanding the grammatical context.

With Christmas over, on the evening of 28 December we became increasingly conscious of the wind beginning to strengthen. I made certain that all the shutters were securely fastened and settled down for the evening by a roaring log fire. This was perfect until the wind became so strong that there was some movement in the house; the chandelier in the drawing room started to sway, and the noise outside was horrendous. The French had actually predicted that the storm would move across the channel to Britain and, of course, it did. We were soon deprived of electricity and had to make do with candles. Having checked upstairs, we realized the futility of going to bed so continued to sit it out in the warmth of the drawing room. At one point, we heard a crash outside but made no attempt to investigate; we just waited apprehensively for the nightmare to end.

Next morning, when we looked outside, we were relieved to see that at least the roofs were intact. The crash we had heard in the front garden was a tall cedar standing a good way from the house, but nevertheless it had hit a wall as it fell. Fortunately, it was not in line with a window, but it did scrape away the plaster (*crépi*). Our gardener came to the rescue with his chainsaw, though the wood was never of any use for burning because of its smell. Getting rid of the roots was quite another matter.

2000

While still getting back to normal after the storm, we received bad news in January concerning my father who had been moved from the 'Lawn' to the Derbyshire Royal Infirmary with a bladder infection. After visiting him, we returned to France but only to be recalled on 26 April as he was now more seriously ill following a stroke. I spoke at length to the doctor in charge who said that he thought he would remain unconscious and that we should go back to France. He would alert me if he thought I needed to be there. On his assurance that he would treat him exactly as he would his own father, we returned to France on 1 May, but six days later were summoned back to his bedside. We had previously arranged to stay with Ken and Monica the next time we came to Derby and, being a consultant physician, Ken was keeping abreast of events. I called him as we approached only to learn that my father had died that morning. He was 97 years' old. The funeral took place at the same crematorium where my mother had been laid to rest, and the minister of Junction Street Baptist Church, where my father had been a deacon for so many years, led the service. The minister had spent many hours with my father in his last days at the 'Lawn'. Ken and Monica kindly invited all my friends and relatives to their house for the wake. The following day, I took them to dinner at the Izaak Walton Hotel in Dovedale. It had been one of my father's favourite places and many sketches and watercolours remain as reminders of his frequent drives out there. We took a brief walk down to the stepping stones before our excellent dinner.

Later in May, after arriving back in France, I learnt from Gilles Clergeaud that La Schola Gregorienne had disbanded, which left only me if there were to be more concerts. I knew that my old colleague John Solum was interested in our move to France, so invited him to pay us a friendly visit, whilst seeing his son Andrew in London, adding that, if he wanted to, he could also play in three concerts for old time's sake. Having now met the Evetts, I asked Judith if she would provide the substitute for the Gregorian chant choir so that I could arrange recitals for voice and organ. Gilles wanted three concerts in August, so I immediately informed Judith and John of the dates and they both kindly agreed to perform. John, who I must say was always an excellent programme creator, suggested a Bach cantata with flute obligato and Thomas Arne's Shakespeare songs, which also feature the flute. It was left to me to build a programme around these ideas to include the organ because they would be performed in three churches. However, organs are not always of recital standard and it occurred to me that our two manual De Blaise harpsichord could provide the answer, but it needed work. Discussing this with Judith, who grew up with the Dolmetsch family, the problem was immediately solved by dispatching it to their workshop in Sussex for renovation. It arrived back just in time.

One of the concerts was to take place in Chaillé-les-Marais, and I was told that there was a good pipe organ there that I could use to rehearse. I now had the use of a reasonable instrument but without sophisticated stop changing action. This is now an accepted luxury and, in its most sophisticated form, it is possible to have a repertoire of stop changes that would require an index to remember, all of which in the past would have been done by hand, usually guided by pencilled notes on the score.

While John and Penny were staying with their son in the new Docklands area of London, John came over to France on his own in time to rehearse for the three concerts on 11, 12 and 14 August in Nalliers, Bazoges-en-Pareds, and Chaillé-les-Marais respectively.

PROGRAMME

WALOND	Voluntary, Adagio and Allegro	Organ
TELEMANN	Die Landrudt	Voice and Flute
HANDEL	'Cuckoo and Nightingale'	Organ
HANDEL	Sonata in E minor	Flute and Harpsichord
MOZART	Two French songs	Voice and Harpsichord
VIERNE	Carillon	Organ
HOTTETERRE	Echo	Solo Flute
ARNE	Shakespeare songs	Voice, Flute, Harpsichord

We had a family reunion to celebrate my seventieth birthday on 28 August, having arranged for all my family to stay at a château in Thoursais-Brouildroux. We had met the owners, courtesy of Gilles Clergeaud, on a previous social occasion and had entertained them for dinner in Nalliers. I received a welcome gift from my daughters in the form of a complete up-to-date Hi-Fi set, no longer so, but still in use at the time of writing, despite progress!

In September, the Lyttons invited us to meet an English couple called David and Margaret Hagues. Like me, David was an Old Centaur. I remembered a classmate at school having the same name and he turned out to be one of his older brothers. I did not remember David, but he knew of me because I frequently conducted the Sinfonia in Derby. David had had a successful tiling business in Derby and we subsequently saw some of his work in the entrance hall of the Royal Crown Derby china works.

More organ recitals followed – Chaillé-les-Marais on 29 September and Montmorillon in the Vienne department on 30 September then Parthenay on 3 November.

PROGRAMME (Montmorillon)

GUILMENT	Grand Choeur in D major
BALBASTRE	À la venue de Noël
FESTING	Largo allegro and variations
ELGAR	Organ Sonata No. 1
Pietro YON	Echo and Humoresque
WIDOR	Toccata

A respite from music followed with another visit to New York. We departed on 22 November, again from Nantes but this time via Paris, which was included in the fare. This was our second visit together to see Gré, Nick and family in New Canaan, and it coincided with Thanksgiving. Celebrations (always on the fourth Thursday of the month) were in full swing the day after we arrived and Gré and Nick's friends Jamie Grant (brother of Hugh) and his wife joined us. While in France, John Solum, who lives in Westport and knew of our intended visit to New Canaan, had suggested we meet up at a concert he was giving close to home and have dinner with them afterwards. It was a Sunday afternoon concert and in a church on our way to Westport. Nick drove the four of us to the venue in time for the concert and I recall entering the church, finding four seats, and waiting patiently for what was clearly going to be a full house. Scrutiny of the platform revealed a set of drums, better described as a drum kit, plus the odd saxophone waiting to be played, all of which made me very suspicious. Furthermore, the audience did not seem to be the kind one would expect to see at a baroque concert, so I sought out an attendant to ask for a programme. There were none available and, on closer examination of the stage, realized that we must be at the wrong venue. Voicing my doubts to the attendant, she did not even flinch, but just smiled and said, 'You want …,' and then gave me the name of another church several miles further on. We arrived there late and patiently stood behind a glass panelled door listening and watching the performance before moving into the auditorium during the applause. There were reserved seats waiting for us, a measure of John's thoughtfulness! We laughed about the matter over dinner that evening and it was such a pleasure to see John and Penny on their home ground. Later the following week John drove over to see us before we left. Although still in touch with each other, the Atlantic still divides us.

2001

After a brief trip to England, work continued on our *grande dépendence*, which was soon to provide us with a sitting room with wood burner, entrance passage with spiral staircase to the music room, sliding patio windows to the study, toilet and shower room at the rear, and finally a kitchen. On the first floor, there was a large music room, similar to the one in Adam and Eve House right down to the music cabinets and bookshelves, and a bedroom above the sitting room.

A special mention must be given to the restoration of the iron-framed glass conservatory entered from the courtyard. There are approximately 600 glass panels on the roof, which, fortunately for us, John Pate was able to replace. It was fortunate because he had been trained as a glacier. The glass panels in this three-sided conservatory were, as in most windows, kept in place with putty and, being subject to expansion in hot weather, many got broken. In the past, panes were probably replaced annually, but if neglected the reglazing could turn into a major job, as it did for us. My old school friend Denis was a great fount of knowledge and, although I did not for a moment think he would have the answer to my problem, if there was one, he was the best person to ask. He quickly discovered that the National Trust in Britain had solved the same problem some time before by using a foil-backed bitumen roofing tape known as Flashband, which entailed placing the glass on a flexible mastic and then covering it with the tape. For all his knowledge, John had never heard of this technique but was, to say the least, very impressed with the result, not to mention the ease of fitting. For my part, I measured the parallel runs of iron, of which there were several sizes, and the number of panes that would be required for each run. From memory, I think there were around 600 of them. In some trepidation, we went to Mr Bricolage, the local DIY shop, which accepted the order and, to our surprise, made no charge for cutting the glass – incredible! The following week we took the trailer to Luçon to pick up the load. When John came to reglaze the structure it was a team effort as Chris painted the metalwork ahead of him. The only nightmare arose from John knocking the old glass out of the frames onto the *verrière* floor, thereby occasioning a few more trips to the *déchetterie* (dump).

* * *

We made a second trip to El Puerto de la Selva in Spain, once again to stay with the Lyttons. We visited some wonderful places, including an incredibly beautiful village called Pals and some wonderful botanic gardens on the coast towards Barcelona. On returning home, we went via Vinca, this time to stay with John and Françoise Wilkinson. Before his retirement, John had been a colleague of Ken Gurling's and we had met him on several occasions in England. He had moved to France with his French wife and, like Ken, was a music lover. John ran a music club for several English friends in the area, but it was also open to the French. They would meet in each other's houses, or in a small hall, to either listen to a talk on music or play recordings. They were due to attend one such meeting at a friend's house high in the mountains and invited us to join them. Because Christine was feeling unwell, John and I went to the house without her and watched a video of Bernstein conducting a recording of his *Candide* (which was based on Voltaire's novel). Before going back, I just had to buy a copy for myself! There have been many versions and I understand the revised one was in 1989. It was a thoroughly enjoyable evening.

Christine and I were still attending French classes at the AVF (Accueil des villes françaises) in Fontenay-le-Comte, but I was beginning to lose interest. People came and went and there was no continuity. Every time a newcomer arrived we went back over the same ground. I was looking for an escape and saw my opportunity when the leader of the school came into our class and asked if anyone would be interested, particularly someone with a teaching background, in teaching English to a French group. I volunteered – not for me but for Christine. Chris was taken aback but did not have time to recover before being accepted. Twenty years later at the time of writing, the remnants of that first class are still with her.

* * *

My reputation for playing the organ had spread and André Casseron, who lived in L'Aiguillon-sur-Mer, approached me to feature in a series of organ recitals he organized each summer. I asked about the organ, but on being told that it was electronic, I declined his invitation, but he at least managed to persuade me to drive over and play it. Seeing no harm in spending a day at this attractive seaside resort, I acquiesced. The church in which we met impressed me from every angle, as it had been beautifully restored. The organ console was to one side with the speakers either side of the choir – a three manual with English RCO pedal board and fully programmed, but how did it sound? I did my usual extemporization building up to full organ and was left without a moment's doubt. After all, Carlo Curley, one of the world's leading organists, had toured the world playing one.

From then on I played every year until the series was halted, sadly because of the appointment a new *prêtre* who believed that churches were for worship and not entertainment. Following an invitation from Père Joseph Vité I gave my first organ recital in Notre Dame church in Fontenay-le-Comte on 19 May.

PROGRAMME

William HARRIS	Flourish for an occasional
FESTING arr. BALL	Largo, allegro, aria and two variations
BACH	Prelude and Fugue in A minor (BWV 543)
Vaughan WILLIAMS	Prelude on 'Rhosymedre'
Edward ELGAR	Sonata No. 1 in G major

On 2 June, our French friends Achille and Madeleine Faucher, who owned a *cave* in Luçon, invited me to play the organ for their son's wedding in the Luçon cathedral. I knew the organ by reputation, for it was a Cavaillé Coll four manual and one of the largest examples of this great organ builder's work in France. It is an awesome instrument and I quickly organised a meeting with Guillaume Marionneau, resident organist, to arrange to see it. I learnt the secrets of how to gain entry to the organ tribune and who to contact to establish when the cathedral was available for practising. It is, however, a difficult instrument to play. It is a tracker organ, which means that everything is mechanical, so basically, to put it crudely, the more stops you use the heavier the action gets. In England, such an organ would almost certainly have been brought up to date in terms of its action, even to the extent of mounting the console away from the pipes. The English generally believe that only the pipework and voicing are worth preserving. The French, on the other hand, literally preserve everything as it is, but in full working order. I would be reluctant to give an organ recital on the Luçon organ because it would require having one or two assistants on each side to help with the stop changes. Simply reaching for the stop and withdrawing it, or pushing it back, requires effort and it is difficult to manage more than one stop at a time. The marriage service went well and Guillaume came up to the organ loft to assist me when I played the bride and groom out after the service to the famous Widor Toccata. It was a joy playing the piece, however, as Guillaume did every stop change for me. I just played. There are foot pistons in the form of levers in front of the pedals, which when forcefully pressed down will bring out a particular group of stops. When needed, he would slide his leg under the keyboard and neatly with his foot press one of the levers at the precise moment to effect the changes. It was a wonderful team effort.

Continuing our concert schedule, Judith and I gave a concert in the church at L'Hermenault. She, however, wished to sing lieder for a change, which I welcomed, so had the luxury of a piano hired from Philippe Caute in Niort. I had met Philippe when I had my Bechstein piano brought over from England. He then regularly tuned it for me and was always present whenever the piano was subsequently moved, even being in charge when I had the piano craned up to the music room in the *grande dépendance* (and down again when we left.) At that point, he supervised the packing and loading of the piano, which was to go back to England for Gré, as I was buying a new Kawai grand. More of which will come later.

I gave my first organ recital at L'Aiguillon-sur-Mer on Monday 13 August, and started the programme with William Harris's Flourish for an occasion. I confess to falling back on a well-tried repertoire with Bach's prelude and fugue in A minor (BWV 543), Guilmant's Grand choeur and Widor's Toccata from his Fifth Symphony plus several less demanding quiet pieces. Returning to Nalliers, we had a visit from Gilles Clergeaud who at that time was involved in compiling a record of historic properties in the Vendée and had visited a house in Saint-Laurent-de-la-Salle that had been photographed during the English owners' absence and required their written consent. He knew that the owner was a retired musician responsible for producing programmes specializing in baroque music, including those of the well-known American William Christie, now living permanently in France. In fact, Christie is in Thiré, the next village and about five kilometres away from our present house, La Noue, in the Vendée. Towards the end of August each year, Christie holds an arts festival in his magnificent gardens in Thiré featuring baroque ensembles, opera and orchestral performances. His orchestra, Les Arts Florissants, is well known internationally for its recordings and broadcasts. When Gilles asked the couple (Nicholas and Alison Anderson) if they knew me, Nick confessed to knowing my name but not yet having met me. As a result, we very quickly did so and a short time later had dinner with them in Nalliers. We now meet up whenever they visit their *maison secondaire*, which is only a short distance away from where we are now living.

2002 Never a dull moment

At the end of February, Rachel rang me from England to say that they had itchy feet and had decided to follow us and live in France. Rachel had apparently been looking at French properties, including châteaux, and was astonished by the difference in property values between France and where they lived in Kingston upon Thames. An unfair comparison it may be, but still true even if compared with provincial England. I said there was no need to buy a château as I knew of a very beautiful *logis* (dwelling) not far from the Vendée. I was asked to ring the owners, John and Laura Poole. John is a musician and conducted the BBC singers before his retirement, but I could only speak to Laura as John had already departed for America where he had taken up an appointment at Bloomington university in Illinois. Literally two days later, Dick and Rachel flew to La Rochelle where we picked them up to stay with us over the weekend so that they could view the house. We drove over and looked around and they immediately agreed to buy. Twelve days later the *compromis de vente* (sales agreement) was signed with completion scheduled for August.

On 21 March, we travelled to England to see Shore Hall, which Gré and Nick, now back from their 13-year sojourn in the States, had recently purchased. Actually, it was more than just seeing as we were providing them with a useful purpose because their move had seriously interrupted their skiing plans, for which they required a dog sitter. It is a well-known fact that my daughters thought of me as what Clare had called 'a no pet parent', which I might say I thought rather unfair since I had bought her a most beautiful red setter called Rufus, though she really wanted a horse. I believe that the epithet was more likely to have derived from my objection to having a dog in the drawing room, dining room and most certainly the kitchen, but I suspect this only applied during my presence. We were impressed with Shore Hall, and above all its garden. There was a long drive to the house through a line of poplar trees, with a paddock on the right and gardens to the left. A centre terrace led to a parterre garden on one side and beyond this a very large lawned area. There was a sunken rose garden leading to the tennis court. At the side of the house was a parterre garden, pool and pool house. On the opposite side were stables and a coach house. I think what impressed us most was the standard of maintenance, which I suppose was less surprising when we learnt that the gardens were frequently opened to the public. They kept the gardener, who never ceased to amaze me with his ability to maintain this high standard.

My Uncle Eric's daughter Valerie and her husband Brian had friends they were visiting in the neighbouring village of Great Sampson, so knowing that Gré now had a house near by, they chose to pay us a visit. I was glad about this because Eric had recently died and it provided an opportunity to share with her my fond memories of the uncle who had so inspired me to play the piano. Chris had a hard job with Gré's dog Dillon, which had to be taken to the vet several times, but both survived. I think Dillon got rather fond of Chris as she was always very popular with him on all our subsequent visits.

It will come as no surprise at this stage that we had for some time been keeping our eyes open for a suitable property for Rebecca and Glenn to buy locally, but had not told Rachel about it at the time because she had already decided to buy the *logis*. After viewing several houses on Rebecca's behalf, we revisited a house in Petosse and met some of the members of the owner's family who lived next door. Rebecca and Glenn eventually purchased the property and continue to live there at the time of writing. It was now time to tell both sisters that they would be living relatively near each other in France.

The sad news of Ken Gurling's death reached me on 17 June. Ken had been a close friend since we first met after a concert in Ilkeston in Derbyshire, and readers will remember that he toured with the orchestra on many occasions. He was at that time, and until his retirement, a senior consultant at the Derbyshire Royal Infirmary. As a matter of interest this building was closed in 2009 and moved to the site of the old City Hospital which had been extended and now given the new name of the Royal Derby Hospital. However, he was also dean of medical studies at the Queen's Medical Centre in Nottingham, part of Nottingham University, and during my time with the Sinfonia we would occasionally meet for lunch on the campus when I was visiting the Sinfonia office.

On 19 June, Rebecca and Glenn came to France to sign their *compromis de vente* for the house in Petosse, and on the 28th Rachel and Dick brought over their two daughters, Sophie and Lara for an intensive course in French at Carel, the language school in Royan. Over three consecutive weekends, we drove to Royan to see and entertain my granddaughters and it was a pleasant and rewarding time for all. Then, later in the summer, Rachel and Dick also moved to France.

* * *

I had been booked to give an organ recital in L'Aiguillon-sur-Mer on 26 August. I was also asked to fill a gap with another earlier one at the end of

July, but was reluctant to do so because I knew I would be preparing for a concert with Judith in Nalliers three or four days later. I suggested that instead of the organ recital, I repeat the Nalliers programme, though it would involve them hiring a piano, to which they agreed.

The concert on 29 July at the Église Saint Nicholas, L'Aiguillon-sur-Mer, consisted of chants accompanied by piano, 'Mon cœur s'ouvre à ta voix' by Saint-Saëns, Wolf's Verschwiegene liebe, Elgar's Sea Songs, and piano solos, Schubert's Impromptu Op. 90, Debussy's Deux arabesques and Grünfeld's Paraphrase on Die Fledermaus.

The Nalliers concert, which followed on 2 August, accidentally laid the foundations for our future as, for an encore, I had prepared a piece for Judith that included Adrian. I understood that, on coming to live in France permanently, Judith had bought Adrian a new bassoon. He had learnt to play the instrument at school and became a member of the Welsh National Youth orchestra. He then continued his studies in London at the Royal College of Music, and it was only later that he opted to go into administration after playing in the Welsh National Opera and BBC Symphony orchestra. For the encore I arranged the Percy Grainger setting of 'The London Derry Air'- 1st verse, bassoon solo, 2nd verse soprano solo, and the 3rd verse 'tutti' (all together). My organ recital at L'Aiguillon-sur-Mer and another at Fontenay-le-Comte completed the summer concerts.

We had also found ourselves in a spasmodic monthly routine of spending the weekend with Rachel and her daughters at the *logis*. Dick had generously been allowed to continue his work with the computer company by working online and periodically returning to London. Apart from enjoying our company, she was a little nervous in the *logis*, which was remote in the country. No complaints, however, as the house had an excellent cellar and it was a joy to see Sophie and Lara. They are both 'animal lovers' and I cannot help thinking their experience of looking after a local farmer's lamb, which they kept in one of the barns, contributed to this.

They decided to have a house warming party on 23 December, by which time they had purchased a new Yamaha grand piano from our friend Philippe Caute in Niort, so this was yet another event at which I would be expected to perform. Philippe really scored with this instrument, which I found superb. He has that rare skill of setting up a piano (particularly a new one) to suit the needs of a jazz or concert pianist, or, if required, one suited to accompanying lieder.

2003

It is an inescapable fact of life that we make mistakes, but on reflection, what we learn from them should make us more knowledgeable, more patient with others but above all give us better judgement when making future decisions. I mention this as I must confess to yet another change of boat when we sold *Cru Classe* in the Spring.

July saw the permanent arrival of Rebecca and Glenn in France. For a short period, I now had two daughters living in France, but sadly Rachel and Dick had decided to return to England. The girls had found it difficult to settle and they all missed the socialising and buzz of London. The *logis* sold quickly and at a profit, unheard of in France. They left in August so had spent exactly one year here. The two sisters made the most of the two months during which they were able to meet up.

This had one compensation for us as East Molesey where they were living was a perfect stopping off place for us when we were in England, and had some good local pubs. I love a pint of English real ale.

By this time we had come to know David Forsyth and his wife Michelle who lived in Le Langon, close to Nalliers where I had given a concert in the church. David sang tenor in a Fontenay choir and, following an invitation to his house, met several future friends and one in particular. I was introduced to Guy and Annick Robin who confessed to wanting a favour from me. They were members of the church, Notre Dame in Fontenay, and I think had attended my last organ recital there. Would I play for their daughter's wedding on 6 September. I agreed and, as usual, asked him to let me know what music they would like. I mention this because in this case the bride wanted Elgar's 'Nimrod' variation for her entry and walk to the altar steps. Marching or indeed walking is usually to the accompaniment of a 2 or 4 beat measure, 'Nimrod' is in 3 and very slow. I think this explanation made Guy a little nervous and he asked me if they could rehearse the walk in the church. We did. She wanted the whole movement to be played, and when I explained they would be left standing by an impatient priest when they arrived it was agreed I would start at the beginning but they would delay the start of the procession until I had reached a particular point in the score. Having timed their walk, it would have been a simple matter to signal the start from the organ, but of course the organ was high on the tribune above their heads. We devised a method that worked perfectly at the rehearsal but alas not at the ceremony, so I was left to my usual escape route of extemporization. No one noticed but I hope Elgar forgave me.

2004

In April we were left in charge of La Fromarderie, Rebecca and Glenn's house in Petosse, while they flew to Sweden to take delivery of their long awaited Halberg Rassey sailing boat, which was ready for launching and trial sails – always an exciting time. They had named the boat *Onyva* (*on y va* in French translates into 'let us go'). This was perhaps an indication of their intentions, but nothing emerged at this time, whilst at the boatyard in Sweden they met a Greek who was buying a Halberg to sail round the world on the Blue Water Rally, the seed was sown.

In June we were in England to welcome them at the Royal Harwich Yacht Club. The voyage from Sweden actually took them a total of three months to complete, for they took their time cruising in the Baltic before crossing the North Sea and now docking in Woolverstone Marina. They too were members of the Royal Harwich Yacht Club. For their arrival in France, we had organised a temporary berth in Rochefort where they told us of their decision to join the Blue Water Rally, a bi-annual event that could be accomplished in stages if desired by joining up with the next rally two years later for the following leg of the voyage.

Chapter 15

Music's in the Air

2005–2007

A busy year, La Noue, birth of Music Box

2005 A busy year

We were in England in early April, so were able to attend a Kettering Symphony Orchestra concert, in my role as president. I was astonished to meet several players, including Yvonne Bowness, the leader of the orchestra who dated back to the period when I had been conducting it. However, the orchestra now had many more members and could justify its title as a symphony orchestra. I suggested to the chairman, John Peck, that for old time's sake they might like to visit France and play in a concert under my direction. Thinking of Judith as the soloist, I would include Berlioz's Nuits d'été in the programme. They were enthusiastic about the idea and said that it would solve the problem of their summer-term rehearsals, which had hitherto failed to result in a concert. I completed the programme for them and promised to fly over and conduct two rehearsals before their visit the following June and July.

On returning to France, we immediately started rehearsing for a charity concert in aid of the Ligue pour la Protection des Oiseaux (LPO). We called it the birds' concert. It had come about after meeting Ian and Marianne Carr at the home of Jean and Christiane Guillard. Jean was the last member of the family to have inherited La Graineterie and was in fact born there. They now lived in a *logis* in open country a kilometre or so down the lane. We frequently met them as they had fond memories of the house, and Jean enjoyed recounting its history and liked giving us friendly advice on it maintenance. We of course responded by updating him on the upkeep of the *verrière*!

The 29 May music is (literally) back in the air for the bird's concert, later affectionately known as the 'wet bird's concert'. I must say that, in all my years of programme planning I had never found one quite as demanding as this one. My thoughts immediately went to Messiaen, who used an almost literal orchestral imitation of birdsong in his various works, one being 'The awakening of the birds' for piano and orchestra, which was clearly out of our range. Judith came to my rescue with songs relating to what I would imagine was every bird in existence, and dating back to the fifteenth century. Being inspired by this I looked more closely at a volume of early keyboard works in my library and was relieved to find there was no shortage of titles involving bird names, so we were not short of ideas for our baroque repertoire. The Carrs rented a *logis* in extensive grounds and we had driven over the previous day to take the harpsichord and rehearse. It was clearly to be a big event, for there were various stalls associated with nature, a meander round the large garden, and a nature walk through the woods. There was also a working bread oven and a buffet planned for the evening. This we saw before rehearsing on a beautiful, warm, sunny day. In the unlikely event of a shower, a large tent without sides had been erected for the buffet to follow the concert. The day of the concert arrived and it was probably the wettest day of the year, but judging from the number of people who turned up with umbrella and wellies, was a very successful event. The concert was moved to the largest room in the house – where the harpsichord had spent the night – and the hall doors were left open so that the audience could see or at least hear what we played. At the end of the afternoon the rain finally abated and people were able to venture outside to the open-sided marquee to enjoy the buffet. In spite of everything, it was a great success (see programme on facing page).

On 14 June we were once again guests of David and Michelle Forsyth, through whom we had met Guy and Annick, for whose daughter's wedding, it will be remembered, I had played. Both David and Guy were members of the Fontenay-le-Comte Lions Club and they invited me to join its ranks. I promised to think it over, hiding my thoughts about these clubs which I had studiously avoided, we carried on enjoying the evening. Then, later, I decided that I would be delighted to accept and was duly elected to the club in the autumn, relieved it wasn't a complicated inauguration and found myself amongst a friendly gathering.

It took me, from that moment, some time to use the friendly 'you' in French (*tutoyer*) which is a sign of true friendship. It had been 'drummed' into me at school to observe that the second person singular 'tu' could not be used in the singular for anyone unless they were related, close friends or

Programme

Chansons 1

Ombra Mai Fu	HANDEL
Come Alla Tortorella	(1685–1759)

Clavecin

Premier mouvement Concerto en Fa Majeur	HANDEL
Le Coucou et le Rossignol	

Chansons 2

L'Amour de Moy	ANON
C'est à ce Joli Mois de Mai	(15 siècle)
Cantique des Petits Oiseaux	
Oiseaux, si tous les ans	MOZART
Dans un bois solitaire	(1756–1791)

Clavecin

La Linotte effarouchée	F. COUPERIN
Le Rossignol-en-amour – Double du Rossignol	(1668–1733)
Le Rossignol-Vainqueur	

Chansons 3

About the sweet bag of a Bee	Henry LAWES (1596–1662)
Amidst the Mirtles	
Gather your Rosebuds while you may	William LAWES (1602–1654)

Clavecin

Les Coucous Bénévoles	F. COUPERIN
Le Coucou	L.C.DAQUIN (1694–1772)
Air con Variazioni 'Le Forgeron gai'	HANDEL

Chansons de Shakespeare 4

Under the Greenwood Tree	ARNE
When Daises pied	(1710–1778)
Where the Bee sucks	

infants. So if addressing a single person, 'vous' is necessary in spite of it referring to more than one person.

About this time, I received an invitation through my Fontenay friend Josef Vité to join a team of four organists playing for Mass each Sunday in the Notre Dame church, not in Fontenay-le-Comte but in the small town of Sainte-Hermine. This interested me because, at an orchestral concert by the Salzburg Chamber Orchestra there, I had noticed the organ, like so many other French organs, on a tribune over the west entrance to the church. It transpired that one of the organists had retired and that the priest was keen to replace him. I was surprised they needed four organists, but on reflection decided it was better than the English practice of having one, plus an assistant if lucky, to carry the entire workload, especially given that in my early days organist fees were pitiful. I drove over to meet the priest at the church and played the organ – a two manual instrument with pedal board and well-balanced choice of stops, well suited to a carefully chosen repertoire for organ recitals. He seemed delighted when I accepted his invitation. I arranged to attend Mass the following Sunday to meet the lead organist, Alan Prezeau. There was a choir of mixed voices, but I confess it was a while before I became aware of its existence because its members sit at the front as part of the congregation and an *animateur* or *animatrice*, a sort of conductor, leads the services. The lead singer runs the rehearsals for the service and, in Sainte-Hermine and I think many other churches, also goes through the settings of the Mass with the organist immediately before the service, and before the members of the congregation arrive. I must mention that it was a very well attended church, so a pleasure to play. I was given full details of the hymns and settings for the Mass in advance and, from then on, was left to get on with it. Since they knew everything backwards, I was the only one who needed to worry! I quickly got into the routine and usually played about once a month.

It may be a surprise to readers, but at this time we decided to put La Graineterie on the market. Our decision to leave Nalliers partly came about through searching for a house for Rebecca and Glenn, which tempted us to consider a change, although the main reason was that, with the *grande dépendance* completed, we had two houses, which was great in the summer when we had guests, but in the winter having the piano and all my music in a separate building was not ideal. We thus decided to find one house that would accommodate all our needs. Property does not sell quickly in France, so although we started to look around, we were certain it would take some time.

We were also in the countdown to Rebecca and Glenn's impending two-year sailing trip around the world and I invite readers to recognise the enormity of this undertaking. First, their Halberg Rassey, which had been new two years earlier, had sailed in the Baltic and across the North Sea to England and down to La Rochelle. Now, ashore over winter in Port-Bourgenay, they had to be thoroughly prepared for 12 months at sea, before even reaching half way. Charlotte, Glenn's daughter from his earlier marriage, who was taking a gap year before going to university, would be helping them with the preparations. The boat was fully equipped with electronic navigation radar, a ship to shore radio and a 220-volt generator. Safety equipment included a life raft, flares, inflatable dinghy, lifejackets and safety harnesses. However, preparation goes much further than that as an EPIRB is required to automatically indicate distress and location, and GPS (latitude and longitude) which when plotted on a chart shows where you are in relation to the land. The scale of a chart dictates the accuracy of the position and has a bearing on the total number of charts you need. Charts are not cheap! They had joined a rally and travelled back to England several times for briefings, which from conversations I had with Glenn, impressed me. They were given lectures on first aid and a list of required vaccinations, which were expensive and I gather surprised their GP here in France. Finally, several weeks at sea means organizing provisions and, importantly, knowing where you have stowed them. Here ends the lesson.

On departure day – 31 August – *Onyva* was brought into the old harbour in the centre of La Rochelle and a farewell party held to see the boat and say *au revoir*. A cine film I took of the occasion has since been included in their DVDs of the two-year cruise. My final shot was of the boat sailing between the famous two towers in the Vieux-Port for their departure. However, and this is supposed to be a secret, they only went as far as Les Minimes marina where they had booked a berth for the night and where Chris and I drove to meet them for a final briefing on our role in looking after their house and interests in France. The next morning, they sailed across Biscay to La Coruña, which they completed on 1 September without any problems. In fact, a few years earlier they had crossed Biscay to the north coast of Spain in *Foxy Lady*. The next leg of the journey took them to Gibraltar where the rally was due to assemble before making a combined start to the two-year voyage.

On 30 October, Rebecca and Glenn left Gibraltar on course for the next stop, Tenerife. During the few days they spent there, Charlotte had been feeling unwell, so had a change of heart and left the husband and wife team to continue the remainder of the two-year journey alone. I should say at this point that most boats sailing across the Atlantic make this their departure point, since it affords them time to wait for the trade winds and their anticipated variations to decide on exactly what sailing course to take. In the event, the weather was unpredictable, so some boats sailed south towards the Cape Verde islands while others went further north. I gather that either way meant a rough crossing, but they all arrived safely. They had two daily radio checks between all boats to make sure no one was in difficulty. There was good camaraderie between the boats. I should add the companionship of the rally has continued to this day with a reunion taking place bi-annually in the host's country.

The Lions Club Ladies Night for members and their wives took place on 20 December, but to my surprise, part of the dinner was still devoted to discussing business. About this time, we heard that Rebecca and Glenn, following a very rough Atlantic passage, had arrived safely in Antigua in time for Christmas.

2006

By 2 January, Rebecca and Glenn had, after a short time in Antigua, now sailed to Martinique. We had earlier said we would probably join them for a holiday in the West Indies and now decided to do so. We left Nantes on the 10th, changed airports in Paris, which is worth mentioning because an airport official took Chris out of the boarding queue to question her nationality as her passport said that she was born in Boston. To my relief, she was returned to me after a short delay. There were smiles all round – it was Boston UK! We decided against staying on *Onyva* and had booked a hotel and car, not only to afford ourselves some independence, but also to give Rebecca and Glenn an opportunity to see more of the island. We were also able to meet other couples from the rally and recall a particular memorable evening dining aboard another Halberg Rassey.

Lions Club meetings were held each month and, for the January one, my services were called on to assist at an inter-club event, also with wives, to be held at the Isamba in Fontenay-le-Comte. Each club was given an after-dinner entertainment slot and I, though nothing to do with my daughter sailing round the world, was called on to rehearse a selection of sea shanties, as the Lion's contribution was to have a sailing theme, which of course had to be in French and which I did not know, so had to learn. (I suppose I should at least have known La Mer, but I did not.) However, I had an additional, I think bright, idea, which was certainly new to the French. I suggested asking the audience to clap at the appropriate times when invited to do so. Consequently, as the final item of the evening, the famous sea shanty, like the final night of the Proms, with everyone clapping from pianissimo to fortissimo, lento to prestissimo, rounded the evening off to thunderous applause.

The house search became more urgent when we suddenly had a buyer for La Graineterie. Chris and I had a slight disagreement over location. I favoured the country, which was not Christine's first choice, so we decided to compromise and go for a village. The search continued and included La Noue (in the country). My first impression from the garden was favourable, but I refrained from giving an opinion until seeing inside the house. Though both tentative, it was now yes or no and, simultaneously, we both said 'yes,' but we knew that there was a hell of a lot of work to do, but importantly the basics were there.

* * *

Back to boats briefly as we had heard from Rebecca and Glenn. They would be passing through the Panama Canal on 13 February and apparently we could watch their transit on Google Earth. Their passage was regulated and we had the timings, which was the middle of the night for us, so a sleepless time ahead. It was fascinating to see the canal in this way and to watch the movement of ships, but alas we did not see *Onyva*. It transpired that there had been excessive movement that day, which meant that their transit (tied to another ship) had to be delayed by one day. Once through the canal, they sailed on to the Galapagos Islands and later Tahiti. We gather that rules are strict there and although allowed ashore by dinghy to view the habitat, fires and picnics were not allowed and they had to return to their boat for the night, but they are beautiful and fascinating islands. Eventually leaving the islands, they were now faced with their longest seas passage across the Pacific.

* * *

Through my recent link with Sainte-Hermine, we had met Laurent and Anne Poultier, who lived in the château next door to the church. Laurent was president of the Sainte-Hermine Festival and he had invited Christine and me to his home. We arrived at the appointed time, but were clearly still not entirely cognisant of what awaited us. However, as expected, we were invited to take drinks. The table nearest to me was full of bottles, mainly of Scotch whisky. I suppose I should not have been surprised because the French are known to be the largest importers of our whisky in the world, but he was

227

certainly surprised when I opted for something French. The next surprise came when asked if we preferred red or white wine with our *blanquette de veau*. There had been no mention of dinner at the time of the invitation and we had eaten before arriving, so the thought of another meal was not exactly welcome.

We were subsequently accompanied to the dining room in which there was a lovely open fire and beautifully laid table. While the dinner was delicious and consisted of several courses, we could only manage tiny portions. After covering the usual formalities, the conversation moved to Laurent's role as president of the Sainte-Hermine Festival and he asked if I would be interested in adding my musical weight to it. Since its inception, each festival had centred on a different period in French history and this, the fourth one (to be held on 5, 6 and 7 August), was to be devoted to the reign of Louis XIV. Would I play in the festival and help plan a concert for each of the three nights? Having been involved in something similar in England, Music of the Royal Courts, I was of course delighted at the prospect and told him that I had a harpsichord I would be happy to use if he could provide transport for it. He then mentioned that Isabelle Douillard (soprano) and Jean François Bart (French horn) from the music school would be joining us after dinner. By this stage, I realized I was hooked, but was warming to the challenge. It was decided to call the programme 'Musique des Courts royales, Versailles et Londres', and later, after receiving some suggestions from our hosts, I was able to draw up a programme to fit the period.

* * *

As we would no longer have a designated music room at the new house and I wanted Gré to have the Bechstein, to which she had been looking forward, on 14 April I had arranged to have it shipped to England. Philippe Caute supervised its craning out of the window and loading into the removal van. Gré was delighted and it fitted perfectly into their drawing room at Shore Hall.

Shortly after this we flew to England for a few days to rehearse the Kettering Symphony Orchestra, now due to visit France and play in the large multi-purpose hall in Nalliers in August. It came as a shock to find myself rehearsing a mere handful of instrumentalists who would not even qualify as a chamber orchestra. I found it embarrassing to have to say that with so few players it would be impossible to go ahead with the concert. Seeing the disappointment in their faces, I suggested a music workshop holiday instead. The music school in Nalliers is adjacent to the hall and as there are no classes in August, I could use its practice studios. It is not unusual for even quite small villages to have an *école de musique* where pupils can have instrumental lessons. Pupils in France also have to attend compulsory theory lessons, which are quite demanding. We finally agreed that the KSO would arrive at the beginning of August and we booked accommodation for the musicians at the Hôtel Le Fontarabie in Fontenay.

La Noue

After almost ten years in Nalliers, on 4 May we completed the sales on both houses and moved to La Noue at La Chapelle-Thémer. Although only about twenty minutes away, La Noue is in a completely different landscape. Whereas Nalliers is on the edge of the Marais, La Chapelle-Thémer is at the start of the Bocage, thus more wooded, with rolling hills. Actually, La Noue is two kilometres from the village but only 500 metres from the hamlet of L'Orbrie, so is not completely isolated. Chris wanted to live in a village when she first arrived, but now that she is more comfortable with the language and loves nature, she is completely content. The house, an old farmhouse set within an acre of ground nestling in the countryside, has plenty of space but, as I have said, needed a lot of work to bring it up to our standards.

The garden was in a sad state when we arrived as the lawns were completely overgrown. We knew the previous owner had been sadly widowed, which explained why so much work was still needed on the house. She had, however, contracted a *paysagiste* (landscaper) to maintain the grounds and took responsibility for having this work done, but there was a delay as he was waiting for some new equipment. I fell back on my experience of previously owning three acres of ground at Tixover and our first purchase was a tractor. We took on the same *paysagiste* in the early days to plant hedges and put up a boundary fence where the property had previously been open to the surrounding field. Work on the inside of the property had already been agreed before we decided to buy and this started in the autumn. Our contractors, both of whom had previously worked for us in Nalliers, were Serge Gatteau for the woodwork, plastering and floor boarding, and Technibat, for the electricity and plumbing. It was going to be a busy year as there were also several concerts for which I needed to prepare.

229

On 3 and 4 June we were introduced to Henry and Christiane Lewis who invited me to provide a musical background to an art exhibition in their moated château at Puy Chenin in Xaintray in Deux-Sèvres. Our harpsichord and *flûte à bec* trio was our first real ensemble in the true sense of the word, for it marked the first occasion of Christine joining Judith and Adrian. Strangely, I had never accompanied Christine playing the flute or recorder. In her days of full-time teaching, we thought of our evenings as a time to relax. She had bought two lovely Dolmetsch recorders for her retirement in France, but John Solum's visit seemed to have sown some seeds that were now about to take root. Going back to the concert, in many ways for all of us it was a rehearsal, as there was no programme and our task was simply to provide interludes of music while the public walked around the exhibition, or alternatively just sat and listened. The music was chosen but not rehearsed. The exhibition, called 'Ecritures de Parfums', was of the work of Catherine Willis, who had been a member of the Bloomsbury set in London – a group started in the first half of the twentieth century of English writers, intellectuals, philosophers and artists and including people such as Virginia Woolf, Vanessa Bell and the Stracheys. Afterwards, the Lewises invited us to stay on at the château for the night.

* * *

The beginning of August was certainly hectic because the Sainte-Hermine Festival coincided with the workshop for the Kettering Symphony Orchestra. For the festival, I met up with the musicians at the start of the school holidays and I was agreeably surprised by the extent of the talent with which I would be working. However, just before the first concert, and with very little notice Isabelle, our soprano, fell ill. I immediately contacted Judith and she magnificently, and without hesitation, came to my rescue, not only taking Isabelle's place but also singing exactly the same arias. To provide variety, there was a change of programme each night in the hope of encouraging listeners to attend more than one concert, and it was this that inspired me to invite Adrian to play his bassoon at the third. In other words, the first concert was an organ recital, the second soprano, horn and harpsichord, and the third, soprano, bassoon and harpsichord.

Those members of the Kettering Symphony Orchestra who had agreed to come to France, arrived on 3 August. I had arranged day classes for them at the Nalliers music school and tutors were made available to give them friendly advice and to play in an ensemble at the end of each session. The Kettering players stayed in Fontenay and were transported daily to Nalliers by coach. On the Sunday lunchtime, before their departure the next day, we entertained them with a buffet lunch on the lawn at La Noue, the new house to which we had moved in May. Several of them attended the festival concert in the evening, which they thoroughly enjoyed, in fact they had a very memorable time with us.

Having sent my Bechstein to Gré, I was anxious to replace my piano with a smaller grand and decided on a Kwai, which was proving a challenge for Steinway. Indeed, I learnt that contestants in world piano competitions were being given a choice of piano for their pre-final performances, and many were choosing Kwai. I approached Philippe Caute, who had recently opted to trade in Kwai rather than Yamaha pianos. However, comparing prices between France and England prompted me to look in the UK. As we were planning to be there in November, I made an appointment to view the range of pianos in St Neots near Huntingdon, where I could try out different models and, importantly, learn more about them from talking to specialists. The full concert grand I saw there was certainly comparable to my Bechstein, and I was told that it had just returned after being played by John Lill.

I immediately questioned that information because I knew that John Lill was contracted only to use a Steinway, but apparently that stipulation no longer applied. The warehouse was prepared to sell me the piano of my choice without the cost of shipping it to France. At the time I thought the offer generous, but in fact the main European warehouse was in Germany and of course my piano would not have to be brought to England. On return-ing to France, I rang Philippe in Niort and he suggested I give him 24 hours to come up with a better offer. My journey had still been worthwhile on two counts. First, I learnt that improvements had been made to the action by changing to using carbon fibre for certain parts of the instrument and, second, when a friend later bought straight from the warehouse in Germany, I discovered that the piano needed regulating before going out to the cus-tomer. In the end, Philippe supplied the piano for me with the new action and for the same price as in the UK, and included his final adjustments to the action and tuning.

By October, Glenn and Rebecca had reached the north coast of Australia where the boat was required by law to be taken out of the water. They took the opportunity to antifoul and fit out for the remainder of their cruise and took a flight to Sydney to see the southern part of the continent. The next part of their journey would take them to Bali.

It is well known that clubs like the Lions and Rotary devote a great deal of time to raising money for charity. On two occasions (in 2006 and 2007), I arranged Christmas concerts for this purpose, with the money raised going to the Campaign SightFirst II. To begin with, I wanted to introduce the French to the traditional English service of Nine Lessons and Carols, but this was unknown to the French clergy, so it turned into a concert of carols with Advent readings. For this concert, Judith Harris, the former member of the BBC Singers mentioned earlier, arranged for some of her former colleagues to fly over and sing under the title of 'The English Singers'. This was, of course, just like working with professional orchestral players as a three-hour rehearsal sufficed to prepare for the concert, which, played to a packed church and partly televised, was an amazing success.

On 23 December, we received a telephone call from Philippe to say that he would deliver the new piano that evening. True to his word, he did, but not until 9 p.m. I could not have wished for a better Christmas present.

2007

Now in receipt of its latest list of members and diary of monthly meetings, I felt very much part of the Lions Club team and was enjoying their friendship. In the past, I had never wanted to be involved in such clubs, but this one fitted in with my resolve to come to France and retire from music. However, it was becoming increasingly evident that music was still occupying a large part of my life. As I write this, I am reminded of an amusing story related to me by Adrian who heard a bassoonist colleague say, 'you know it's not the music, it's the inconvenience!' which certainly proved to be true in my case, 'the inconvenience being the politics'.

Birth of Music Box

Early in the year, when Judith and Adrian came round to see the new piano, Adrian suggested holding a concert in the house featuring Judith (mezzo soprano), Christine (*flûte à bec*), Adrian (bassoon) and me (piano), and then finishing it off with a social event at which we would serve wine. The more we discussed the project the more we warmed to the idea. If one concert, why not more? It was also Adrian's idea to have a music club and he suggested we call it 'Music Box' – a date was fixed and the invitations went out.

The first performance of 'Music Box' for friends at La Noue took place on 20 May.

PROGRAMME

HANDEL	Arrival of the Queen of Sheba
GRIEG	Three songs
FINGER	Sonata No. 1
CHOPIN	Scherzo in B flat minor
ELGAR	Three sea songs
GODFREY	Lucy Long

We presented all our guests with a questionnaire on which we explained that if people were sufficiently interested we would put on a concert every two months, but added that the venue would be flexible. Anyone with a piano and enough space to hold an audience could volunteer to host the concert and those with space but without a piano could still qualify because, with our two manual De Blaise harpsichord, we could put on a 'baroque' concert.

The response was positive and we invited our friend Chris Skerry to act as our secretary. We now had administrative help and the addresses (postal and email) of those interested.

* * *

To return to Glenn and Rebecca who had earlier in the year sailed round into the Gulf of Aden, into the Red Sea and finally through the Suez Canal into the Mediterranean, this was by far the most dangerous part of the voyage, not because of bad weather but because of the risk of piracy. This part of the rally had been carefully organised, with boats travelling in pairs and staying in close contact. They were certainly relieved when they arrived in Crete. They were now on their way home and stopped off to meet Gré at her villa in Portugal. Finally, on 11 July, they completed their 28,000 nautical-mile journey round the world arriving *à l'heure* in La Rochelle. I had filmed their departure and I now filmed their return – an emotional moment for all and celebrated with breakfast together. Well done those two! We drove them back to La Noue to see our new house for the first time.

22 July

The Music Box concerts got off to a flying start with another visit to Ian and Marianne's *logis* to play in the same salon as we had for the wet bird's concert. Eugène and Simone Oger, who were among our earliest French friends, hosted the September Music Box at La Richardière. Also in September we were invited back to the château at Puy Chenin to play for another exhibition, again as a harpsichord recorder quartet. Then, our 25 November concert was at La Noue. I should perhaps have mentioned earlier that all these concerts were scheduled for a 4 p.m. start on a Sunday.

* * *

Following the success of our Lions Club Christmas concert, I was to arrange a second one this year, again for the 'Campaign Sight First II'. Our reputation, however, had spread and we were invited to play the same programme at the Collégiale de Saint-Marc-la-Lande in Deux-Sèvres, this had to be on a professional basis which was accepted and took place just the night before the Lions Club concert in Fontenay-le-Comte. I was able to engage our English Singers, and fortunately the receipts from the Lions Club event more than covered their fees. As a thank you for the Fontenay Christmas concerts, Lions presented me with its Melvin Jones Fellow Award for dedicated humanitarian services. I felt very honoured.

Chapter 16

Musical Highlights
2008–2010
More music, Holland

2008 More concerts

This year started with a Music Box concert in Deux-Sèvres, which Colin and Pat Cook hosted at their large modern house in Champdeniers. Colin and Pat were interested in theatre and, before coming to France, Pat, whose special interest was musicals, had performed with the Leicester Theatre Group. Colin had a powerful voice and, I believe, had been the perfect Professor Henry Higgins in the group's performance of *My Fair Lady*, the part Rex Harrison had played in the original film. They particularly wanted a concert of theatre music, so we agreed to start the New Year with 'Music from the Shows'.

I decided to invite Mike Rayner to fly over with his wife Joy to join us for the New Year, for I knew that he would never turn down an opportunity to sing. Readers will remember that he had been my principal baritone in the Opera da Camera before moving to the Birmingham School of Music as a mature student, then to the Welsh National Opera, followed by an Arts Council promotion to Opera For All. He was finally appointed principal baritone in the D'Oyly Carte Opera Company. Pat had a boudoir Steinway piano, which I had played before and, being in a large drawing room, was ideal for the concert, for which there was a very large audience. Needless to say, Mike, with all his talent, was a huge success and Colin was lavish with his refreshments afterwards.

Des Veillées musicales approached me on 24 February with a view to giving a concert in our village, La Chapelle-Thémer. I decided that fulfilling such a request required a level of professionalism that Music Box, which was in effect a music club, lacked, so decided to give it the new name of L'Ensemble de la Chapelle and its first of many concerts marked Christine's début as a flautist.

Strangely, there are considerably fewer churches in France than in England. Stamford in Lincolnshire, where I lived for a number of years, had seven Anglican churches, and this was over and above the Catholic and Protestant ones. France, of course, is principally a Catholic country, but it does contain a handful of Protestant churches. Fontenay-le-Comte, once the capital of the Vendée, has only two Catholic churches and, I believe, just one Protestant one, and this is the general pattern. I was therefore surprised when Music Box was invited to give a concert to the Friends of the Temple (Les Amis du Temple) in Sainte-Hermine. All Protestant churches go under the name *temple* but I had never come across this building as it is tucked well away from the town centre. We agreed to play there and continued to do so on an annual basis, giving our first concert on 16 May. The building is beautifully restored, small but friendly. However, it has no organ, so our concerts there were inevitably baroque and we never played to other than full houses. The grassed area at the front of the church allowed for socializing after the performance. I think my colleagues would agree that performing there gave us as much pleasure as I know we gave them.

By now an annual event, L'Ensemble de la Chapelle duly gave three concerts at the Festival de Sainte-Hermine. It was traditional for the stallholders filling the square opposite the church to wear period costume during the festival. There would also be a late evening performance of a period play in the grounds of the château. Given that the period of this year's festival was the reign of Louis XV (1710–1770), we were asked to dress in the appropriate costume. This was like old times for me, so with the help of my colleagues we took the opportunity to create a programme for each of the three concerts to represent the transition of music from the baroque to classical period. Since the composers popular at that time included Charpentier, Purcell, Handel, Gluck, Haydn and Mozart, we had a wide range of music from which to choose.

Even before the Sainte-Hermine Festival, we were having to rehearse for four different concerts as we had already started rehearsing for our now annual concert in La Caillère, which Des Veillées musicales organised. Bernard Cottreau, who was closely associated with the church there, very efficiently managed these events for the town. We needed to replace Chris Skerry as our secretary for Music Box, both because the workload had grown and because Chris was only in France six months a year. Now, knowing Bernard so well, we invited him to take over, which he was happy to do.

The La Caillère programme on 8 August included an aria from Bach's cantata No. 119 *Preise Jerusalem, den Herrn*, accompanied by organ with flute obligato. There was also an Adagio from Mozart's Bassoon Concerto, and 'Pie Jesu' from Duruflé's requiem ending with Widor's organ toccata from the Fifth Symphony.

The Music Box had really caught on and we found ourselves being invited to a wide range of venues, often for a celebratory reason. One concert was to commemorate Frank and Jocelyn Fort's discovery of an early fireplace of great historic interest, which they had accidentally unearthed while attempting to update their existing one.

Another interesting engagement was to perform for the opening of bee-keeper (*apiculteur*) Franck Alletru's large new boutique. He has hundreds of hives in the Bocage, the Plaine and the Marais, some just down the road from us, and his honey is excellent. It was an enjoyable concert despite a few bees flying around!

The Lions Club took over the theatre in Antigny for a Christmas concert for which I used L'Ensemble de la Chapelle. I was determined to involve a few fellow members of the club in the programme and took it upon myself to find six members to play toy instruments in Haydn's Toy Symphony. I had directed this work with the English Sinfonia on several occasions, so was aware that famous people (I won't mention names) could present a challenge to achieving a musical performance. Needless to say, it was a wonderful finale.

On a slightly more serious note, on 23 December, Christine and I were invited to give a private flute and piano recital to Philippe de Villiers and his family at their home in Les Herbiers. Philippe de Villiers was at the time president of the Conseil Général of the Vendée, but retired in 2010. He also founded the world famous theme park, Puy du Fou, in 1977. It was a most agreeable and intimate evening, with all the members of the family sitting around the fire drinking champagne while they were being entertained.

2009

I believe there is still a website on the internet referring to our Music Box. We had a very keen member, Charles Antoine Verly, who set up this blog for us, but alas since he moved to Nantes some time ago, it has not been updated, but it is perhaps still of some historic interest (the-music-box.over-blog.com).

* * *

On the family front, after visiting us the year before, Clare had decided to move to France and, in June, arrived to view a couple of houses that we had shortlisted for her. This also gave her an opportunity to meet French agents who could show her properties that might interest her. She particularly liked a cottage we had shortlisted for her in Saint-Maurice-des-Noues, near La Châtaigneraie and, in the autumn, she bought it. By October, having at last decided to take the plunge, she was living here permanently. Arriving ahead of the removal company she was able to get the house ready for her mostly antique furniture, including some fine paintings and clocks. I was happy about her being able to cope with the language, since she had spent nearly a year here after leaving school, but I was less happy about her negative attitude to life, which had become increasingly evident since the breakdown of her marriage to Neil, quickly followed by a relationship with an accountant called Iain and the birth of their son, Ben. Iain's mother, who had previously been married to a doctor in York, had taken over Ben's care shortly before Clare came to France. There was no doubt that Clare was a devoted mother, but although I thought the world of her, we were not on the best of terms. To make matters worse, having promised to make ends meet in France by running a B&B, she instead brought a lodger with her, who was living rent free but with whom she assured me she did not have a relationship.

* * *

To return to the musical world, on 6 June L'Ensemble de la Chapelle was invited to play for the Association of Parks and Gardens of Les Pays de Loire at the Parc de l'Anneau in the commune of Chantonnay. The concert was divided into two parts – in the afternoon a moveable *flûte à bec* consort to entertain the public wandering around the beautiful grounds, and a full programme of songs, instrumental solos and ensembles of works from Pachelbel to Mozart in the château in the evening.

Not surprisingly, Music Box also put on a concert for Laurent Poultier in the château in Sainte-Hermine, barely a month or so before our next festival concert in the town.

It was a relief to the ensemble that this year for the first time we would not need to dress in period costume for the Sainte-Hermine Festival scheduled for 1, 2 and 3 August, for the period chosen for 2009 was 1944 to 1958. At the annual meeting earlier in the year, I had warned the committee that to cover this period we would need a piano. Thankfully, they left it to me to arrange one for the three performances and, with the help of my colleagues, we drew up a varied repertoire of vocal and instrumental music to include reasonably popular works that would have been played during those fifteen years. Clearly, on this basis we could play anything written before 1944, which we did, but the emphasis was decidedly on the twentieth century. I include a few titles from the programmes to illustrate:

WINKLER	Neapolitan Serenade	Ensemble
HONEGGER	Danse de la Chèvre	Flute
VILLA-LOBOS	Bachianas Brasileiras	Soprano
R. GRAVES	Waltz Romantique	Bassoon
ARTHUR BENJAMIN	Jamaican Rumba	Piano
	'Jealousy'	Voice and ensemble

Two days after the festival, and not giving us much room for turning round, we had an ensemble concert at Bessay for the Association des Gardes de la Tour de Bessay. The concert actually took place in the beautifully restored sixteenth-century *pigeonnier* in the park of the Château Colombier. The *pigeonnier*, which was declared an historic monument in 1990, contains 3,000 *niches à pigeons*. I have to say this was a remarkable concert as every single piece we played, vocal and instrumental, referred to birds, and I might add it was not a short concert. Composers included Vivaldi, Haydn, Handel, Couperin, Saint-Saëns, Mozart, and Arne.

A few days after this, on Saturday 8 August, we had our seventh annual concert at La Caillère for which I recall my main contribution, apart from all the accompaniments, being the Bach 'St Anne' Fugue. This was followed with my annual organ recital at L'Aiguillon-sur-Mer and, looking back at the programme, am reminded that I shared the concert with Christine, which takes the pressure off a tiny bit but still requires a great deal of concentration. However, it was basically a repertoire programme, but from many years of experience I knew that this did not mean that it was time to relax. From earlier recitals, I knew that the organisers would have liked me to talk briefly about the works I was to play, but I declined on the grounds that my French was not good enough. Christine was happy to speak about the works she had chosen, and did so admirably. I put her considerably improved French down to the female sex having a greater need to communicate. (I enjoy writing bold statements like that when I cannot be challenged.)

After a short break in Moissac, we gave an ensemble concert in Saint-Juire-Champgillon, where I was able to accompany the ensemble on the organ. This concert was particularly memorable for me because a member of the audience, a nephew of Clifford Curzon, one of Britain's most renowned concert pianists with whom I had occasionally worked in England, made himself known to me at the end of the concert. Indeed, Clifford would have made his last appearance with Philomusica apart from the fact that, although booked to play with the orchestra, we could not get his agent to inform us of his choice. We waited until the last moment before being advised that Clifford was indisposed. He died on 1 September 1982. There were two concerts requiring a piano soloist at that time, notably Richard Watkins and John Ogden, but I cannot recall which of the two was the replacement. Fritz Curzon and his wife Joanna talked with us after the concert and Fritz took a photograph of the ensemble, which I think we all rate as the best we have. This was taken in the roadway down from the church in Saint-Juire.

Ensemble St Juire

2010

The year began with a Music Box concert of Viennese music at La Noue. For this I took a bold approach towards arranging the music for the talent that surrounded me. I was aware of what a string trio, violin, cello and piano could achieve and resolved to try my hand at arranging some Viennese music. We already had experience of playing palm court music using flute, bassoon and piano, but since there were no arrangements for what I had in mind for our impending concert, I set myself the task of arranging Tales from the Vienna Woods, Perpetuum Mobile, and the Thunder and Lightning Polka, for which I already had the full scores. These works went into rehearsal and proved extremely effective. Using a bit of imagination, I decided to go further subsequently adding well known overtures and even going to the extreme of arranging Richard Strauss's overture *Der Rosenkavalier*. The reader should bear in mind that the attractive thing about the piano is that it is capable in terms of notation of covering every pitch of sound in harmonic terms which, in the orchestra, has to be shared by individual instruments each playing basically one line of music. A keyboard player on the other hand has the benefit of being able to hear every sound in terms of pitch by himself. I will digress briefly to say the downside to this is, unless playing in an ensemble, practising by oneself proves to be a lonely occupation. All other instruments found in the orchestra will invariably be played by musicians with either an accompanist or other instrumentalists to form an ensemble. The ability of a keyboard player being able to 'realize' the entire repertoire of other instruments was apparent in eighteenth and nineteenth century particularly in Britain as they built and installed large pipe organs in city and town halls which could feature the entire repertoire of a symphony orchestra as well as providing accompaniments for all the great oratorios and even opera to be performed with the sound colour and indeed volume one would expect to hear from a symphony orchestra. Historically this was not necessary in Europe as, going back to earlier times, the legacy of Royal Courts in each of their kingdoms would have a court musician and indeed orchestra a tradition which has continued to this day.

The 'Palm Court Trio' Violin, Cello and Piano in contrast to the 'classical' trio was Britain's other compromise at the same time as city organs relying on the tonal colours of the violin and cello and the harmonies of the piano for popular music and music for dancing. Going back we could complete a varied programme with Judith singing popular arias by Strauss and Lehár. To give even more variety, Christine and I played a four-handed arrangement of the Blue Danube together on the piano. The concert was followed by mulled wine and mince pies. Need I say more? The venue for Music Box in July was in the *orangerie* of the château at La Sicaudière, near La Caillère. It was a perfect summer day and, like all Music Box concerts, was on a Sunday, started at 4 p.m. and ended with drinks in the grounds.

A busy summer of concerts followed. We finalized our programmes for the next Sainte-Hermine Festival, which involved the usual three concerts (7–9 August). I can no longer recall the period for this festival, but from looking at the programmes, I assume it must have related to the Napoleonic Wars circa 1800 because the works were all classical edging into the romantic period. Once again I had a piano. Some of the works chosen for the festival were Beethoven's Piano Trio theme and ten variations; Devienne's Sonata for Flute and Bassoon; Mendelssohn's 'Suileka', and 'Auf Flügein des Gesanges', and Schubert's Marche militaire.

The festival was followed by the annual Ensemble de la Chapelle concert at La Caillère and, on 16 August, we were once again in L'Aiguillon-sur-Mer, where, following the success of our flute and organ recital the year before, were invited to work to the same format this year. Warming to the challenge, Christine became more adventurous in her choice of pieces, which included the Vivaldi 'Il Cardelina' concerto and the unaccompanied Honegger Danse de la Chèvre.

Holland

Our annual break followed and this year it was to be in Holland. I need to update readers to the fact that we were once again boatless and so I decided to revisit some of my old haunts there. I had never owned a steel boat, though I had once sailed one, which had been a bruising experience. However, we had admired several cruisers in various Dutch marinas and had never failed to be impressed. I knew the three main builders by reputation and settled for Pedro. In June, we had decided to visit his factory in Groningen far up in the north of the country and drove the 2,390 kilometres it took (I hasten to add not in one day) to get there. The long and short of it was that we bought their 30-foot cruiser.

On 19 August we once again set off on the long drive to Groningen to take delivery of our Pedro 30. We spent several days in Pedro's marina where his sales team and workers looked after us admirably. We were taken on a trial run and I benefited from several useful tips, not least a valuable one concerning the bow thruster that was completely new to me. On returning, I could see that my first attempt to reverse into the berth we had left was not going to work, so I quickly put the boat into forward motion and, on clearing the berth, positioned it for another attempt. I immediately realized just how useful this bow thruster was but, to my surprise, my tutor instructed me to take the boat out of the marina back into the river and make the attempt again from there. He explained that, having disturbed the water with the failed attempt, it was necessary to let it settle before trying again. This time it worked. How often since have I seen helmsmen making this same mistake!

While in the marina we victualled the boat, transferred our personal belongings and a considerable amount of boat gear – tools, charts, navigation aids, the list is quite long – and finally made arrangements to leave our car until we could retrieve it once we had found a berth nearer to the area I knew so well from earlier visits. We finally departed and made our first passage along the Winschoterdiep canal from Pedro's yard at Zuidbroek and, passing under eight bridges, to Groningen. The wind was blowing strongly and, since there was no space on the town quay, we motored into the Motor Yacht Club, where we were kindly assisted into a berth. On leaving the next morning, we entertained a group of onlookers to our safe passage under the very low bridge on which they were standing; privately, it had me sweating! Over the next few days we travelled along the Noord Willemskannal passing through Assen and berthing in Smilde in the late afternoon. We had gone through 25 bridges, which had all opened as if by magic. We learnt that the bridge keepers were kept up to date on the movement of boats along the canal, though not so at Spiersburg Bridge the next morning, which remained firmly closed! Eventually, on creeping up to it, the bridge keeper appeared and explained that he only knew if we were there if we got close enough, 'cautious Neville'. Then it was onwards through Mettel, Zwolle and Hattem where there was a very pleasant marina; we had done 100 kilometres since leaving!

The next morning we went into the town and, on hearing the carillon, which reminded me of Veere, we visited the church where the organ was playing. On seeing me looking up at him, the organist asked if I was interested and, if so, said I was welcome to join him. I performed my usual extemporizations and was impressed with the instrument. Warming to me, he revealed that there were two other organs in the church, one of particular historic interest that I must see and play. This was on another gallery and, having climbed the narrow steps to the organ loft, he showed us the huge platform on which he walked. The platform collapsed as he walked across it and continued to do so until he reached the far end. He was in fact compressing the bellows, which reminded me of my early days when my mother used to hand pump the little pipe organ in our Baptist church. These bellows, however, were capable of providing sufficient wind for the large number of stops I was to see on entering the organ loft overlooking the church. I gather that in the years before the new organ was installed, the organist would walk the plank, so to speak, which would provide sufficient wind to accompany only a few verses of a hymn. However, for recital purposes, two people would definitely be required to walk the plank. I was not warned that the instrument predated equal temperament tuning introduced by Bach in his lifetime. Discovering the problem to the amusement of the organist, and being told the keys I could play in, I was able to continue, but only with considerable forethought.

I will digress at this point to say a few words about 'pitch'. Possibly the first discovery to be made was the octave. Two voices could sing what sounded like the same note even although one sounded higher. This is explained in scientific terms as registering twice the number of vibrations. Getting from a given sound at the lower end and rising to the same sound higher was found to be best achieved by dividing what we call the scale into two halves – C to F and G to the higher C on the piano keyboard. This progression produces a semitone between the third and fourth notes and is perfectly matched with a similar semitone between the seventh and eighth notes. However, any hope of copying this starting on another note required introducing a new semitone to be inserted between the new third and fourth notes. This is clear on a keyboard instrument as, I said earlier, it is possible to see the sounds being made. This will work only for a limited number of scales and did so until Bach introduced 'equal temperament'. While of no material significance, it is worth pointing out if a singer or violinist is asked to play a scale pitching each note perfectly to achieve the octave they will arrive at a very, very slightly higher pitch. Thus, orchestral players who tune their own instruments to an agreed pitch will tell you if they are playing with a 'fixed' pitch instrument, such as a piano or organ, that they consciously have to adapt. This can be evident in the case of a piano concerto where the orchestra starts with a long introduction and is eventually joined by the piano, which is not immediately in tune. I hastily add that this is not evident in the best orchestras because they will already have allowed for the difference. So subtle is this difference that I can assure readers if I look at the chord of D flat major on a piece of manuscript, I will not hear in my mind the same sound as a written chord in C sharp major. I remember as a boy learning Bach's C sharp major prelude and fugue and struggling with every note being a sharp, which is how I heard it in my mind, and therefore played with a feeling for the sharps. I later discovered the Associated Board published the 48 with an alternative exact copy of the C sharp written in D flat. I would have played it very differently if I had learnt it in that key!

On 28 August, while continuing our journey through the Overijssel towards Deventer, with the driving rain seriously affecting our visibility, I received a telephone call from my old friend David Cound, who had remembered that it was my eightieth birthday. At this moment, the sky suddenly turned black, the heavens opened, and there was an horrendous thunderstorm. In fact, the whole trip so far had been rather wet. Where were the warm, sunny summers I remembered in the past? We finally reached Deventer, where we dined in the clubhouse to celebrate my eightieth on Vienna schnitzel, Dutch beer and champagne. After a night in Doesburg, we joined the Gelder IJssel where we began to see many huge barges. A night in Wageningham followed on the Nederrijn, which was certainly the best marina so far in Chris's opinion, with excellent showers and clubhouse. Even the sun came out and we were finally able to put up the Bimini and bring out the deckchairs. Passing close to Arnhem the next day we joined the river Lek, having passed through an enormous lock, and we were the only boat in it! On this stretch of water we had to be careful of oversized barges that took up more than their beam when on 'tight' bends. They showed warning signs and effectively took the bends on the wrong side of the river, which was quite scary at times.

After joining the Nieuwe Maas, our passage became turbulent. It was like being at sea, with boats travelling fast in every direction, and everything being flung around the cabin; even the glass of our treasured oil lamp, which had survived many channel crossings, got broken. Finally, on reaching Rotterdam marina, we took a berth. We were dreadfully disappointed by the state of the pontoons, which ducks had left filthy, so Chris had to set about cleaning both the decks and the pontoon. The facilities, however, were superb, but a very long walk away. This was certainly not the marina of our dreams, but our main priority was to return to Pedro's by train the next day to collect our car.

We were only able to get a train as far as Zuidbroek, which still meant a long walk to Pedro's, but at least it was dry. Now, with the car at our disposal, it was not long before we found Barendrecht, which had a better marina with plenty of space, so we signed a contract for an annual berth there and arranged to bring the boat the following day. An official in the marina office kindly rang for a taxi to take us back to Rotterdam.

* * *

Back home and with little time to waste, we started rehearsing for our next concert, which was to be at Le Prieuré in Réaumur on *la journée du patrimoine*, the day in France when people can visit buildings, monuments and historic sites not normally accessible to them.

On 5 December L'Ensemble de la Chapelle gave its Christmas concert – soon to become an annual event – at La Caillère. A week later, with the same programme, we were in Saint-Marc-la-Lande, which was where we had been before with the English Singers.

Chapter 17

Twilight Years

2011–2020

A whistle-stop tour to retirement

2011

January saw the start of our 2011 schedule with the customary Viennese concert at La Noue – and as usual we played to a full house. Then, after a concert on 15 May in the Sainte-Hermine Temple, we drove to Holland for our main holiday.

From where we had left our boat in Barendrecht on the Oude Maas, we undertook several day trips and visited the lovely town of Brielle on the banks of the Brielse Meer before heading east to Dordrecht. There we joined the Beneden Merwede stretch of river that passes through De Biesbosch National Park, an area of outstanding natural beauty in which walks and cycle tracks meander past waterways and through forest. Continuing on, we cruised to Gorinchem, locked into the beautiful Linge river, and found a bankside mooring just past the yacht club in the pretty town of Arkel. The sun finally broke through and was strong enough to warrant putting up the Bimini. The following day, after spending the night at another bankside mooring at Oisterwijk, the temperature reached 30 degrees centigrade.

The following day, we continued on to Leerdam where, being Christine's birthday on 28 June, we spent two nights. We explored the town, which was attractive, and were enjoying a superb meal in an Indian restaurant when we were suddenly interrupted by a viscous storm that soon flooded the streets up to the level of people's car doors. Fortunately, the restaurant was a few steps up from the street, so unlike many of the shops, was not flooded. After finishing our meal and waiting a while for the rain and wind to abate, we were able to return to the boat. The roads were strewn with leaves and branches from trees, so we were relieved to see the Bimini cover still intact, but unfortunately we could not sleep in our bed because the rain had entered through

247

a partly opened hatch. We returned to Arkel to spend the following two nights in the marina, which has a welcoming clubhouse. Later we took the opportunity to embark on a long walk along the bankside to explore the town. Despite the storm, Leerdam impressed us, and we returned there for another night to drink to *Azimut*'s anniversary (5 July) before retracing our steps back to Dordrecht and Barendrecht.

* * *

Back at La Noue, my July organ recital at L'Aiguillon-sur-Mer this year included the Ensemble de la Chapelle. This involved more work for me because organ recitals usually last for about an hour, whereas a group as varied as ours insofar as it featured solo soprano, flute, bassoon, and organ, then combining forces, certainly called for more preparation and a longer programme.

The Sainte-Hermine Festival followed as usual (in costume) on 6, 7, and 8 August. This year's theme was *La Belle Epoque* (1879–1914), so covered Elgar, Debussy, Johan Strauss, Grieg, Scott Joplin, Lehár, Satie, and Mascagni. I have to say that, looking back at the festival programmes, they make interesting reading. It was always a joy to play at these concerts, and certainly rewarding to do the arrangements.

* * *

Two days after our annual concert in La Caillère we left for Holland again but our stay there was unhappy. The following turn of events is difficult for me to write about and I crave your indulgence. My daughter Clare had now been in living in France for nearly two years and we had naturally seen her from time to time, but the lodger she had brought with her made us feel uneasy. He tried and did obtain some work in France and, indeed, I had also helped by giving him some maintenance work at La Noue, which he did well but I was anything but happy about their situation. On the boat and on our return journey, late at night I received slurred telephone calls from Clare, which suggested to me that she had been drinking heavily and, at one point, she even said that she wanted to die. I thought she was suicidal, but despite her intoxication, she assured me that she would not ever take that step.

On our return to France, all seemed well until my other daughters discovered that for some time Clare had had a large lump in her breast, for which she did not want any treatment. On hearing the news, Christine immediately said we must move Clare to La Noue where we could look after her and arrange proper care. Naturally, we instantly drove over to see her and, on our arrival her lodger insisted on me seeing her alone. She was in bed and clearly very ill. She told me not to worry, but adamantly refused any help from us. I think she would have been happy to die at that moment. Fortunately, her son Thomas took charge and returned Clare to Manchester where she was well looked after in the hospital.

Following a Music Box concert in September at the home of M. and Mme Houdart in Luçon, the Ensemble de la Chapelle started rehearsing for our first 'tour abroad'. This was how we jokingly described our impending trip to England for a charity concert organized by my daughter Gré. The concert, at the invitation of Lady Ruggles-Brise, was booked to take place at Spains Hall in Essex. However, it had to be cancelled at the last moment because, the day before our departure, I had a chest pain, which I decided to have investigated before attempting the journey the following day. It was late evening and Chris drove me to the A&E department at the Fontenay-le-Comte hospital. The condition was clearly more serious than I thought it would be and, at 3 a.m. that night, I was driven to the hospital in Niort and literally, on arrival, given two stents. I was happy that Christine chose to visit me daily. I recovered sufficiently well to play for the carol concert at La Caillère, which, growing in popularity all the time, went ahead with the usual mince pies and mulled wine.

2012

It was not a good start to the year. I was inundated with medical appointments and this was only to be made worse by the sad news of Clare's death on 25 January. She was in her 53rd year, so her life was only five years longer than her mother's had been. Four days later we had our Music Box concert at La Noue, which I dedicated to Clare and at the end of which I played my recording of Percy Grainger's arrangement of the 'Londonderry Air'.

Clare had made it clear that she wanted to be buried alongside her mother in Tixover and listed the hymns that she had wanted sung. She particularly asked for the Barber Adagio, which I arranged for the organ and played in the church with considerable difficulty, and I weep as I write this. We had travelled to England the previous day and, due to snow during the early part of the route on the A1, faced a very hazardous journey. I determined to try and complete the drive and remember Chris checking vantage points to which we could return if necessary to find a hotel. Fortunately, there was less and less snow the further north we travelled, and we finally arrived, long overdue but safe. The next day the church was full and I met the present owner of Tixover Hall, who was a churchwarden. He invited us to call on them on our next visit to England, which I will mention later. Following the funeral, we met at the George Hotel in Stamford for the wake. There I grasped the full measure of her friendship with her old school friends and indeed many other friends, but was unable to avoid the great sadness of the occasion.

* * *

It is with particular affection that I remember our Music Box May concert in the Temple this year as I had prepared a performance of Bach's 4th Branden-burg Concerto using two recorders, exactly as Bach had specified but, not having a violin, required Christine to take over this part.

A real highlight came on 9 June when we hosted the Stamford Singers for a concert in La Caillère. The choir came over on 7 June and stayed at the Hôtel Le Fontarabie in Fontenay-le-Comte. Before his retirement, Paul White, its conductor, had been director of music at the Stamford Endowed Schools and had for many years conducted the Stamford Choral Society, which I believe was closely associated with the schools. In his retirement, he had formed the Stamford Singers, a chamber choir with some good readers. The choir had visited Europe on several occasions, but the majority of its work was in Britain where it has sung evensong in almost every cathedral and abbey in the country, including Westminster, which is no mean achievement. The main part of the concert consisted of the choir, which had its own accomplished organist in the form of David Lovell Brown. As David would be playing for the choir I sent him a copy of the specification of the three manual organ in the church. Paul, however, was insistent that the Ensemble de la Chapelle should also be involved. It was a memorable occasion and came to be known as 'the cupboard concert'. This was because, after taking several bows, Paul left the platform through the door to a cupboard rather than the vestry. Finding himself confronted with a formidable wall of shelves, he retreated to the adjacent door and made his escape to a noticeable increase in the applause and to much laughter. In the second half, the choir sang the Vivaldi Gloria, with Judith singing the solos with the flute, bassoon, harpsichord continuo and organ (www.stamfordsingers.org). The following day we hosted the Stamford Singers to a buffet lunch at La Noue before their return home.

* * *

Shortly after this we spent ten days in England visiting family and renewing our brief encounter with the present owners of Tixover Hall, Tony and Maureen Slipper. I had brought a whole lot of press cuttings with me that a former member of the O'Brien family (the MP who took part in the Corn Law debates) had accumulated over the years. Although I had meant to leave them at the hall, they had got packed up with the rest of my papers, so were still in my possession.

I will divert for the moment to explain that all the books I had at the time, plus full scores, as well as piano and organ music, created something of a dilemma for me when I left Easton. However, knowing that I was going to Adam and Eve House, I solved the problem by buying ample glass-fronted display cabinets with adjustable shelves that were ideal for storing both books and scores. They came to occupy the end wall in the music room at South Luffenham and, subsequently, were in the music room at La Graineterie in France. To the best of my knowledge, they are still there because I decided not to bring them to La Noue. Instead, until I could find a way of disposing of them, we would store the full scores, which filled several crates, in our attic at La Noue. Sargent, who had not only full scores but also 'band' parts, had told me that he intended to bequeath his to the Royal College of Music. For my part, however, Christine managed to find a second-hand bookseller on the internet who specialised in music and seemed interested. Since all the full scores were indexed, I could email him a copy and he kindly agreed to buy the lot, including an almost duplicate set of miniature scores. Some of the full scores had been signed by visiting artists with whom I had worked, and there were also some original manuscripts of first performances signed by their composers. As these would add to their value, it was necessary for me to sign my permission for him to buy the collection. Returning to our visit to Tixover Hall, Christine was able to see every part of the house and garden during our guided tour, which she loved.

At the beginning of July, my heart specialist did a second stress test on me and diagnosed another blockage, so it was back to Niort. To my relief, this was quickly sorted out, but unfortunately not quite in time for me to take part in our next concert. I must briefly go back some years to when I met Jean André who lived in Luçon. Jean was interested in music, had attended some of my concerts, and invited me to join the association, Sur les pas de Richelieu, of which he was president, which initiates, promotes and participates in anything related to Richelieu and his period. Christine and I, who had attended some of its functions, enjoyed the company of its members, but I regretted that my French was not up to sitting through meetings and lectures. The association had booked the Ensemble de la Chapelle to give a concert (in costume) of sixteenth-century music in the historic Chapelle des Ursuline in Luçon. The programme, arranged some time earlier, was virtually unchanged apart from a harpsichord solo and the first item being a recorder consort. Christine undertook to play all the other accompaniments on the harpsichord and played Purcell's Air and Hornpipe for Flute without accompaniment. Our reputation did not suffer.

The year came to its musical end with our Christmas concert in the church at La Caillère. Again I had to hand over to Christine who, due to my absence, played the organ for the congregational carols. My problem was my arrhythmia. I had a pacemaker fitted, which meant another short spell in hospital in Niort, where coincidentally Ken Lytton, mentioned several times previously, was undergoing the exact same treatment. I just made it home for Christmas and enjoyed a good but quiet end to the year.

2013

I recovered well, but concerts did not start immediately. While I was not being over cautious in relation to my health, there was a shade less activity generally, primarily because, following the breakdown of his marriage, Laurent Poultier was leaving the Vendée to go and live in Paris. The festival turned out to be the last for the Ensemble de la Chapelle, for we learnt that a considerable deficit had accrued over the years.

We did, however, receive an invitation to play in the church in Olonne-sur-Mer in aid of La Fondation Raoul Follereau. For this we had the organ and were able to play a repertoire programme to a full church. Still in church mode, Radio France decided to broadcast mass from Notre Dame, Sainte-Hermine, and I was called on to provide the incoming and outgoing organ voluntaries. I was struck by the way the sound engineers made their timings, using a stopwatch in the short time they had before the service started, and the somewhat vague arrangements they made with me to know when to start. No sophisticated lights were flashing, just a wave of the hand to me perched high on the organ gallery at the opposite end of the church.

This year's theme for our concert at the Temple in Sainte-Hermine was to be opera, and included the Mozart Impresario Overture, arias from the *Marriage of Figaro* and *Cosi Fan Tutti*, plus some Gluck and Purcell.

* * *

A family event now dominated our movements as Christine's mother Evelyn reached her ninetieth birthday on 6 July. We went to the UK to celebrate the occasion and, while staying in her home, were astounded by how many people were choosing to visit her. There was a constant trickle of friends coming round with presents and she had already received more than a hundred cards. The following day, we had arranged a luncheon for her family at the Normanton Park Hotel overlooking Rutland Water, and followed this with a drive round Rutland visiting many of the villages we knew so well. This was enjoyable for Evelyn and certainly a trip down memory lane for Chris and me.

* * *

The usual summer concerts took place again at Le Temple, La Caillère and Luçon, but with the loss of the festival in Sainte-Hermine, things were slowing down. There were of course the traditional Christmas carols, along with mince pies, in La Callière and we now had some members of the choir from the parish to help with the congregational singing. It was a challenge for them to sing in English, but they took on the task with great enthusiasm and enjoyment. In the build-up to Christmas, this is always a joyous occasion.

* * *

It is time to return to the subject of boats. I had by now covered an enormous area of Holland and Christine had also seen a great deal, but we both agreed that the car journey to Barendrecht was just too much of a marathon. We guessed that our boat was worth more in sterling than euros, so decided to take her to England and put her on the Broads, the only waters in and around the UK in which I had not sailed. We hired a delivery skipper to take her to Yarmouth, but due to bad weather at the point of departure, he had to postpone his trip. In the end, we resorted to returning the boat directly to Wayford Bridge marina by road and arriving in August. Because she was chocked up, we decided to leave her there for the winter and fit her out for the following year. It was from there that we made our first cruises on the Norfolk Broads and found the experience very satisfying – in many ways much like Holland but on a smaller scale. The greatest bonus of all was that there were no locks. As it was our intention to sell the boat in England, we put her on the market at the end of the season, confident from our previous experiences that we would still have her the following year. We were thus slightly disappointed when she suddenly sold before Christmas.

2014–2020

The concerts carried on as usual with some new venues for Music Box, one, at the invitation of David and Jo Wilds, a light programme with, as we explained for the benefit of the French, '*une touche d'humeur*'. Le Temple concert in May is always a difficult one to programme because (a) the building is small, and (b), with its ancient harmonium organ, we are left with no option other than to play from a baroque repertoire. I decided this year to arrange all four of Vivaldi's seasons and to start with 'Spring'.

For the La Caillère concert, we included works by Honegger, Butterworth, Debussy, and Elgar, and Music Box continued its 'Four Seasons' with a performance of 'Summer' in Luçon. 'Autumn' followed through the invitation to their country home of our former secretary Chris Skerry and his wife Angela.

Christmas came and went and in 2015 Music Box remained popular and, over and above its regular venues, performed in Longèves, Antigny, Fontenay-le-Comte, and Luçon. I think we were all wanting to reduce the number of concerts each year and I remember saying to Chris that we seemed to be living our lives in two-monthly intervals, and as soon has one concert was over, we were starting to prepare for the next. Perhaps 2016 would be a little different; it was, but not in the way we expected.

2016

I would like to mention a Music Box concert we gave at Badeau, the residence of Adrian and Judith, which included the first performance of Burlesque, a bassoon and piano work by Errol Matthews. Although we expected him to be present at the performance, we were disappointed that he was unable to be there, especially since we found the piece challenging, but more importantly he would have enjoyed hearing his music played live.

In May, after a Music Box concert in the Temple at Sainte-Hermine, Yves Dooghe, who I was to learn had set up a series of organ recitals at Notre Dame in Fontenay-le-Comte, approached me. Throughout my time in the Vendée, I never ceased to be astonished that, with its fine organ, this church had never had an organist to match either the instrument or the size of the church. Readers will recall that I had met Père Josef Vité at my first recital in the church at Nalliers, and that we had become friends. He had further invited me to play the organ in Notre Dame whenever I chose and I had subsequently played several organ recitals in the church. Now at last there appeared to be someone in charge as I understood there was to be a series of organ recitals in the summer under the title of 'Festi d'Orgue'. Having heard our Music Box concert in Le Temple, he explained his intention to supplement the organ with a soloist whenever possible, but would I extend this to my ensemble. I explained this would be L'Ensemble de la Chapelle and was confident we could perform as an ensemble with the organ on the tribune. I should mention at this point that it was customary to reverse the seating in the nave so that the audience could view the organist. Now they would also see the ensemble.

* * *

There is of course more to life than concerts, so yet again I am returning to boats. I have to confess that, having sold *Azimut* so quickly, we were disappointed not to have more time to explore the Norfolk Broads, so decided (in 2016) to charter a boat to do so. Another factor was that Christine's mother was needing more help, so we needed to visit England more frequently. We therefore decided to combine our next visit to Bourne with a few days chartering. During our charter, we noticed many small cabin cruisers with only two people on board, and thought that it might be nice to own something similar. So, at the end of our charter, Christine suggested we call in at Norfolk Yacht Agency on our way to Southampton to look at a boat she had seen advertised on the internet. It seemed perfect, but since there was no time for a trial sail, we expressed our interest and left without making an offer. We then returned to France and thought no more about it until July, when Chris read on the internet that it was still for sale. I rang the brokers and said that if the owner would accept my offer subject to a trial sail, we would fly over and complete the purchase. We flew to Stansted, hired a car, bought the boat, found a marina next to where we had kept our previous boat and, within three days had returned to France as boat owners. I arranged for the agency to skipper the boat to its new home at Wayford Bridge on the River Ant. *Nauti Buoy* is a comfortable 26-foot cruiser affording us a double berth in the fore cabin with comfortable seats and TV. The saloon has seating, collapsible table, galley with gas cooker, refrigerator and seating for two at the wheel. The heads has shower, wash basin and toilet, and the interior is heated by warm blown ducted air. The cockpit with seating has a canopy. We subsequently discovered that the owner of the marina in which we found a berth had owned it in its earlier days.

Very sadly, Christine's mother Evelyn died suddenly on 13 August 2016 aged 93. We had no reason to expect this turn of events and were committed to the Festi d'Orgue concert in Notre Dame, Fontenay-le-Comte, to which we had agreed in May. The final rehearsal was that afternoon, and a very difficult time for Christine; my admiration for her professionalism was unbounded and shared by all.

Chris inherited Evelyn's bungalow in Bourne and we decided, after making the necessary renovations, to offer it out as a rental. However, this entailed rather more work than we had originally anticipated – not only was complete re-rewiring needed but we had also decided to install a new kitchen and redecorate throughout. The bungalow was finally ready to let to a retired couple the following year in April 2017.

* * *

Now that the Festi d'Orgue in Fontenay-le-Comte had become an annual event, its organisers asked me to give further organ recitals in Notre Dame (2017), while indicating that they would welcome another soloist to add variety to the series, so happily Christine was now also part of the team.

I had been aware of my failing eyesight due to macular degeneration and had been receiving specialist treatment for it for some time, including periodic injections of Lucentis into my right eye, which has the wet form of the problem. I was experiencing particular difficultly reading small print and was finding it increasingly hard to read music, although still having a good memory I could get by comfortably. When the restoration of our church in La Chapelle-Thémer was nearing completion, I was invited to give a concert to raise money to help cover some of the deficit. Although the concert was a success, I was not happy about it, and at that moment decided that it was time to stop playing.

Driving was still possible, so nothing was preventing us taking trips to England to explore the Norfolk Broads and visit family. However, I was not spending as much time in the garden as previously, and since we have a large number of very mature trees, which require the skilled attention of a landscape gardener, we now employ a regular *paysagiste*. Fortunately, I can still drive our tractor mower, so our lawns are not neglected.

* * *

A little over a year before, my grandson Thomas had sent us an invitation to his wedding where he was to marry his partner Darren, which was to take place in Manchester. He, the first of my grandchildren to take the plunge, had always been well organized, which probably accounts for his considerable success in business. The invitation set out all the details of the event, right down to asking us to decide in advance which dish we wanted for the evening meal. It was a memorable occasion and, as the photograph shows, one that really brought my family together again.

While cocktails were being served after the ceremony, a solo violinist, accompanied by a full symphony orchestra playing from a sound box, entertained us to a range of Viennese and popular classics. I was impressed and, on talking to her during the interval, was astonished to discover that she was playing an electronic violin. Her technique convinced me that she was worthy of greater things than this, so I suggested she could at least play in the Hallé. She replied that first she had a young family to care for, which would not fit in with rehearsals, travel and concerts, and second this work was infinitely more rewarding in financial terms.

We had visited Thomas and Darren the year before their wedding and had combined this trip with a visit to see my cousin Jean (Brown) living near to Huddersfield. It was also an opportunity to meet up again with Mary (Harding) her sister who was over at that time from Canada with her daughter-in-law, Andrea. Sadly the year previously both sisters had lost their husbands within six months of each other.

After Thomas's wedding we took the opportunity to stay with Jean again and on this occasion met Julien her son for the first time.

Jean and Ken had visited us several times in Nalliers and Mary with Arthur from Canada, after our move to La Noue. Ken was in education and had connections in local politics, Arthur, a geologist, had been involved in surveying and advising on motorway routes worldwide.

I sadly had to step back from taking an active role in the series of Festi d'Orgue recitals that the Association Chamade was arranging for the summer of 2018 in Notre Dame, Fontenay-le-Comte, but did direct and play in the end-of-year carol concert in La Caillère.

Music had more or less ground to a halt in 2019, but I was persuaded to do the Christmas concert and programmed this to include Haydn's Toy Symphony, which I argued had to be in keeping with the idea of Santa Claus, but took the precaution of using my three colleagues in the ensemble to play the most exacting toys and the best amateurs we knew to play the remaining three. This was an impeccable performance featuring, in addition to the ensemble, Rebecca my daughter who plays the oboe, Jo Wilds who plays the piano and recorder, and Danny Cottreau, wife of our secretary, who also plays the organ.

The emergence of the coronavirus in early 2020 put an end to any thought of struggling on, so I do not feel the slightest bit guilty about saying that I have finally retired.

Postscript
It's not the music, it's the politics

I left the English Sinfonia at the end of the concert season in 1980, 'it wasn't the music, it was the politics'. Following my departure I was soon to learn the orchestra had ceased to operate in Nottingham after the Arts Council of Great Britain had withdrawn their support, thus finally depriving me of my dream to have an orchestra of quality in the Midlands giving regular concerts in that region of England.

My work soon became primarily with Philomusica but I had the occasional pleasure of guest conducting the Sinfonietta and the Sinfonia following the players taking back the original title of their orchestra but would wryly add there was usually a 'guest' leader!

My personal relationship with John Cruft remained on friendly terms and indeed went further when he later 'seconded' my sponsor to become a member of the Royal Society of Musicians. With regard to my personal relationship with the Arts Council, suffice it to say that during the entire period of my conducting career their support for my work never ceased. This covered the period from 1958 to 1990 first with the Kettering Symphony Orchestra through the National federation of Music Societies and subsequently directly to Opera da Camera, Midland and subsequently English Sinfonia and finally with Philomusica through the Eastern Authorities Orchestral Association.

To sum up, perhaps I should be happy with the 'Glory Years' and the enormous success we achieved at that time, but it was not just my dream that was destroyed. It was the dream of many other people in the Midlands who were to be deprived of the many concerts we had played, from small ensemble to a symphony orchestra depending on the size of the venue. Nottingham and the Sinfonia had been the beating heart of the Midlands, but sadly not all dreams come true.

APPENDIX

1. Orchestral works recorded by Neville Dilkes

English Sinfonia

Bax	Dance in the Sunlight
Bridge	There is a Willow grows aslant a Brook
Butterworth	The Banks of Green Willow
	A Shropshire Lad
	English Idylls Nos 1 and 2
Grainger	In a Nutshell Suite
	Molly on the Shore
	Irish Tune from County Derry
	Danish Folk Music Suite
	The Immovable 'DO' (or The Cyphering 'C')
Hamilton Harty	A John Field Suite
Honneger	Concerto da Camera for flute and cor anglais (with John Solum, flute and Anthony Camden, cor anglais)
Ibert	Flute Concerto (with John Solum, flute)
Ireland	The Holy Boy
Jolivet	Flute Concerto (with John Solum, flute)
Lambert	Concerto for Solo Pianoforte and Nine Players(with Richard Rodney Bennett, piano)
Leigh	Concertino for Harpsichord and Strings(with Neville Dilkes, harpsichord)
Moeran	Symphony in G minor
	Two Pieces for Small Orchestra
	Lonely Waters
	Whythorns's Shadow

Philharmonia Orchestra

Arnold	Concerto for Flute and Strings (with John Solum, flute)
	Flute Concerto No. 2 (with John Solum, flute)
	Sinfonietta No. 1
	Sinfonietta No. 2
*Doppler	Bird in the Wood (L'Oiseau des Bois) Idylle, Op. 21
*Fürstenau	Rondo Brillant, Op. 38
*Kummer	Divertissement, Op. 13
*Popp	Scherzo Fantastique, Op. 423
*Saint-Saëns	Romance, Op. 37
*Tulou	The Angelus (L'Angélus), Op. 46

*A Bouquet of Romantic Flute Music for Flute and Orchestra (with John Solum, flute). This recording was released in 1979.

2. What the music critics say:
(copies of press releases 1973 and 1974)

1973

'Spontaneous … an effect was achieved which gripped the imagination … marvellously done.'   (*Leicester Evening Mercury*, March)

'This programme was among the most exciting of the season and certainly the most adventurous.'   (*Derby Evening Telegraph*, March)

'Scintillating … hit just the right mood … king size reception for Viennese spices … full of exhilaration.'   (*Derby Evening Telegraph*, March)

'Dynamic … full of variety and contrast. … This orchestra gets better every time I hear it. Nottingham is lucky indeed to have it based here.'
                                                      (*Nottingham Evening Post*, November)

'From the outset … the Orchestra played with competence and enthusiasm … rhythms were crisp and incisive.'   (*Manchester Guardian*, December)

Tour of Spain, 24–30 March 1973

'A major success.'

(*Libertad Valladolid*)

'Richly inspired and with a delicious sentiment, full and suave.'

(*El Diario Vasco*, San Sebastian)

'A large number of chamber orchestras exist in Europe; the English Sinfonia can be perfectly placed amongst the best of these.'

(*La Vanguardia*, Barcelona)

Tour of Bermuda, Canada and the United States, 5 October–6 November 1973

'A highly satisfying and polished performance of Bartok's Divertimento, charged with tautness and rhythmic intensity. ... I was impressed with the conductor's ability to convey each change of mood and character; every nuance was exploited, every mood brilliantly conveyed.'

(*Bermuda Mid Ocean News*, Hamilton, October)

'One of the most exciting evenings ... a stimulating programme which interspersed contrasting styles of music all perfectly suited to the size of the group ... the artistes were of a high calibre with a harmoniously coordinated interaction.'

(*Bermuda Sun*, Hamilton, October)

'The English Sinfonia deserves considerable credit ... breathtaking ... what a wealth of colour and sound.'

(*Mail Star*, Halifax, Nova Scotia, October)

'The English Sinfonia played with precision and faultless intonation under its dynamic young conductor ... romantic depths were beautifully realised.'

(*Keene*, New Hampshire, October).

1974

'A confident involving performance.'

(*The Times*, January)

'Neville Dilkes did wonders in coordinating the ensemble ... but even more remarkable was the richness of phrase, the lack of inhibition which carried one to the end in exhilaration.'

(*Guardian*, January)

'Their conductor Neville Dilkes has over the past dozen years established a solid and capable rapport with his band of players ... always worth hearing. ... Well articulated, clear and honest ... even without all of its deeper shades of nostalgia, it took fire; the shrill accents, the marvellous surge and contrapuntal counter-surge, the relentlessness, all held firm.'

(*Financial Times*, January)

Tour of Spain and Portugal, March 1974

'This English chamber Orchestra was presented in Valencia preceded by an extraordinary reputation which, listening to it, was confirmed to us. ... The performance of the English Sinfonia greatly delighted the very large audience which admired the visiting artists from the first downbeat, stirring up great enthusiasm.'

(*Jornada*, Valencia)

'The English Sinfonia is a model of technique and of expressivity. ... From the beginning, the hall had the impression of being overwhelmed by the magic of an ensemble of exceptional quality.'

(*Norte Exprés*, Vitoria)

'Their technique comes finished like gilt swords and gives the impression that it would take a conscious effort to play badly, since they carry absolute dominion over their instruments, as well as possessing rhythm and high expressivity within themselves.'

(*El Correo Español*, Vitoria)

'Once again our Philharmonic Society has been visited by the English Sinfonia ... whose previous performance here we recall with notable pleasure, since we regard it as one of the most gifted of the "pocket-size" symphonic ensembles.'

(*La Voz de Asturias*, Oviedo)

'The English Sinfonia, which left such a good impression in its concert this year ... has reached a distinguished level amongst the many orchestras of the same type which now exist.'

(*La Nueva España*, Oviedo)

'The English Sinfonia proved itself to be an excellent instrument. ... The conductor and the orchestra were greeted with prolonged and well-deserved applause.'

(*Diario de Noticias*, Lisbon)

3. Copy of email from John Solum about our last recording,
'A Bouquet of Romantic Flute Music'

Dear Neville

I've been thinking about the Romantic Music album which you and I recorded for EMI in 1978. You mentioned you like to listen to it. I think it is an outstanding recording, and I have some observations about it. First, nothing on that record had ever been recorded before. Moreover, neither you nor I had ever performed it. Yet, we went into the Abbey Road studios of EMI and made that recording in three sessions. What daring! You and I had worked a great deal together before then and understood each other's signals or body language. We were in complete agreement about tempos. I appreciated the freedom and flexibility of tempos that you gave me, the music breathed and had a narrative quality. Each piece tells a story. Although the composers had strange names like Popp, Kummer, Tulou and Furstenau, neither you nor I were in the least bit condescending to them. We gave them their full dignity. As for myself as a flutist, I was 43 years old for those sessions and still had the full measure of my technical virtuosity. Moreover, I had also reached my musical maturity. And I had had enough experience making recordings that I knew how to use the sensitivity of the microphone, rather than belt it out as if we were in a concert hall. As a result, the recording is filled with subtleties, nuances, and tonal beauty. The virtuoso aspects of the music do not overwhelm the music; rather, we treat them as genuine musical gems, little masterworks by minor master composers. Those are my thoughts that I want to share with you and Christine. Thank you, Neville, for being a superb conductor during those years we worked so successfully together. It was always a pleasure. Stay safe! Love to you and Christine – John.

4. Letters of appreciation
(See following page.)

ENGLISH SINFONIA

Extracts from letters of appreciation from members of
the English Sinfonia Association, Summer 1980
to mark the occasion of a presentation to Neville Dilkes
on his termination of office as Music Director to the
English Sinfonia 1961 - 1980.

*"For Neville Dilkes, with much gratitude for his
wonderful music making".*

*". . . a small token of gratitude for all the pleasure Neville
Dilkes has given me throughout the years".*

*". . . a small contribution to the Sinfonia Association Fund
with all our very best wishes to Neville".*

*". . . I, together with other members, will miss Neville at
the Sinfonia concerts, but I wish him well in his
future . . ."*

*". . . he has given us many hours of musical pleasure and
we shall miss him very much".*

*". . . in appreciation of Neville Dilkes's service to Music
and the City over the past years".*

*". . . very sorry to learn that he is leaving the Sinfonia. I
have enjoyed many concerts over the years . . ."*

*". . . a small appreciation towards a gift for Neville Dilkes,
with every good wish".*

*". . . I am sure that he will be greatly missed and the
pleasure he has given to very many people over the
years is immeasurable".*

*". . . gratitude and appreciation for his long period of
service . . . without his initial ideas the orchestra would
never have existed".*

*". . . a tribute towards a gift for Neville . . . we were
surprised and dismayed . . ."*

INDEX

Printed in Great Britain
by Amazon